M

CALIFORNIA PUBLIC GARDENS

California Public Gardens

A Visitor's Guide

Eric Sigg

John Muir Publications
Santa Fe, New Mexico

John Muir Publications, P.O. Box 613, Santa Fe, NM 87504

First edition. First printing

Library of Congress Cataloging-in-Publication Data
Sigg, Eric.
    California public gardens : a visitor's guide / Eric Sigg. — 1st ed.
    p. cm.
    Includes bibliographical references and index.
    ISBN 0-945465-56-4
    1. Gardens—California—Guide-books. 2. Botanical gardens—
California—Guide-books. I. Title.
    SB466.U65C28 1991
    712'.025'794—dc20   90-23866
                                                                          CIP

Cover Design: Sally Blakemore
Text Design: Abraham
Typeface: Schneidler
Typesetter: Copygraphics, Inc., Santa Fe
Printer: McNaughton & Gunn, Inc.

Distributed to the book trade by
W. W. Norton & Co., Inc.
New York, New York

Cover photo: San Francisco Conservatory of Flowers

CONTENTS

ACKNOWLEDGMENTS

In my remarks on the gardens, I name most books and other published works that I have relied on or that offer more detail to those interested. Authors appear in the index. A few other sources should be acknowledged here. *Pacific Horticulture* and *Sunset Magazine* regularly offer valuable treatments of California gardens. Robert Smaus writes in the *Los Angeles Times* with strong local feeling, firsthand horticultural experience, and interest in style and design. I have also referred to Jellicoe, Goode, and Lancaster, *The Oxford Companion to Gardens*; William L. Kahrl, *The California Water Atlas*; Loraine Kuck, *The World of the Japanese Garden: From Chinese Origins to Modern Landscape Art*; Christopher Thacker, *The History of Gardens*; Graham Stuart Thomas, *Climbing Roses Old and New* and *The Old Shrub Roses*; Edith Wharton, *Italian Villas and Their Gardens*; and *The WPA Guide to California*.

Because of their intelligence, wit, and attentiveness to the gardens, the indispensable books by David Gebhard and Robert Winter, *A Guide to Architecture in Los Angeles & Southern California*, *Architecture in Los Angeles: A Compleat Guide*, and with Eric Sandweiss, *The Guide to Architecture in San Francisco and Northern California*, have been a source of inspiration.

I wish to acknowledge Patricia Sigg and Michael Mackness, who contributed photographs to this book. All other photographs are by the author.

Besides the encouragement of my parents, Robert and Patricia Sigg, I am pleased to have this chance to thank Chet Boddy, Charles Coburn, Steven Cutting, John Hall, Gail Matteson, Charles J. O'Neill, Phillip Robinson, Roger Stutts, Tom Tillotson, and Steven Timbrook and to express my gratitude for the contributions of my friends Sherwin Carlquist, Verlyn Klinkenborg, Michael Mackness, Tori Smith, and Linda Venis.

INTRODUCTION

Each word of the title, *California Public Gardens: A Visitor's Guide*, describes something about the goals of this book and how it is organized. This is the first book discussing all major (and many minor) public gardens throughout California. Although they are not necessarily owned by a public entity, the gardens are open to visitors on a scheduled basis. As distinguished from the many sites in California owing their beauty and interest to nature alone, this book emphasizes the garden, consciously placed, planned, and planted by human effort. Instead of offering horticultural advice to gardeners, the book accompanies visitors enjoying gardens prepared for the public. Finally, by including critical, descriptive commentary and practical information, the book guides readers and visitors through the gardens and around the state.

The chapters divide California into twelve regions. Within each chapter, the major gardens receive more lengthy commentary, while a concluding "Briefly Noted" entry or a grouping of city gardens ("Pasadena Gardens" or "Fresno Parks and Gardens") treats smaller gardens of local interest, botanical curiosities, and historically significant horticultural sites. Although it is hoped that the critical discussions and descriptions will help visitors set priorities and plan itineraries, most of the gardens contain more plants and other features than my comments could possibly record. I have tried to report matters of general importance as well as to record my own responses. I point out in passing that this book was not written by mail; I have paid at least one visit to every garden I discuss.

Following each treatment of a garden, there is information for visits: address; directions, if necessary; price of adult admission (admission for children, students, or senior citizens may be less); days and hours when the garden is open; whether it is necessary to make a reservation in advance; facilities (book, plant, or gift shops, libraries, eating facilities, etc.); tours, classes, and other public programs; and telephone numbers. This information is accurate at the time of writing, but some particulars inevitably change. As a practical matter, it is advisable to avoid disappointment by telephoning before a visit to confirm, for instance, the hours that a garden will be open. This is especially true where a reservation is required.

Visiting public gardens, that is to say, requires a bit of self-reliance. It is crucial, for instance, to have good street maps; the excellent American Automobile Association maps and Thomas Brothers Guides label many of the gardens. Most large public gardens offer maps of their grounds, and some have detailed plant lists and other information; inquire about these publications as you enter.

The public gardens vary in botanical quality, design interest, and horticultural maintenance, but each one has something worth seeing. (I saw little reason to include dull, unkempt, or poor-quality gardens and less reason to dwell on their inadequacies in print. Such gardens have been silently omitted, as have one or two downtown gardens for which access was unreasonably difficult.) The estates of philanthropic owners, arboretums, botanical gardens, and landscaped city parks that emphasize horticulture form the core of California's public gardens.

Aspiring to inclusivity, however, this book also welcomes gardens at museums, zoos, a theme park, a cemetery, a courthouse, a historic Chinese temple, a winery, an office complex, at college campuses, and at several California missions, as well as sculpture gardens, demonstration gardens, and local garden centers. The list includes gardens for pleasure, entertainment, education, historical preservation, worship and meditation, water conservation, science and botany, and commerce. It also mentions books about the trees, plants, or gardens of a particular California city and occasionally focuses on individual plant specimens of merit. With a few exceptions, I omitted nurseries. Although California has many places of natural plant beauty, I mentioned only those groves or stands of native trees located conveniently near a public garden.

What is a garden? At its simplest level, a garden comprises the plants that grow in it, and I have tried to mention something of the botany, taxonomy, horticulture, and cultural history of plants. I have also recorded impressions made by the plants: color, fragrance, shape, habit, and so forth. To an extent, a garden is in the details, which has made necessary some listing of plants. Such catalogs have their value, if only to indicate typical plants or where to find a rare one. But my discussion has also sought to go beyond individual specimens; the most interesting garden comprises more than the sum of its botanical parts. Besides the plants, that is, a garden involves a place and a plan.

For better and sometimes for worse, California is a different place, disorienting to some and delightful to others. To take the instance of climate, most of the state has a long summer, though not an endless one. It has confused many who came from four seasons to encounter the actual California climate, which has two: one cool and rainy, the other warm and dry. Complicating this ambiguous simplicity, the state's long coastline, alternating mountains and valleys, and hot interior create dozens of microclimates and refinements from place to place. As its public gardens reveal, California turns out to be quite other than an escape from weather, proving instead to be an immersion in climatic nuance.

A garden exists in the natural world, subject to the sun, humidity, rain, winds, and frost, and to the soil and native vegetation. Thus I have mentioned climate, geology, topography, and natural history. Yet if it is set in nature, the garden remains a piece of human design and work. People want gardens where they live, learn, teach, worship, play, work, and relax—in city parks, around churches, schools, and museums, and enclosing their dwellings. I have approached gardens in these contexts, commenting on architecture, urban planning, and social purposes. And because gardens satisfy the need for beauty, style, ornament, and pleasure, I have linked them to literature, aesthetics, history, and design, viewing the garden as a fine art as well as a humane one.

I have also tried to connect the gardens to the people who made them, to the history and myths of California, and to its landscape. On the last point, the antithesis between pleasure and use, between horticultural beauty and agricultural utility, must in one sense be false. Anyone who has viewed Sonoma County vineyards, passed by tidy fields of broccoli and lettuce along Monterey Bay, or seen citrus groves set against Ventura County's bare mountains will have encountered crop and orchard landscapes of exceptional beauty. Quite other than untamed nature, the natural beauty arising from human activity infuses vast expanses of California with the look and spirit of the garden.

Where possible, I have identified the people who made the gardens—owners, landscape architects and designers, and the gardeners themselves—and have tried to link them to a garden plan. A design usually involves an intention, a functional purpose or a stylistic effect that the garden maker wishes to achieve. Intention sharpens the distinction between the garden and the site of natural botanical splendor. Nature produces wild beauty at its leisure, almost as if by accident. A garden, by contrast, requires deliberate artifice and conscious effort. The best ones seem to flow from a plan that expresses an original intent about an ultimate goal, whether it is to cultivate a lavish monument or simply to call forth the *genius loci*. (This is not to overlook the role of circumstance and accident in a garden, but design, plus labor, are what urge constant change to take the shape of growth instead of the disarray of decline.)

If the plants are the details, in appreciating a garden it is important to step back, to ask how they contribute to an overall scheme, and to remember how the garden had its first existence in an idea. Often this exercise can reveal a personality and human presence that makes a return to the individual plants all the more satisfying. Keeping attentive to design, style, and plan helps to complete the experience of a garden, lifting it out of fleeting sensory experience and fitting it into a larger world.

It is the great temptation of gardens to withdraw into a cultivated perfection. (The word "paradise" comes to us from the Greek for park or garden. The Greeks got it from Old Testament Hebrew, which took it from Persian, and so on. It is not without significance that several religions have linked the garden to paradise, however ambivalent the connection, as in that brief but eventful afternoon in Eden.) So many gardens are places of retreat, scanty plots of private pleasure and accomplishments, that a public garden is something of a paradox. Although compromising its privacy, the act of opening a garden to the public widens the vision of a good and happy life by making some aspect of a garden's beauty and value available to all. It is a social act, and the place, plan, and plants of public gardens have a social context, joining culture and horticulture. Many of its gardens realize ideas about what California society might become, trying in a small way to materialize the great promise the state has always seemed—and still seems—to hold out to the imagination.

Public gardens offer one measure of how seriously a society desires to become a good society, of its commitment to becoming a commonwealth. California now finds itself wealthy, crowded, and still officially committed to growth without limitation. It remains to be seen whether these facts will prepare the way for a better future, a blandishment of the California myth that until recently formed its most enduring feature. Even as urbanization and an immense population might seem to jeopardize the existence of public gardens, however, they make them all the more valuable and necessary. Visit and appreciate them.

I
San Diego

The Alcazar Garden and California Tower, Balboa Park

BALBOA PARK

California's third great coastal city, San Diego bears comparison with San Francisco not only because of its protected harbor and maritime tradition but also because it has one of the state's two great urban parks. Balboa and Golden Gate parks both have outdoor musical facilities, science and art museums, specialized indoor botanical gardens, and diverse horticultural displays. Soon both will also contain Japanese gardens, as Balboa Park's long-awaited facility is now under construction.

Horticulturally speaking, the two parks are entirely artificial creations from San Francisco sand dunes and San Diego's semi-desert. The difficulty in establishing a green park in San Diego's arid conditions has passed into the city's lore, but early photographs (such those in Florence Christman's *The Romance of Balboa Park*, 1985) confirm how forbiddingly bleak the terrain was before trees began to be planted around the turn of the century. Although farsighted civic leaders had set aside land in 1868, the park suffered many attempts to develop its 1,400 acres and floundered for decades before taking shape around the 1915 Panama-California Exposition.

Of the many leaders instrumental in protecting and developing the park horticulturally during its formative decades, a single figure towers above the rest. As early as 1889, Kate Sessions led a party that planted a small area on the park's west side. In 1892, Sessions established a nursery on thirty acres, planting, as rent, 100 trees annually inside the park and supplying 300 trees for planting elsewhere in the city. (In 1900, Sessions joined noted botanist T. S. Brandegee's expedition to Baja California which found the *Brahea brandegeei* palm. She returned to San Diego with seeds of the slow-growing palm, and north of Sefton Plaza, dozens of the seedlings survive as mature trees, marking the site of Kate Sessions's park nursery.) Many of these old trees—eucalyptus, Monterey cypress, pepper trees, Torrey pines, jacarandas, and others—continue to beautify Balboa Park. Until she died in 1940, Sessions was so closely involved in the financing, planning, planting, and irrigating of park horticulture that she became known as "the mother of Balboa Park." In 1957, the city dedicated land on Mount Soledad overlooking San Diego's two bays as Kate Sessions Park.

Only after 1909 was the identity of Balboa Park finally established. That year saw the approval of a proposal for an exposition to celebrate the opening of the Panama Canal, whose first American port of call would be San Diego. The park received a name in 1910, when it was decided to commemorate Vasco Nuñez de Balboa, the first European to sight the Pacific Ocean in 1513. Despite a rival world's fair in larger, wealthier, and politically more powerful San Francisco, the San Diego Exposition went forward, concentrating on Latin American countries, establishing the Spanish Colonial architectural style that continues to distinguish the park, and transforming the terrain into a verdant landscape. Many of the 100,000 eucalyptus and other trees could be planted only by drilling or blasting holes in the park's hardpan. Installing over two million plants for the exposition established a green canopy throughout much of the park and a foundation for its landscaped areas. Even the San Diego Zoo can trace its beginnings to the exposition.

After World War I, a question arose which would continue to create civic controversy for generations: should the temporary exposition buildings be torn down or restored? Fortunately, San Diego has usually chosen to protect the park by restoring its buildings. It has also added notable new structures such as the *moderne* Deco-Pueblo complex southwest of the historic core for the 1935 California Pacific International Exposition. A third wave of restoration began in the 1960s, and the work continues.

Not all of the park's early horticulture has survived: Kate Sessions's cactus garden behind the Balboa Park Club suffers badly from neglect, and no trace remains of a "formal garden" behind the Natural History Museum. Fine old plantings nonetheless persist throughout the park, offering surprises around nearly every corner: a grove of *Dracaena draco* shades the entry to the Balboa Park Club; huddling for warmth against the south facade of the Natural History Museum, a pair of African tulip trees (*Spathodea campanulata*) bloom brilliant orange in September; and acanthus, splendid *Howea forsteriana* and Senegal date palms, and clipped *Syzygium paniculatum* shrubs line the arcades and florid facades of buildings along El Prado.

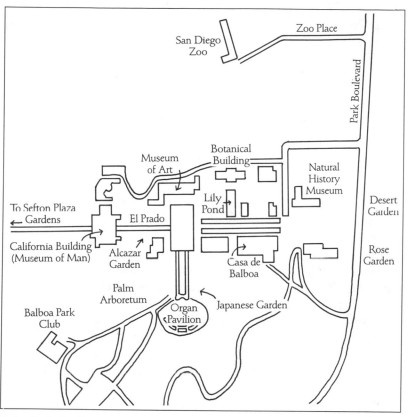

Balboa Park, San Diego

Each El Prado building surrounds a courtyard. The California Building's grilled balconies, tiled dome, and ornate tower overlook the most dramatic courtyard, the Alcazar Garden, laid out during the term of Richard Requa, architect of the 1935 exposition. In this courtyard, patterned after gardens of the Alcazar Castle in Seville, Spain, an arcade's beige planes and curves, twin fountains tiled in deep blue, green, and mustard tones, and symmetrical flower beds surrounded by squared and cubed box hedging suggest a Latin formality and precision. It nonetheless remains primarily a flower garden, whose winter Iceland poppies and calendulas and summer zinnias and marigolds are planted in a style not unlike carpet bedding, more lush and colorful than is usual in Spanish gardens. The Alcazar Garden presents fine views to the north, with its simple but graceful arcade planted with tree bird of paradise and king palms and a view of the romantic California Building tower framed by Canary Island palms and eucalyptus.

To the south, spreading ficus trees shade a pair of grand portals, regrettably leading only to a parking area that should really be used horticulturally. The asphalt overlooks Palm Canyon, marked by a screen of fans, fronds, and columnar trunks, and especially by a pair of superb *Caryota urens*, unique among palms for their bipinnate fronds, doubly divided in a fishtail shape. A wooden footbridge crosses the canyon, weaving between blue fan palms (*Brahea armata*), shaving brush palms (*Rhopalostylis sapida*), *Chamaedorea* (their trunks like bamboo until the eye alights on their pale green fronds), a *Trachycarpus fortunei* grove, and two queen palms, a species that grows magnificently here and in older districts of San Diego. Under the palms and beneath massive *Ficus macrophylla* (their gray trunks buttressed by exposed roots that flow down the canyon slope) are clusters of crinum lily, ginger, tupidanthus, and other subtropicals.

The footbridge presents a view down the canyon, into which a path descends under several dozen *Washingtonia robusta* palms, leaning to catch the sun. The *robustas* have lived here for many years—the 1915 exposition map described the area as "La Cañada de las Palmas"—but in the 1980s palm plantings have resumed, with canyon slopes thickly planted with young *Chrysalidocarpus lutescens*, pygmy date palms, sentry palms (*Howea belmoreana*), and innumerable plants of the gracefully pendulous *H. forsteriana*, now the dominant palm when viewed from within the canyon. The tone is tropical but cool, with clivia, philodendron, miniature bamboo, and elephant ears underplanted in the canyon floor's moist shade. The only flaw in this evocative landscape is that the path descending into the canyon reaches no goal, simply petering out to the noise of the freeway under the eucalyptus trees that are ubiquitous in this area of the park.

Southwest of Palm Canyon, the Spreckels Organ Pavilion's twin curving, arcaded wings—each crowned with a balustrade and festooned with masks, rosettes, and botanical ornament—spread from a two-story music box housing the world's largest outdoor pipe organ. The pavilion, painted in two tones of beige like the other park buildings, completes an axis it forms with the San Diego Museum of Art. Designed by Harrison Albright, donated by Adolph B. and John D. Spreckels in 1915, and capably restored in 1981, the pavilion and its peristyle (enclosing outdoor seating for Sunday afternoon concerts) seem quite the most sophisticated of the park's oldest buildings. Lighter and less intense than the Spanish Colonial architecture, the composition strikes a note of refinement that suggests Portugal or the French Riviera. To the northeast, after years of delay the first phase of the Japanese Friendship Garden of San Diego—with Mitsuo Yokoyama as design adviser, Takashi Nakajima as Japanese landscape architect, and Kawasaki-Thielacker-Ueno & Associates as San Diego landscape architect—began in 1989. Plans call for the project and its several structures to fill a dramatic, 11.5-acre canyon site partly surrounding the Spreckels Pavilion.

East of the axial El Prado and past a plaza and large fountain, a pedestrian bridge arches over Park Boulevard to a rose garden and a desert area, an unusual pairing except insofar as their thorny inhabitants complement one another's bloom schedules. The desert garden flowers best from February through April; roses bloom from April through early winter. The unlabeled plants of the desert garden include not simply cacti but dracaena, yucca, aloe, agave, succulents, euphorbia, Mesembryanthemum and other ice plant ground covers, desert palms, and flowering trees. Caught in bloom at the right moment—timing is crucial—these dry climate plants produce exceptional flowers, aside from the perennial interest of their habits and foliage. Flowering trees include palo verde, coral, floss silk, and most notably, the _Tabebuia avellanedae_. This small, deciduous tree clothes its bare branches in dark rose trumpet flowers during March. The northern tip of the finger-shaped desert garden also contains several _T. chrysotricha_, smaller but equally spectacular for their canary yellow flowers.

Like the desert garden, the rose garden offers one of the best views inland toward the mountains, a reminder of how large Balboa Park is and how much of it remains undeveloped. The roses grow in a series of circular and crescent raised beds surrounding a fountain and pergola covered with the two-inch, double, cream-white flowers of Lady Banks' rose. Dedicated to Inez Grant Parker in 1975, the garden contains modern hybrid teas and floribundas, mostly labeled, with many All America Rose selections.

North of the Natural History Museum stands one of the largest Moreton Bay fig trees in California, its exposed roots and spreading branches so attractive to children and other explorers that a low fence now protects it. A service driveway north of the Botanical Building contains other unusual trees. These include a _Livistona australis_ palm and a medley of ficus trees: a Zulu fig (_Ficus nekbudu_); next to the Botanical Building's central dome, a rare sycamore fig (_F. sycomorus_), so named for its odd, multicolored bark that flakes off with rubbing; and north of the art museum, a multitrunked bodhi tree (*F. religiosa*), the tree under which the Buddha found enlightenment. Also known as the quaking fig, the bodhi's distinctive heart-shaped leaves—their tails causing them to resemble a sting ray—quiver in the breeze.

Best seen in early spring, a second area of horticultural interest surrounds Sefton Plaza, where El Prado crosses Balboa Park Drive. Along the north side of El Prado near Cabrillo Bridge, a grove of flowering peaches blooms in March and April, accompanied by hundreds of fragrant freesias in a bed east of a bowling green. To the north lies a screen of palms that includes the grove of blue fan palms marking the site of Kate Sessions's nursery. One of many trees Sessions planted, a single *Tipuana tipu* tree rises in the middle of a lawn southeast of Sefton Plaza. A rare South American species, its yellow to apricot blooms appear in late spring or summer. Near the Cabrillo Bridge, El Prado offers a fine view of the eucalyptus forest that Sessions and other foresighted contributors to Balboa Park established and that forms such an important part of the San Diego landscape.

As the exposition's directing architect, Bertram Goodhue was largely responsible for its Churrigueresque style. In his introduction to *The Architecture and the Gardens of the San Diego Exposition* (1915), Goodhue considered the temporary buildings no more than stage scenery, providing illusion rather than reality. Although he questioned whether they would survive, Goodhue deemed a cluster of permanent buildings "the crux of the whole composition," which "should ever remain the focal and dominant point of the city when the Fair, and even the memory of the Fair, had passed utterly." Cabrillo Bridge still forms a causeway into a dream city, tower and dome emerging from a forest beyond the chasm, a landscape conjured from the past to help San Diego imagine its ideal future. As Goodhue foresaw, "when the trees and flowers that grow to such unrivalled perfection in San Diego should have attained their full magnificence, this domain would then become a public plaisance that might well be the envy of all other American cities."

(An information center in the House of Hospitality Building on El Prado has a map and other information on park facilities. Telephone 619-239-0512.)

THE BOTANICAL BUILDING, BALBOA PARK

I n all of Balboa Park's 1,200 acres, perhaps nowhere does more horticultural beauty and expertise concentrate into such a small area than in the Botanical Building. Built for the 1915 Panama-California Exposition from a design by Carleton Monroe Winslow, the Botanical Building is one of the park's historically and architecturally important structures. Many park buildings have benefited from restoration efforts, but only the Botanical Building and a few others from the 1915 Exposition have retained something like their original function.

With a long lily pond that completes it as an axial composition and reflects its dome and the screen of eucalyptus behind it, the Botanical Building forms part of one of the finest park spaces in California, perhaps in the United States. At the pedestrian promenade, El Prado, the lily pond meets three of the park's finest Spanish Colonial buildings. The surrounding vegetation—palms, camellias, and flowering trees— suggests balmy weather, pleasure, and even indulgence. Grimacing masks, quatrefoils, torches, rosettes, urns, finials, sunbursts, seashells, gourds, wheat sheaves, and grape garlands twining up the columns celebrate the exuberance of Churrigueresque ornament.

Whoever classified architecture as a branch of confectionery must have had something like the Casa de Balboa in mind, with its squiggles, as if applied from a pastry gun, slithering beneath naked caryatids with pendulous breasts and chubby waists supporting the cornices. (That these undulations might strike a *noir* note, pitched at the moment ripeness becomes rotten, was not lost on Hollywood, which with its unfailing ear in such matters filmed exteriors for *Citizen Kane* in Balboa Park. The effect might even seem sinister; from a grilled balcony above El Prado one would scarcely be surprised to witness a uniformed figure emerge to announce, from behind sunglasses, that military law would prevail until further notice.)

Yet classical architectural volumes and function—arch and arcade, pilaster and cornice—underlie all of this hedonism. The axial plan and balanced landscaping, each palm or other clustered planting balancing another on the other side of the lily pond, likewise betray a fundamental Latin rigor and symmetry, the tension being that of leisured sensuality based on a diligently rational plan. Although it would be unwise to claim absolute Hispanic cultural authenticity for buildings designed by people named Bertram Goodhue, Carleton Winslow, and Frank P. Allen, Jr., their splendid creations make it clear that here we are well outside the Calvinist culture area.

Besides celebrating the completion of the Panama Canal, the 1915 Exposition was conceived as a gathering of the Americas, the countries of the western hemisphere. San Diego's site and history, as well as the Latin American nations participating in the exposition, supported the logic of choosing this architectural style. Most buildings were intended to last only during the two-year exposition, but several have been restored more than once since then. The Botanical Building has undergone several restorations, perhaps made necessary because of its unusual materials and engineering. The Santa Fe Railroad originally intended the structure's metal arches to form the skeleton of a train station. The exposition directors purchased it unassembled and engaged Winslow to redesign it to display exotic plants.

Although its domes and balustraded bridge across the lily pond link it to surrounding architecture, the Botanical Building expresses a peculiarly twentieth-century classicism. Its twin entrances flanking the pond, its central dome and cupola, and its two wings' symmetrical, curved volumes speak in the classical idiom. Yet the Botanical Building uses twentieth-century materials and engineering, with the abstraction of redwood lath strips—a structure yet not a skin, providing shelter from sun, wind, and frost yet admitting light and air from outdoors—fitted over a steel superstructure, bolted and welded into place for all the world to see. The beauty derives not from ornamental overlay but from the structure, its materials, curves, and proportions. This beauty, intellectual in the best modernist sense, propounds a fine set of paradoxes: an indoor space remains open to the weather; classical symmetries and volumes fuse with modern structural materials and methods; and the straight lumber of lath accommodates the building's curves and domes.

Inside, similar paradoxes recur. The plants grow in a series of raised concrete block beds between beige cement paths. As it penetrates the lath *treillage*, the sunlight casts striated bars and rectangles of light and shadow. Shining silver on glossy tropical leaves, especially seen from below through lacy tree fern fronds, these stripes contrast with organic filigree. The meeting of translucent vegetation and precise engineering composes a marvelous aesthetic effect, a true unity of opposites.

The 1915 plantings by Paul G. Thiene and John Morley (superintendent of the park) contained the bananas, tree ferns, philodendrons, and palms that grow today, although an ornamental *Vitis utilis* grapevine in a glass-enclosed tropical area and an *Isolepsis* ground cover are no more. In keeping with the exposition's hemispherical theme, the horticulture was intended to evoke the Central and South American jungles. Today the planting has become more open, artful, and disciplined. Symmetrical, raised beds follow the building's lines: curving beds under the dome, rectangular paths and beds under each wing. Four tall king palms mark each corner of a square within a circular central bed; philodendrons fill in the middle level, their ropy aerial roots ascending the palms' gray trunks; while at ground level, the staff installs seasonal plantings of orchids, epiphyllum, begonias, caladiums, poinsettias, or other potted color. Throughout are the ferns for which this collection is justly famed.

The ferns are not the tallest plants in the Botanical Building; the king palms retain that honor. Nor are the ferns the only plants of towering stature; their rivals include the slender trunks topped by leafy foliage of

Lily pond and Botanical Building, Balboa Park

Cussonia spicata, an enormous umbrella of *Ficus roxburghii,* clumps of pink-ribbed bananas, and a false aralia (*Dizygotheca elegantissima*) in a shady corner. But the tree ferns grow to such size that they dominate this garden: no other California public garden offers comparable specimens. Particularly notable are the New Zealand *Cyathea dealbata,* with ten-foot trunks; its cousin, the black tree fern (*C. medullaris*), so called for its purple petioles persisting on the thirty-foot-high trunk; and even taller, resembling the black tree fern in shape, frond, and stature but having a light beige trunk, the *Alsophila australis.* Besides these tree ferns, the high, arched lath structure shelters ferns of every other size as well: six-foot Tasmanian tree ferns (*Dicksonia antarctica* and *D. fibrosa*); superb ground growers such as *Asplenium bulbiferum,* lacy and pendulous; and its very different relative, the bird's nest fern, *A. nidus,* whose four-foot, undivided fronds almost resemble banana leaves in this ideal habitat.

The palms repeat a similar size progression, from tall king palms to decades-old clumps of rhapis, their diminutive fronds topping hairy, spindly stems that lean out of shady corners. A raised bed contains two superbly grown butterfly palms (*Chrysalidocarpus lutescens*), their smooth, pale yellow-green trunks as tall as ten feet in clumps of as many stalks, part of a fine composition composed of coleus, begonias, and the pale pink, cream, and muted green foliage of the snow bush (*Breynia nivosa*). Throughout the Botanical Building appear the miniature Central American *Chamaedorea* palms: Guatamalan *C. Glaucifolia,* Honduran *C. Radicalis,* and *C. tepejilote,* its olive green, shiny trunks resembling bamboo.

Because of the shelter it offers tender tropicals, the Botanical Building refines the landscaping of the park outside with philodendrons, heliconia, ligularia, elephant ears (the rare, pale green "New World taro," *Xanthosoma maffafa,* from Ecuador), anthuriums, and several bananas (*Musa nana cavendishii; Ensete maurelii,* the Ethiopian banana, with wine-red midribs on enormous maroon and green leaves; and the vivid *Musa sumatrana* 'Zebrina' with its copper variegation). The plantings nonetheless avoid a jungle's coarse chaos, instead carefully providing foliar variety, with the striping and purple underleaves of the zebra plant (*Calathea zebrina*), the glossy, cream-and-olive variegation of *Heimerliodendron brunonianum variegatum* from Tahiti, and the hot pink and purple "blood leaf" (*Iresine lindenii*) from Ecuador.

Small but intensely hued flowers relieve this lush verdure. *Cordyline stricta* blooms in sprays of tiny lavender flowers in spring; *Ligularia gigantica* produces yellow daisies; *Pachystachys lutea* sends out golden bracts with tiny white floral tongues; cymbidium and cattleya orchids appear

Lath magic inside the Botanical Building in Balboa Park

in several groupings; and suspending potted begonias from a shady wall reveals not only their fuzzy pink and red flowers but dark red veins visible on underleaves.

Through its varied plants, the Botanical Building makes a statement about a place and a climate. The highly wrought style of surrounding buildings, axial plan, and the existence of this indoor garden argue in favor of placing Balboa Park among other fine public gardens of Europe and the Americas. The building's curving volumes gently echo the great greenhouses at Kew and the Jardin des Plantes in Paris. Its lath construction, however, indicates that the warm winters and cool summers of the San Diego climate—subtropical, marine, and said to have the lowest variation in mean temperature from winter to summer of any city in the world—do not require an artificially heated, enclosed structure. (Acknowledging the structure's paradoxes with one of his own, Winslow's *The Architecture and the Gardens of the San Diego Exposition* [1915] termed it an "open conservatory.") Other than their protection from wind and from sun, these plants are—more or less—living out of doors.

So the Botanical Building describes a friendly climate—the cool tropics, if such an oxymoron is possible—through its horticultural capabilities.The collection is enormously popular, and overheard comments by visitors reflect a widespread public knowledge and enjoyment of the area's botanical possibilities. Of course, it is quite artificial, dependent on imported water and tropical plants carefully selected to exclude rank, poisonous, or otherwise uncivilized species. These plants, moreover, do not require sweltering heat; perhaps their refinement arises from a preference for a half-shaded life under the lath. Their qualities of controlled lushness, subdued proliferation, and clean fertility produce a remarkable and splendid garden.

(The Botanical Building, Balboa Park, San Diego; admission is free; open 10:00 a.m. to 4:00 p.m.; closed Mondays, Thanksgiving, Christmas, and New Year's Day.)

SAN DIEGO ZOO

P erhaps San Diego's best-known attraction, the San Diego Zoo also contains plantings of botanical and horticultural distinction. Renowned though the zoo is for its size, innovations in housing, care, and display of wildlife, and research in zoological science, it has been said that the value of its plants exceeds even that of its exceptional animals. If the plantings remain in a supporting role, they seem destined to move closer to center stage as the zoo redesigns itself into "bioclimatic zones," displaying animal and plant species that share the same habitat in nature. Besides reflecting a shift in zoo design, the technique seeks to heighten public awareness about the futility of protecting animal species without simultaneously preserving their botanical habitat: the plants animals use for food, shelter, defense, play, mating, and nurture of the young. Already a true zoological garden, the San Diego Zoo has undertaken to become a certified botanical garden.

In *Animals and Architecture*, David Hancock termed the difference between a menagerie and a zoological garden as one of intent. The former simply offers animals to entertain the public or satisfy its curiosity. A zoological garden assumes a more serious, scientific, and socially conscious role. Besides its entertainment value—not to be disregarded, but only one of several purposes—a zoological garden maintains a research program, makes efforts to improve conditions for zoo animals, and views its own animals as linked to their wild counterparts. Through conservation, habitat protection, breeding programs, replenishment of wild animal populations, and other means, the modern zoo acts as a kind of ark to prevent extinction of endangered species, one goal of the breeding program conducted at a second facility, the San Diego Wild Animal Park.

Like so much else of interest in Balboa Park, the zoo traces its origins to the 1915 Panama-California Exposition, which assembled a small menagerie on Park Boulevard. A physician who served as surgeon to the exposition, Harry Wegeforth, is credited in 1916 with the idea of creating a zoo and forming the San Diego Zoological Society to support it. By 1922, the City had granted Balboa Park land for zoo use.

As it developed, the zoo took advantage of what had been regarded as a difficult site of mesas and canyons. The topography proved adaptable to what was then a new idea in zoological garden design. The goals of the "barless zoo," first attempted in 1907 at the private German zoo of Carl Hagenbeck, still guide contemporary zoo design: to display animals without cages through the use of moats, changes of level, pits, and other means, and to pay attention to landscaping, sight lines, and visual settings. Balboa Park's benign climate also helped realize another of Hagenbeck's principles: unlike cold-climate zoos, in San Diego many animals could be seen outdoors, another step toward a more "natural" zoo environment for both animals and people.

The San Diego Zoo's botanical wealth elaborates this naturalistic principle. Today the zoo finds itself in the midst of changes that will update the presentation of its splendid wildlife collection (3,200 animals of 777 species) and alter the landscaping (incorporating over half a million plants of some 6,000 species) of its 100-acre property. Two completed areas, Tiger River and the East African Kopje exhibit, point the way to the new zoo's bioclimatic zone principle, integrating plants and animals that would live together in the wild according to a "landscape immersion" approach.

At Tiger River, a naturalized, sloping canyon simulates a humid tropical rain forest with densely planted bamboos, palms, aroids, ferns, orchids, ginger, rarely seen tropical trees (such as the China lace tree, *Radermachera sinica*; Indian tulipwood, *Harpullia arborea*; and the medicine tree, *Rauvolfia javanica*), and vines and creepers (such as glory bower, *Clerodendrum fragrans*; Rangoon creeper, *Quisqualis indica*; and the intensely fragrant Chinese *Jasminum polyanthum*). The Tiger River plants, international in origin, are also reminders of the continuing loss of the equatorial rain forest, the world's oldest and most varied ecosystem, nurturing 40 percent of all living species packed into only 7 percent of the earth's land area.

This jungle also displays web-footed tropical water cats, the Malayan tapir, the Sumatran tiger, and underwater exhibits of turtles and an alligatorlike reptile, the false gavial. As its 9,000 plants deriving from 500 species mature, they will likely leave much of Tiger River in deep shade. With the computerized misting system—a water feature that embellishes the tropical light-and-shade under the broken canopy—the effect will seem mysterious, enclosed, and remote from other parts of the zoo. Besides preserving endangered animals, the San Diego Zoo conserves and propagates endangered tropical rain forest plants, such as mahogany, teak, orchids, palms, and ferns.

A sun-baked acre of rocky outcrops, the East African kopje—Afrikaans for "little head"—could not be more different. Designed by the firm of Jones & Jones and winner of an American Association of Zoological Parks and Aquariums design award in 1987, the kopje re-creates an isolated, geologically exposed "rock island," the head of an underground mountain emerging from the silt of surrounding plains. A haven for trees that survive on water collected in bedrock during the rainy season, the kopje's distinctive plants provide food, shade, and concealment for specialized, plant-eating birds, insects, and mammals (such as klipspringer antelopes and hydraxes, the latter a tusked, rodentlike animal that is the elephant's closest biological relative) that in turn attract unusual carnivores. The kopje's plants range from several coral trees (such as the "lucky bean," _Erythrina caffra_) and the Natal plum (_Carissa grandiflora_), a workhorse California landscaping plant here seen in something like its natural habitat, to the the storksbill or _Pelargonium_, from which the garden geranium descends.

More unusual are cycads such as _Encephalartos arenarius_, "Pride of the Cape" (_Bauhinia galpinii_), a small, twiggy, shade-growing shrub related to the more common Hong Kong orchid tree, and the candelabra tree (_Euphorbia ingens_), whose branches the Africans break off and place in streams, where its toxic sap stuns fish for an easy catch. A large "fever tree" (_Acacia xanthophloea_) marks the entrance to the kopje. So named because it grows where malaria is common, the fever tree also provides the favored retreat of leopards, who secure convenient camouflage in its yellow bark and filtered shade.

Eventually, nine areas will be redesigned along bioclimatic principles. Many of the zoo's traditional areas nevertheless contain horticulture to be enjoyed along with the animals, such as in the aviaries, the palms and eucalyptus of elephant mesa, and the beautifully matched and maintained Canary Island palms that ring waterfowl ponds containing blush-pink southern pelicans (_Pelecanthus onocrotalus_). Not surprisingly, some of the zoo's plants help feed its animals; koalas, for instance, can only sustain themselves by consuming certain eucalyptus species.

One area seems exclusively horticultural, perhaps created consciously by zoo designers as a place where visitors may retreat from animals, people, or too much sun. A steep descent into Fern Canyon from the zoo's busy entrance leads through another kind of tropical forest. Here a *Jacaranda mimosifolia* canopy creates a microclimate by shading ferns during summer and fall heat and losing their leaves by late winter to admit warmth when the ferns need it most. A watercourse runs from top to bottom, where a *Dombeya cacuminum* blooms superbly in March with pendulous, dark rose bell-flowers.

Many other plants besides ferns inhabit the canyon, mostly familiar garden plants (acanthus, *Monstera deliciosa*, clivia, bananas, callas, and camellias) but also epiphytic plants and gingers (*Hedychium gardneranum*, the kahili ginger; *Zingiber officinale*, the edible ginger found in grocery stores; and *Alpinia zerumbet*, the shell ginger). Besides some familiar ferns, the canyon also offers rarities: the epiphytic *Aglaomorpha coronans*, protected by an orchidarium housing miniature, cattleya, cymbidium, and other orchids; the Hawaiian "manfern" (*Cibotium chamissoi*); several staghorn fern species; and the exceptional black tree fern (*Cyathea medullaris*), the tallest tree fern, reaching up to sixty feet.

Unusual plants appear throughout the zoo, but even near the entrance there is an abundance of unusual specimens, such as a rare *Thunbergia mysorensis* vine hanging in ropes from an eave and blooming continually with yellow flowers marked with maroon. Across the plaza near a clichéd but fascinating flock of pink flamingos, note how the horticultural staff has grafted and otherwise encouraged aerial roots to form on a Moreton Bay fig and Kaffir fig (*Ficus nekbudu*), which ordinarily decline to assume this habit outside the tropics. Sometimes concentrated and otherwise dispersed throughout the grounds, the zoo maintains extensive collections of palms, gingers, cycads (particularly near the Warner Administration Center), bamboo, bananas, cactus (in "Dog and Cat Canyon"), eucalyptus, ficus, bromeliads, aloes, erythrinas, euphorbias, and many others.

Although not always consistent, labels appear on many plants. The vast changes that the zoo will undergo during the next decade may delay any comprehensive treatment of the plants for visitors, but the horticulture department conducts worthwhile botanical tours. The zoo's plantings fulfill many functions—shading the animals, protecting them from visitors, providing familiar surroundings, and offering a chance to browse between meals. For zoo visitors, the plantings provide education, beauty, and a sense of strangeness, even danger. That feeling concentrates the mind wonderfully, and also opens it. Modern zoos have come to see cultivating those inner, mental responses as one of their most prized achievements.

(The San Diego Zoo in Balboa Park, Park Blvd. at Zoo Place; open 365 days a year 9:00 a.m. to 5:00 p.m. in the summer, closing at 4:00 p.m. during the rest of the year; adult admission $10.75. The zoo offers animal shows, concerts and special attractions, tours, visitor services, and eating facilities. To confirm hours and for general information, telephone 619-234-3153.)

QUAIL
BOTANICAL
GARDENS

Quail Gardens offers an assortment of rare flowering plants made possible by a favored site overlooking the Pacific Ocean in northern San Diego County. In 1957, San Diego County accepted Ruth Baird Larabee's donation of her home, a twenty-five-acre parcel about a mile from the ocean, and her large collection of drought-resistant plants. (Later gifts enlarged the parcel to about thirty acres.) Like many other public gardens, Quail Gardens is located in an area supporting many horticultural businesses, some renowned and very specialized. (A single local business, for instance, supplies nearly all the world's trade in poinsettias.) The proximity to such businesses (clustering in the immediate neighborhood and up the coast as far as Vista), the fine climate, and a high level of horticultural interest among north county residents all contribute to the remarkable range of unusual plants grown at Quail Gardens.

Drawing freely on the state's mythic climate, many California gardens make the claim that something blooms every month of the year. Although seldom utterly false, often the truth must squeak in under the guise of little more than a floral technicality. Quail Gardens, however, can claim a genuinely year-round floral display, as shown by plants near its entry lawn: the "poor man's rhododendron" (*Impatiens oliveri*), with light violet flowers; *Dombeya walichii* from Madagascar, its spherical pink flowers reminiscent of hydrangeas but suspended overhead in a small tree from late autumn through January; the Ecuadorean "purple tobacco" (*Iochroma cyaneum*); and fragrant kahili ginger (*Hedychium gardneranum*) from tropical Asia, blooming with pale yellow flowers through November.

Besides these rarities, Quail Gardens displays more common plants such as azaleas, camellias, aloes, crimson Turk's cap (*Malvaviscus arboreus*), the Hong Kong orchid tree, and *Mandevilla* "Alice DuPont." Most fill beds around the central lawn, shaded by southern magnolia, the Australian dammar pine (*Agathis robusta*), Monterey cypress, Cook's pine (*Araucaria columnaris*), and the African tulip tree, blooming in dense clusters of deep, brilliant orange trumpet flowers in autumn. In addition to low-growing, flowering plants such as Pride of Madeira and *Crinum moorei*, the beds also contain tropical bromeliads; two immense *Anthurium schlechtendahlii* with five-foot-long leaves; a rare traveler's tree (*Ravenala madascariensis*), making a fan of bananalike leaves above a palmlike trunk; and a "Maguey del Cumbre" (*Agave atrovirens*) from Mexico.

The path from the lawn follows the sound of water: a deck overlooks the falls and rocky watercourse of the Mildred McPherson Waterfall, which forms the first phase of a projected pan-tropical section. Tropical plants cover each bank of a small gorge with cycads, bananas, *Ficus religiosa* and *F. duriculata*, philodendron, king palms, Australian tree ferns, tupidanthus, bromeliads, and an outstanding Kashmir cypress (*Cupressus cashmeriana*), whose evergreen, weeping habit perfectly suits this tropical dell. Unlike the plants around the entry lawn, this display achieves a tropical effect not with rare species but with the cumulative effect of familiar plants, massed dramatically in a gorge of rushing water.

A staircase descends into the small canyon along the watercourse, where Tasmanian tree ferns, elephant's ear, and other palms, ferns,

A cool fern garden beneath Hollywood junipers, Quail Botanical Gardens

philodendrons, and aroids extend the tropical theme. The lower canyon offers blooming plants: a white-flowered angel's trumpet; *Abutilons* such as "Tangelo," flowering bright orange-red; *Osmanthus fragrans*, the East Asian "fragrant olive," whose tiny white flowers belie their powerful, sweet-and-spicy fragrance; and red-orange, tubular blossoms of the Mexican fountain bush (*Russelia equisetiformis*).

Below a bridge across the creek, the path enters a palm canyon that concentrates many rare palms: the Mexican (*Sabal mexicana*) and Santo Domingo palmettos (*S. unbraculifera*); the saw palmetto (*Serenoa repens*); the Himalayan *Trachycarpus wagnerianus* and *T. takil var. nana*; the Taiwan fish tail palm, *Arenga engleri*; and the Egyptian gingerbread palm, *Hyphenae thebaica*. The palms are interplanted with *Rhododendron laetum* (producing golden blooms on small trusses); the Himalayan "mandarin's hat" (*Holmskioldia sanguinea*) bearing copper bracts and rusty red tubular flowers; and Philippine violet (*Barleria cristata*), a mounded shrub covered with one-inch single violet flowers.

At the property's western edge, a desert garden overlooks the greenhouses of Encinitas to the Pacific Ocean, making an unusual backdrop for desert plantings of palo verde; a massive tangle of garambullo (*Myrtillocactus geometrizans*); the Mexican *Cephalocereus polylophus*, a columnar cactus resembling the giant saguaro; and "spurge" (*Euphorbia canariensis*), an eight-foot-wide clump of 100 slender stems. Other specialized collections include what has been called the best bamboo collection in the United States, cultivated by the American Bamboo Society. Its species range from the unusual "square bamboo" (*Chimonobambusa quadrangularis*), so named for its distinctly four-sided stems, about twelve feet high but only half an inch thick, to the vigorous *Bambusa beecheyana*, with green and light gold trunks five inches in diameter and thirty feet tall—a monster.

From this western, seaside exposure a driveway curves through a well-regarded hibiscus collection. A subtropical fruit garden, sponsored by the California Rare Fruit Growers, contains unusual fruit and nut trees to illustrate the possibilities for edible home landscaping, from the increasingly well known macadamia to the less familiar East Indian carambola (*Averrhoa carambola*), the candlenut or "Kikui" (*Aleurites moluccana*), and the "Jambolan plum" (*Syzygium cumini*) from India.

Near this area, an exotic herb garden contains South Asian culinary herbs. Under a spreading Mysore fig tree, an old-fashioned garden displays bedding annuals and a few old roses (such as "Madame Alfred Carrière" (1879) and "Duchesse de Brabant" (1857). On Quail Gardens' western slope, local begonia and fern societies have planted a walled garden, shielded from ocean winds by a barrier of old Hollywood junipers. Begonias fill hedged beds on three sides of a small lawn, accompanied by a bank of _Ceratozamia longifolia_ cycad and ferns: the bird's nest fern with its undivided fronds, a tangled bank of the contrasting, deeply divided leatherleaf fern (_Rumohra adiantiformis_), a great staghorn fern suspended from a weeping bottle brush (_Callistemon viminalis_), and black tree ferns (_Cyathea medullaris_).

This small walled garden has interesting proportions, even if the junipers screen the ocean view. Here and elsewhere Quail Gardens has not yet realized the aesthetic potential of its excellent site, although development continues. Nevertheless, it has used the property well in other ways, particularly by selecting unusual plants. If this mostly informal garden at present lacks a degree of polish or finish, it nonetheless ranks very high among southern California public gardens as a place where one may encounter plants seen nowhere else in the region. Some public gardens with fine sites remain content to grow what is familiar. Quail Gardens, by contrast, offers something for the connoisseur, making an adventurous and largely successful attempt to grow what is rare and unusual.

(Quail Botanical Gardens, 230 Quail Gardens Dr., Encinitas; exit Interstate 5 on Encinitas Blvd., and travel a half-mile east to Quail Gardens Dr. Admission is free; $1.00 parking. Open 8:00 a.m. to 5:00 p.m. daily, including holidays. Gift shop and plant sales 11:00 a.m. to 3:00 p.m., Wednesday through Sunday. Tours are given Saturdays at 10:00 a.m.; group tours by appointment. For information, telephone the Quail Gardens Foundation at 619-436-3036.)

SAN DIEGO
WILD ANIMAL
PARK

Many of the goals and themes governing the display of animals and plants at the San Diego Zoo in Balboa Park reappear at the San Diego Wild Animal Park, with one important difference. Sited on three square miles in a fairly remote area, the wild animal park is devoted mainly to breeding and raising endangered animals. (The Zoological Society of San Diego operates both facilities.) While it has many of the entertainment features associated with zoos—bird, elephant, and "animal antics" shows—it also features an Animal Care Center (for raising small mammals and orphaned animals), contact with keepers as they care for the animals, and a 5-mile guided rail tour around the park's largest area, which contains over 2,000 animals running relatively freely through several hundred acres.

The wild animal park's botany and horticulture likewise resemble that of the San Diego Zoo in some ways. The plants feed some of the animals, and the landscaping tries to provide natural surroundings for the animals and evoke the wild habitat for visitors. In some ways, however, the wild animal park emphasizes its plants more strongly than the zoo. Besides a retail nursery selling rare plants, the wild animal park devotes considerable space to permanent horticultural and botanical exhibits that are presented without reference to animals.

Visitors enter through the double doors of the Borthwick Flight Cage, containing brilliantly colored rare birds that whizz and dive through a free-form aviary composed of wooden telephone poles and netting. The aviary also offers the first glimpse of the park's tropical vegetation: fishtail and king palms, and tree ferns, ginger, bananas, philodendron, ficus, tupidanthus, and other trees in whose limbs and crotches birds make their nests.

Beyond the aviary lies Nairobi Village, the busiest part of the park, with shops, the Nairobi Plant Trader nursery, a children's petting kraal, live animal shows, and the rail tour departure area. Nairobi Village mixes garden-variety flowering plants (geranium, red salvia, ageratum) with vining _Bauhinia punctata_, the cape chestnut tree, and a grove of African fever trees (_Acacia xanthophloea_), whose smooth, golden green trunks support fierce thorns on upper branches that shade a dining area called Thorn Tree Terrace. Wooden structures give Nairobi Village a rustic, vaguely African hardscape, with log and pole trellises, huts conically thatched with palm fronds, and wooden staircases, barriers, fences, flower beds, and viewing platforms. Cycads, tree aloes, and proteas appear doubly exotic as they overlook ring-tailed lemurs or a pond containing the exotic "crowned crane" (_Balaerica pavonia reglorum_), whose graceful body is surmounted by a glamorous topknot of golden feathers.

The park contains a wide variety of specialized botanical areas. The Australian Rain Forest Sensorial Trail travels under a eucalyptus canopy past acacia, brachychitons, king palms, the spongy-barked _Melaleuca quinquenervia_, vining _Kennedia nigricans_, and bird's nest, staghorn, and tree ferns, many labeled in Braille. Bronze bird sculptures correspond to plants and birds exhibited in cages. Nearby, across from the cheetah enclosure, lies an intensively cultivated herb garden containing myrtles, sweet woodruff, Mexican tarragon, peppermint geranium, and many other herbs on a terraced hillside.

A hiking trail leads through the Helen Chamlee Native Plant Garden, which supports thriving evergreen Torrey pines, California ironwood, incense cedar, and Monterey cypress. The path leads past the Sumatran tiger enclosure and a timber bamboo screen before reaching Simba Outpost, where a young protea collection in a sunken amphitheater forms a landscape almost like a rock garden.

Up another hill, the park's primary horticultural area, the Kupanda Falls Botanical Center, covers twenty-five acres and is expanding, with a California Nativescape area under development. Each existing unit is marked by a plaque and other information describing the specialty and sponsorship provided by local horticultural societies. The Nicholas T. Mirov Conifer Arboretum honors the botanist and author of _The Genus Pinus_ (1967) and with Jean Hasbrouck, _The Story of Pines_ (1976). Its 1,500 specimens include not only pines, but also cypresses, cedars, sequoias, several _Araucarias_, and other evergreens. It contains many beautiful specimens, both familiar and rare, such as the weeping Kashmir cypress (_Cupressus cashmeriana_), the Italian cypress (_C. sempervirens_), the majestic cedar of Lebanon (_Cedrus libani_), and tropical pines such as the West Indian _Pinus caribaea_.

Leaving the evergreens, the trail arrives at a rushing stream lined by dwarf conifers, where a creek trail passes several plant collections. In the Epiphyllum House, iridescent, ten-inch-wide flowers make an exceptional display during May and June. Hundreds of these tropical, epiphytic cacti—relatives of the spiny desert species, a kinship easily observed in their blossoms—grow under shade cloth in pots suspended from overhead pipes, trailing their flat, spineless leaf stems.

A *torii*, the distinctive Japanese ceremonial gateway, marks the Bonsai House. A "tray tree," miniaturized by withholding water and by root and shoot pruning, bonsai tries to achieve an effect of "asymmetrical balance" to evoke the serenity of a natural setting. Any species, not just Asian evergreens, can be bonsai subjects, whether a California juniper, a European olive, or Algerian ivy. With informational plaques describing the bonsai art, tools used for pruning, shaping, and scarring, and several bonsai design types, the Bonsai House displays the largest bonsai collection in the western United States.

Past a row of *Livistona* palms and a cream-yellow *Chorisia insignis*, the Fuchsia House displays some 2,000 fuchsias representing 500 species and subspecies planted in the ground and suspended in pots. The fuchsias are pruned in the fall, although a few remain in bloom later in shades of purple, red, salmon, and hot to palest pink. Humidified by a waterfall and a small creek, the lush Fuchsia House garden also contains cycads, ferns, rhapis palms, clivia, and philodendrons.

Through the conifer arboretum and past an area under development for a bromeliad display, the park's Baja California garden reputedly houses the world's largest collection of Baja California cacti among its 2,000 plants. A collection of Boojum trees (*Idria columnaris*), the dark green, spiny *Agave shawii*, and the salmon-pink, clawlike blooms of candelilla (*Pedilanthus macrocarpus*) show the range of Baja plants grown here.

Several areas in development indicate the San Diego Wild Animal Park's commitment to provide space for local gardeners to create specialized horticultural exhibits to educate and delight visitors. Some of these gardens breed and preserve endangered plants, resembling the wild animal park's animal breeding successes. The extent to which endangered plants and animals alike can be propagated or preserved enhances the likelihood of life surviving on our planet.

(The San Diego Wild Animal Park, located east of Escondido in northern San Diego County; exit Interstate 15 at Via Rancho Parkway, and follow signs to the park. For information on hours and admission prices, telephone 619-234-6541. Facilities include shops and a plant nursery, restaurants, entertainment and educational presentations, photographic, monorail, and children's tours, and hiking trails.)

SAN DIEGO
BRIEFLY NOTED

B efore the eastern facade of the SAN DIEGO COUNTY AD-
MINISTRATION CENTER, a low-water-use garden displays flowering, drought-resistant plants: the cold blue of
California lilac (*Ceanothus* "Julia Phelps"); the deep rose of the
Hong Kong orchid; and yellow, single flowers on a spreading *Fremon-
todendron* "California Glory." The clean planes of the 1930s "P.W.A.
Moderne" building highlight a row of expertly pruned *Podocarpus
gracilior* trees. Underplanted camellia, impatiens, and calla lilies, twin circular ponds in an entry terrace, and lawns candidly suggest, however,
that extremism in the pursuit of low water use is no virtue. Palms,
cycads, and philodendrons contribute to a lushness that the building's
western grounds do not contradict. Indeed, the western garden—views
of San Diego Bay from wide lawns set with leaning Senegal date palms,
yuccas, and philodendrons—offers an essay in simple but elegant coastal
landscaping. (San Diego County Administration Center, Pacific Highway at Cedar Street, downtown San Diego.)

A sense of adventure pervades the NAIMAN TECH CENTER JAP-
ANESE GARDEN, screened from the glass and gray corrugated metal
of surrounding office buildings by coast redwoods and deodar cedars.
The garden offers one solution to the problem of distinguishing these
usually interchangeable office complexes. In the southern part of the Japanese garden, the play of gravel footpaths against a stone-dry riverbed,
manicured lawns and shaggy mondo grass berms, boulders emerging
like the islands of an archipelago in a turfy sea, and flowering azaleas
and magnolias against junipers and small pruned pines suggest a modern, pared-down version of the ancient Japanese garden art: not a stone
lantern or Buddha to be found.

The garden's less interesting middle third, however, trots out the conventional pagoda, bamboo-tipping fountain, and waterfalls that drain
into a koi-filled pond next to a restaurant-teahouse. A fencelike screen

of golden-stemmed bamboo—something of a comment on surrounding, fairly colorless structures—forms one border of the six-acre garden, whose northern third loses focus in two contemporary amenities, a sand volleyball area and tennis court. (Naiman Tech Center, 9605 Scranton Road, San Diego, two blocks north of Mira Mesa Blvd., east of the 805 freeway.)

Although many plants outside MISSION SAN DIEGO DE ALCALA are anachronistic, they sketch the colorful, dry plant lexicon associated with the mission gardening style: pale orange aloe torches, rusty green loquat leaves, scarlet bougainvillea, and blue agave spears. Inside the first and largest of the mission's three courtyards, the silver dollar plant (_Cotyledon orbiculata_) blooms with bell-shaped orange flowers around a stalk near epiphyllum cacti climbing into California pepper trees (_Schinus molle_, a South American species introduced up the coast at Mission San Luis Rey by the mission fathers). The peppers ring the courtyard's walls, which are covered with pink oleander, hibiscus, and the fiery orange flame vine (_Pyrostegia venusta_).

A high-ceilinged, dark sanctuary opens into the second courtyard's bright sunlight, whitewashed and arcaded and with a shrine to St. Joseph, the patron saint of the Spanish expedition to the area and for whom San Diego was named. Canary Island palms shade the garden's climbing bougainvillea, plumbago, and pigeon berry (_Duranta repens_), simultaneously bearing tiny, blue-violet flowers and chains of golden orange berries.

The "Pietà garden," the smallest, shadiest courtyard, contains tupidanthus, tree bird of paradise, _Podocarpus gracilior_, and a single Australian tree fern reaching hopefully beyond the shade cast by high walls. Wax begonias, philodendron, a pygmy date palm, clivia, and callas grow at ground level. Good maintenance and labeling invite visitors to appreciate the mission horticulturally. Father Junipero Serra founded the San Diego Mission in 1769 on a site nearer the coast. (It was moved here five years later.) The environs of this first mission in Alta California are now entirely suburbanized, and though it may not be as evocative as some others, its mild-climate version of the mission style and its differently scaled courtyards are worth a visit. (Mission San Diego de Alcala, 10818 San Diego Mission Rd., San Diego; telephone 619-281-8449. $1.00 adult admission.)

Up the coast in Encinitas, gilded domes and _Washingtonia robusta_ palms mark the Retreat and Hermitage of THE SELF-REALIZATION FELLOWSHIP. Its golden lotus towers recall the sacred _Nelumbo_, whose blossoms incline toward the heavens unsullied by the mud around its roots: an Indian symbol of a soul's progress, by meditation, beyond earth and body into the freedoms of consciousness. Presented in 1936 to Paramahansa Yogananda, the 17-acre property is operated by the religious organization dedicated to his teachings. Yogananda brought India's science of meditation to the West and lived here during his final years, during which he planted many specimens in the small but choice meditation garden and directed its landscaping. (Swami's, a local surfing beach just south of the property, is also named for Yogananda.)

From the entry gate, a beautifully mortared staircase climbs the bluff past a large princess flower shrub, a spreading ficus, and olive trees. People meditate in this garden's corners, within the sound of water from fountains, streams, and ponds. A canopy of ancient Hollywood junipers at the crest of the coastal palisade lifts the fresh, cool ocean breeze above underplanted flowers and ferns and keeps the garden in sun and shade. Flowering cyclamen, plumeria, hawthorne, impatiens, camellias, clivia, and the pink trumpet flowers of *Mandevilla* make an almost showy display under the junipers' tortuous branches and pungently fragrant, dark green needles.

The garden is terraced with pink-beige sandstone that also forms the staircases and paths. It also edges the pools that teem with ornamental koi whose bright orange scales match flaming pyracantha berries during autumn. The garden offers fine views of the Pacific Ocean north and south for ten and twenty miles in clear weather. Whether visited briefly or apprehended with contemplative discipline, this small garden beautifully illustrates the spiritual properties of ornamental horticulture. (Self-Realization Fellowship Meditation Gardens, K St. west of 2nd St., Encinitas. Free admission; open Tuesday through Saturday 9:00 a.m. to 5:00 p.m., Sundays 11:00 a.m. to 5:00 p.m.; closed Mondays and holidays. Retreat office telephone: 619-753-1811.)

II
South Coast
and
Orange County

Sherman Gardens

SHERMAN LIBRARY AND GARDENS

Ample proof that good things come in small packages, Sherman Gardens illustrates a second maxim: it is better to do a few things well than many things indifferently. A small gem, Sherman Gardens offers a botanical collection of the highest quality and beauty on two acres not far from the Pacific Ocean. The garden and library, funded by the Sherman Foundation and named for Moses H. Sherman, date from 1966. Like Henry Huntington, Sherman profited from sales of real estate he made valuable by bringing electric railways from Los Angeles to Pasadena, Hollywood, and—"Sherman's march to the sea"—Santa Monica. Huntington's Pacific Electric later bought Sherman's rail lines, and in 1905 the two joined other well-placed speculators in a syndicate that acquired 108,000 acres in the San Fernando Valley. Los Angeles voters were convinced to pay for a project to deliver water even though the San Fernando Valley was not yet part of the city. The Owens Valley aqueduct arrived in 1913. Property values leaped. Sherman sat on the Los Angeles Water Board throughout the proceedings.

Given these events, the Sherman Library's description of itself as a research center devoted to the Pacific Southwest, emphasizing "the spectacular transformation of this region that has occurred over the past one hundred years," does not entirely lack a disingenuous quality. Historical cynicism aside, Sherman Gardens illustrates a key theme that fueled the southern California myth: the beauty of the climate. With the crucial addition of water, that climate fostered several horticultural styles that symbolized a new way of living: tropical gardening, year-round flowers, exotic plants, and dry climate plants of the desert Southwest.

Sherman Gardens pursues each of these horticultural styles and also presents several fine specialized collections. Its compact scale and garden structures also make it a kind of essay in the suburban garden. (Until recently, suburban living was another theme that the southern California myth seemed to promise.) Sherman Gardens' superb horticulture and garden structures, however, heighten suburban living to something approaching elegance, a rare quality in the usual tract property. Finally, the planting and maintenance at Sherman Gardens attain a level scarcely seen elsewhere, adding another argument in favor of establishing priorities and sacrificing vast extent in order to achieve superior quality.

Somehow myth has come to mean something false, rather than something people believe in and which motivates them to think, feel, and act. But at least one element of the mythic southern California climate is true; the flowers blooming at Sherman Gardens during every month of the year prove it can be done. An emphasis on floral color unites many disparate parts of the garden, from beds crowded with summer marigolds or blue salvia to calendula, varicolored primula, or cream and pink Iceland poppies in the winter. Beds under pergolas and lath shelters display cyclamen, impatiens, camellias and azaleas, and heliotrope. Sherman Gardens also specializes in hanging plants; around a fountain courtyard hang baskets of ivy-leaved geranium, begonia, and fuchsia, the latter especially fine in this marine climate only a few blocks from the ocean.

Flowering vines clamber throughout the grounds, with bougainvillea, cup-of-gold vine, an old wisteria, and *Mandevilla* "Alice du Pont," the latter bearing bright pink trumpet flowers on green, glossy foliage. The garden also contains flowering coral, bottlebrush, and floss silk trees and white, rose, and creamy golden varieties of angel's trumpet. The interest in color extends into varieties planted for their foliage; a particularly fine example appears outdoors at each inset corner of the tropical greenhouse, as the Indonesian "blood banana" (*Musa zebrina*) displays its light green leaves, variegated with maroon splotches worthy of abstract expressionist art.

Inside a greenhouse, foliar color reaches its height. Southern California horticulture has traditionally imported tropical plants. It is true that many steps can be taken in this direction, as illustrated by kahili ginger, pink-stemmed blue Mexican fig (*Ficus petiolaris*), false aralia (*Dizygotheca elegantissima*), and various philodendrons, with their glossy, deeply incised leaves. Yet the climate remains too cool in winter and dry in summer for most true tropicals. Hence this greenhouse provides the warmth and humidity necessary for a splendid show of tropical flowers, bracts, and foliage. The collection offers anthurium species; a bed of bromeliads with bracts of hot orange and cool rose; cape primroses, African violets,

the tiny orange flowers of _Episcia,_ and other gesneriads; and a fine collection of richly flowering orchids.

The greenhouse also sketches the infinite shapes, textures, and
shades of tropical foliage. The outstanding display offers the purple
stems of Indonesian torch ginger (_Nicolia elatior_), bearing leaves veined
and edged with mahogany and beige; the roses, creams, and deep reds
of fancy-leaved caladium; the deep purples of Irisine, the burgundy of
"Prince Albert philodendron," and the purple-stemmed elephant ear;
and the foliage patterns of Alocasias, creamy veins contrasting with

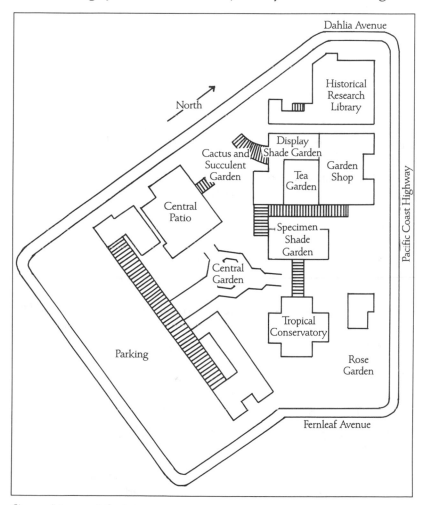

Sherman Library and Gardens

shiny gray-green leaves, a similar variegation occurring in zebra-striped *Vresia* bromeliads. Vines, the fronds of African elephant's ear ferns (*Platycerium angolense*), and the sage green, lacy foliage of Spanish moss overhang this foliar carnival. Croton (*Codiaeum variegatum*), the common houseplant, here achieves an over-the-top extravaganza of yellows, pinks, and oranges.

A wisteria-draped pergola links the greenhouse to its less sheltered counterpart, a similarly proportioned lath house left open to the air save for a clear plastic barrier against the sea breeze. Instead of the greenhouse's added heat, the lath house protects plants against sun and wind. Its ferns are especially fine, less because of their rarity than because in these protected conditions the Australian tree ferns, bird's nest ferns, and blond tree ferns (*Cibotium glaucum*) acquire a size and perfection they seldom do in an outdoor garden. Half a dozen *Howea forsteriana* palms, for instance, have grown through the roof.

The greenhouse, lath house, and pergolas at Sherman Gardens appear to reflect Gertrude Jekyll's ideas on the best color for such structures. She thought the usual white paint produced a glaring, "deplorable effect" and advised instead a "quiet warm gray" or Portland stone color, a suggestion that appears to have been followed throughout Sherman Gardens. One such covered passage extends along the geranium courtyard and its tiled central fountain. It shelters benches of potted begonias, cymbidium orchids, and other shade plants, before reaching a large patio shaded by an ancient California pepper tree.

The pepper's filtered shade above a tiled patio oversees a gradual transition from the cool lushness of ferns to an array of potted epiphyllum specimens hung from a lath wall. These tropical cacti point the way toward Sherman Gardens' dry garden, a small but choice display of desert plants from the arid zones that dominate so much of the Pacific Southwest and south into Latin America. (It also serves as a reminder that Moses Sherman co-owned a 700,000-acre desert ranch extending from the Imperial Valley into northern Mexico.) Among its notable plants are the Mexican grass tree (*Dasylirion longissimus*), a gray-green *Agave parryi huachensis*, and the unusual "Madagascar palm" (*Pachypodium lamieri*), not a palm but a relative of the oleander, a relationship revealed in the topknot of leaves emerging from the tip of its bare, spine-covered trunk.

Across a courtyard to the rear of the garden, another pergola shelters hanging staghorn ferns and a beautifully groomed cycad collection. It includes *Dioon spinulosum* from eastern Mexico, a fine *Lepidozamia peroff-*

skyana, and a *Macrozamia moorei* cultivated in perfect conditions that produce fresh, dark-green fronds on this refined cycad. Elsewhere the gardens display small rose and herb collections, and at every turn its fountains, patios, seating, and structures suggest ideas for residential outdoor living space. Sherman Gardens can be interpreted as a set of cultural and horticultural symbols, extending botanical themes into the history and myth of the region and representing something of its way of life. It can also be approached on a practical level, as it offers plants, design ideas, and structures for use at home. Analysis, however, must not overlook the plain matter of Sherman Gardens' great beauty and finish and its more than 1,000 species, carefully chosen, planted, and maintained. Sherman Gardens remains one of California's most aesthetically lively and satisfying gardens.

(Sherman Library and Gardens, 2647 East Pacific Coast Highway, Corona del Mar; open 10:30 a.m. to 4:00 p.m.; $2.00 adult admission. Sherman Gardens offers light lunches served outdoors under the geraniums and fuchsias; a book, plant, and gift shop; and lectures and classes in horticulture and other subjects throughout the year. For information, telephone 714-673-2261.)

Hortense Miller Garden

Overlooking the Pacific Ocean from a steep coastal canyon, Hortense Miller's garden offers a series of unfolding views and horticultural rarities. Although in a sense this is a backyard garden, the property has little sense of front and back. In time-honored California fashion, the garden surrounds every side of the house (built in 1959), even penetrating the dwelling itself where a breezeway garden intercedes between distinct living and sleeping areas. It is also a more sizable property than that of most residences, and a sloping site with expansive views causes its 2.5 acres to seem even larger. Finally, there is the matter of those views, extending inland across and up an undeveloped, chaparral-covered coastal canyon and down and through eucalyptus to the sailing craft that plough and furrow the rippling blue plane of the Pacific.

The unusual arrangement by which the public can visit also distinguishes this residential garden. Miller lives in the house and maintains the garden, but the Friends of the Hortense Miller Garden (a community support group) and the City of Laguna Beach conduct excellent tours. The tour begins from the highest point on the property, descending a stairway through an area burned in a 1979 fire that raced through the canyon and consumed much of the garden as it then existed. It is part of Miller's philosophy, however, to allow nature to restore what it had so quickly and fearsomely destroyed. And as she wrote in *The Garden Writings of Hortense Miller* (1990), only seventeen days after the fire some forty-five different plant species had already emerged. Moreover, the fire dislodged, fertilized, cooked, and otherwise jolted dozens of wildflower seeds into germination and bloom the following season, a display not seen before—or since.

Experimentalism, the willingness to let natural cycles and processes establish the plants, thus forms a key element of Miller's philosophy.

Although her garden contains far more exotic than native species, the feeling is one of plants that need no coddling and are fundamentally suited to these admittedly favored coastal conditions. Initially, the tour passes such specimens as the blue-flowered _Ipomea leari,_ a morning glory vine growing up a Canary Island pine whose charred bark eleven years later still bears fire scars; fuzzy, pale orange lion's tail (_Leonotis leonurus_); white and gold-flowering rock rose under blue-lavender ceanothus; and the silver-green foliage of _Euphorbia rigida._

As the path descends, the rectangular outlines of the residence gradually emerge. Flat-roofed, perched on the canyon lip with a deck that cantilevers to obtain ocean views, the house opens onto level areas away from the canyon. In the first of these, the finely cut, blue-silver foliage of _Gonospermum canariensis_ and _Artemesia_—Miller calls the latter "plants that catch the light"—establishes a color rhyme with immature gray-blue foliage of a _Eucalyptus cinerea_ waving overhead. Through a bamboo gate, something of this garden's scope and variety emerges as small garden spaces progress successively to larger ones.

Here the house forms a U-shaped courtyard whose fourth side slopes up to a summer house. Not unlike the severe (if refined) style of Miller's house—horizontal lines, glass, straight edges, and flat roof, which is how

A view down the canyon to the ocean, Hortense Miller Garden

they built progressive dwellings in southern California during the Case Study Program years of the 1950s—the summer house and its painted geometric abstractions contrast starkly with surrounding plants. Dark-green Korean grass makes a bumpy apron below a seating area under a western sycamore, a jacaranda, and a pink-flowered locust (*Robinia ambigua "Decaisneana"*). Miller once counted forty-seven climbing plants on her property; the courtyard shelters flowering vines such as star jasmine, bougainvillea, white trumpet flowers of *Pandorea jasminoides*, and from under the breezeway, blood red trumpet vine (*Distictis buccinatoria*) planted against a screen of knotted jute.

The tour route causes the house and property to unfold in something like reverse order. The home's true entrance, ornamented with architectural candor by thick beams and two-by-four lath, a metal screen, and a checkerboard brick-and-gap wall, has a superb weeping red bottle-brush tree (*Callistemon viminalis*). Along the driveway grow a scandent *Bauhinia galpinii*, the stout trunk of an *Erythyrina caffra* coral tree, and the fragrant, weeping gray-green foliage of the peppermint tree (*Agonis flexuosa*).

Under a California pepper tree across the driveway, the Pacific Ocean paints a background as the path curls around a bed of bromeliads, calla lilies, ferns, and *Mackaya bella*, an evergreen South African shrub producing pale lavender flowers marked by darker lines in the throat. Above the yawning canyon, pale yellow Lady Banks' roses clamber over the house, as do the Belle of Portugal rose and the yellow trumpet flowers of cat's claw vine (*Macfadyena unguis-cati*). Just below the house is a perennial flower garden, with *Verbascum*, pink *Dierama*, daylilies, coreopsis, geraniums, crinum lilies and hybrids, Chinese maples, and penstemons. Thus begins the garden's largest area.

Crisscrossed by paths of dirt and redwood rounds, traversed by sandstone or railroad tie staircases, accommodated by sheltered seating areas, and terraced by riprap, the vast slope merges native and exotic plants, offers views of house, garden, canyon, and ocean, and represents a kind of adventure in the space and time of nature, wild and domesticated. Miller's writings confirm that she prizes a garden left alone as much as possible. She does admit both the necessity of added water and the difficulty of gardening with California native plants. These two candid departures from the current horticultural party line prove that Miller gardens, and thinks, for herself. Versailles, her bête noire, belongs to an owner who will not garden, who ruthlessly subordinates plants to an architectural stage set, and whose interest in power and control yields "an enormous plan, a lot of empty space, straight lines, grass flat, trees in lines all clipped, and water confined."

The yang of this catalog of Bourbon horticultural error implies Miller's positive antitheses. Her garden values unusual, distinctive plants; a humane scale; an informal profusion that capitalizes on nature's accidents and serendipity; changes of level and lines that curve, cross, and coil; and water, where it runs, left unimpeded. On reaching the area below the house, the true extent of the garden becomes apparent in a naturalistic planting of California natives—the white flowers of the Matilija poppy, coast redwood, and yellow _Fremontodendron_—and exotics suited to the coastal climate, such as the African linden (_Sparmannia africana_), tree aloes, the blue-lavender trumpet flowers of _Thunbergia grandiflora_, yellow _Spuria_ iris, the pale chartreuse flowers of _Crotalaria capensis_, and lavender, curiously curly flowers of the snail vine (_Vigna caracalla_).

Letting her plants proceed with added water but otherwise with a minimum of interference, Miller has created a garden of considerable beauty. Although she is not infrequently pleased to find the result aesthetic, she keeps other goals in mind. Aware of issues as transcendental as the relatedness of all life as well as the political issues of overpopulation and overdevelopment, Hortense Miller captures much of macrocosmic nature in her garden microcosm. To paraphrase Thoreau, she has traveled extensively in Laguna Beach. The testing of fire and flood, the constant labor and gardening successes and failures, and the hint of pagan, mortal time concealed within each blooming flower and ripened berry exclude any element of sentimentality from Hortense Miller's garden. Besides its qualities of beauty, toughness, and botanical range, her garden also creates the sense—unfortunately fairly rare in southern California—of being suited to its place.

(The Hortense Miller Garden may be visited by reservation only; admission is free. For reservations and directions, contact the Laguna Beach Recreation & Social Services Dept., 505 Forest Ave., Laguna Beach, CA 92651; telephone 714-497-0716. Contact Friends of the Hortense Miller Garden at P.O. Box 742, Laguna Beach, CA 92652-0742.)

DISNEYLAND

Orange County's most famous symbol also happens to have unusual gardens. Few people go to Disneyland for its plants, interesting though they can be; admission is too costly and the park simply too crowded and too busy. But if you do visit Disneyland for fun, pause occasionally to note the skillful main-tenance, expert horticulture, and cunning landscaping. Members of a notable family of Los Angeles plantsmen, Jack Evans and Morgan Evans, originally designed and installed the park's sixty-five landscaped acres. (Morgan Evans, who landscaped Walt Disney's own estate in Holmby Hills, has been associated with Disney parks around the world since Disneyland first opened in 1955.) Any number of effects set the stage for Disneyland's intensively modified reality, especially the ani-mal topiary (Walt Disney himself initiated the topiary program), floral panels of Mickey and other Disney characters near the entrance, and Burle Marx swirls of carpet-bedded annuals.

In *The Poetics of Gardens*, Moore, Mitchell, and Turnbull make a case for placing Disney in the company of Hearst, Huntington, and Getty—wealthy California collectors of art, architecture, and gardens. Those connoisseurs of high art, however, sought aesthetic repose, a timeless atmosphere of beauty in quiet, scenic surroundings. As a showman, Disney craved motion, sequence, and surprise to entertain his audience and thrill it if he can. Disney aspired to a total, even Wagnerian art environ-ment, ideally producing not only dramatic effect but altered conscious-ness. Like the other elements in the Disneyland caldron—technology, speed, lighting, music, architecture, futurism, history, children's literature—horticulture performs an illusionistic supporting role, shifting styles and allusive plant materials to encourage an effect or subliminally enhance an environment.

The park comprises seven "themed lands"—for example, Frontierland, Tomorrowland, and Fantasyland—plotted so as never to confront the visitor with more than two choices. The horticulture shifts as the thematic sector does, dressing the set to elicit the intended audience response. Palo verde and other desert plants recall the parched Southwest around Thunder Mountain's runaway mining train; riparian and forest plants bend lushly into a (circular) Mississippi along a steamboat ride; and deodar cedars (a Himalayan rather than a Swiss evergreen, but true art never lets mere accuracy cramp its style) cluster about an Alpine chalet that suspends passengers in skybuckets and dispatches them along cables through a steel and concrete Matterhorn. The wittiest composition, a sculptural assemblage of chrome and plastic trays at the Main Street entrance to Tomorrowland, holds spears of spiny, stripped-down, futuristic bromeliads and cacti: an ominous warning about the tomorrow our technologies prod us toward, a leafless, prickly future in which only tough, well-armed plants survive.

Some of the rides offer outstanding horticultural set design. Boats entering Monstro the Whale's dark mouth emerge from that potential trauma into the transfigured sunlight of Storybook Land, where miniature characters peep from a landscape of dwarf conifers and tiny succulents embroidered in patterns along the canals. The pastiche of pseudo-tropica—bamboo, coral trees, palms, elephant ears—that envelops a quite different water voyage makes the Jungle Cruise ride the park's strongest horticultural illusion. As rubbery, audioanimatronic amphibians rise without warning from watery depths near the tour boat, the ersatz jungle's menacing, deep shade makes their bloodshot eyes and shivering tongues seem almost real. The vinyl boscage of the neighboring Swiss Family Robinsons' fake ficus tree clarifies the point that even in horticulture, exploring the line between illusion and reality, artificiality and authenticity, seems to be the point of Disneyland.

The park mediates reality in many subtle ways that may seem fascinating or sinister, depending on one's mood and perhaps on one's politics. Whether Disney is subliminally playing around (the nine-tenths scale of Main Street buildings makes adults feel like children and makes children feel taller) or getting serious (the Monorail really could be built and used as mass transit, couldn't it?), it pays to pay attention despite a sense that somebody or something else is really in control. Nearly everywhere there is something interesting horticulturally, whether immaculately kept bedding plants, flowering vines, or scalped-looking trees pruned to within an inch of their lives. (Like the topiary, this grandiose bonsai is another instance of ruthless control, here dictated by technology: lighting and sound systems operate from the branches.)

"The Happiest Place on Earth"—that's putting the rest of us in our places—has things that one can criticize but also offers much to appreciate. (The evening electrical parades and fireworks during the summer, for instance, are marvelous, and it would take a lengthy essay to cover the park's immensely creative and varied water features, functioning as transport, climate control, comic relief, historical allusion, and purely aesthetic landscape ornament.) As summarized by Randy Bright's *Disneyland: The Inside Story* (1987), the park has seen many changes over the years; some of us still mourn the loss of the Monsanto Home of the Future. Yet its horticulture smooths out such discontinuities and upholds the idyllic if stagy illusion that keeps Disneyland so durably fascinating.

(Enter Disneyland from Harbor Blvd. south of the Santa Ana Freeway [Interstate 5] in Anaheim; adult admission $25.50; parking extra; hours vary seasonally; confirm by telephoning 714-999-4565.)

WRIGLEY
MEMORIAL
BOTANIC
GARDEN

Twenty-five miles across the sea, the lyric went, Santa Catalina Island is a small resort on a big island, easily accessible by ferry from the mainland yet with the feeling of being far away from the Los Angeles colossus. The seaside village of Avalon could not have a lovelier setting, huddled around a curving bay under dwellings clinging to steep cliffs on the edges of Avalon Canyon. Avalon's modest cottages, small scale, and proximity to the ocean recall a coastal southern California beach town of the sort that ceased to exist on the mainland several decades ago. Catalina also offers many natural attractions and architectural features; for only one example, the Avalon Ballroom, famed from the big band era, has been restored in a beautiful art deco casino built in the 1920s. With all but 1 percent of Santa Catalina controlled by two large owners (a nonprofit conservancy, devoted to preserving the land in its natural state, owns 86 percent of its 76 square miles), the island has so far escaped intensive development, although a Rio de Janeiro-style behemoth not far up the coast from Avalon suggests that the island's time will come sooner rather than later.

The village lies where Avalon Canyon widens to form a small harbor. At the top of the canyon, a botanic garden and memorial commemorate Chicago Cubs owner and chewing gum magnate William Wrigley, Jr., who purchased the Santa Catalina Island Company in 1919 and during the next thirteen years invested in many improvements that helped bring fame and prosperity to the island.

The botanic garden is approached along Avalon Canyon Road, a lane through a wide valley whose steep sides are thickly clothed in chaparral kept lush by the surrounding ocean and thick cloud cover of May, June, and July. One may choose any of several ways to travel the 1.7 miles to the botanic garden: bus, tram, car, golf cart (the preferred tourist mode), bicycle, horse, or on foot (it is a 3 percent grade). As the lane passes a golf course and a ruined aviary (decorated with antique, locally produced tile), statuesque Canary Island palms tower above fences straining under flowering vines—crimson *Tecomaria capensis,* violet bougainvillea, and cup-of-gold vine. The brilliant colors are reminiscent of a romantic southern California landscape of the sort that has largely disappeared across the channel.

Comprising 37.85 acres, the botanic garden dates from the 1920s, when Mrs. Ada Wrigley established a collection of cacti and succulents in consultation with horticulturist Albert Conrad. The Wrigley Memorial was completed in 1934. World War II began a period during which the garden languished. Since the Wrigley Memorial Garden Foundation was formed in 1969, the botanic garden has been revamped, has added a herbarium and propagation facilities, and has expanded to include native and endemic plants of the Channel Islands.

Avalon Canyon narrows considerably by the time it reaches the botanic garden, whose plan essentially consists of beds on either side of a central path continuing up the canyon to the memorial tower. The lowest beds feature aloes, yuccas, *Dracaena draco,* agaves, cacti, euphorbias, and other succulents, many blooming during the winter in the hot desert colors of coral, yellow, and crimson. The garden specializes in succulent ground covers such as *Crassula falcata,* whose star-shaped, blue-green stems send out carmine blooms speckled with tiny yellow bits of pollen. The southern California landscape would show far more bare earth without such ground covers as the magenta-flowering *Cylindrophyllum speciosa* or the crimson blooming stalks above fleshy green stars of *Echeveria coccinea,* beautifully grown at the Wrigley Botanical Garden.

The botanic garden displays over a dozen *Mammillaria* cactus species, a profusion of columnar and barrel cactus, and some rarely seen yuccas, such as the shiny-leaved, chartreuse *Yucca guatamalensis.* Although containing mostly familiar palms, its euphorbias are outstanding. The bare branches of *Euphorbia regis-jubae* support sparse leaflets not unlike small oleander leaves. The thick trunks of *E. resinifera* send out small flattened branches in the typical flanged euphorbia shape, almost like miniature epiphyllum stems. The most unusual euphorbia is "Medusa's head" (*E. caput-medusae*), named for its dozens of tubular branches, one inch in diameter and eighteen inches long, sprawling and swarming like snakes.

The garden also specializes in California natives: for example, the mountain mahogany (*Cercocarpus betuloides*); the California laurel; and the golden yellow flowers on mauve stems with pale green seed pods of the "bladder pod" (*Cleome isomeris*). Of particular note are the insular

Cactus, succulents, and desert palms at the foot of Wrigley Memorial Tower

endemic species, native only to California offshore islands, clustering at the top of the garden nearest the memorial. The display includes the eight Santa Catalina endemics—St. Catherine's lace (*Eriogonum giganteum*), Catalina mahogany (*Cercocarpus traskiae*), Catalina ironwood (*Lyonothamnus floribundus*), and five others.

A section devoted to insular endemic trees is particularly impressive. Tree species include the toyon (*Heteromeles arbutifolia macrocarpa*); the island oak (*Quercus tomentella*); the Santa Cruz Island pine (*Pinus remorata*), which in a curiously discontinuous habit also grows hundreds of miles north in Marin County; the Torrey pine (*Pinus torreyana*), similarly discontinuous with small habitats on Santa Rosa Island and in coastal San Diego County; and the Catalina cherry (*Prunus lyonii*). The garden also displays native island shrubs, such as the Catalina currant (*Ribes viburnifolium*), the Catalina manzanita (*Arctostaphylos catalinae*), and the superb tree poppy (*Dendromecon rigida rhamnoides*) in full bloom in February with bright yellow, single flowers on sage foliage.

At the top of the canyon, the botanic garden slopes up into the hills, terminating at the Wrigley Memorial Monument, designed by the Chicago firm of Bennett, Parsons and Frost in 1934 and dedicated to William

Wrigley, Jr. Built as much as possible with Catalina Island materials, the imposing, 130-foot-high monument offers a fine view over the botanic garden, down Avalon Canyon, to the village and the ocean. One hundred steps lead to an intermediate terrace and through bronze double doors to the tower, where twin Italian cypress grow in a terrace of blue island flagstone surrounded by tiled walls.

The Wrigley Botanic Garden is a delightful surprise: well labeled and maintained, accessible, scenic, and full of interesting plants. The journey up to the garden through Avalon Canyon is equally agreeable. In fact, a visit to Avalon for the day or for several days offers a relaxing, low-key holiday; the mode is cute, quaint, and (except for the Crescent St. promenade along the harbor) quiet. The island and its clear surrounding waters offer a variety of natural sites and tours to enjoy—buffalo, a glass-bottomed boat tour, and many other features. The botanic garden, Avalon, and the island remain undiscovered treasures that are easy to find.

(The Wrigley Memorial Botanic Garden is located at the top of Avalon Canyon Rd. Adult admission is $1.00; open 8:00 a.m. to 5:00 p.m., seven days a week, although sometimes closed on holidays, so holiday hours should be confirmed in advance. By advance reservation, group tours are available from the Wrigley Memorial Garden Foundation, P.O. Box 88, 1400 Avalon Canyon Rd., Avalon, CA 90704. For information, telephone 213-510-2288.)

UNIVERSITY OF CALIFORNIA, IRVINE, ARBORETUM

The name "arboretum" strictly denotes a specialized botanic garden devoted to trees. Shortly after entering the UC Irvine Arboretum along a kind of street shaded by pines, loquats, pittosporum, abutilon, and flowering *Paulownias,* one nevertheless quickly surmises that this arboretum emphasizes species of all kinds—not restricted to trees—that will survive in full sun in a mild, dry climate. The centerpiece of this ten-acre arboretum is a carefully assembled collection of over 140 aloe species, a large percentage of the more than 400 known to exist. These are planted in gravel beds with succulents and other allied species. Native to southern Africa and flowering from late winter into spring, the aloes grow in many shapes and sizes: *A. striatula,* mounding fifteen feet wide and five high, reveals yellow, chartreuse, and orange flowers; *A. cryptopoda* produces five-foot, branched blooming spikes with glossy, orange tubular flowers; and the bare limbs of the arboreal *A. bainesii* branch from a trunk and terminate with typical fleshy spears at each tip. The aloe collection helps preserve endangered species such as *A. pillansii,* a slow-growing species of which only about 100 specimens remain in its native Namibia.

The aloes also offer exceptional foliar color, not only sage, apple, and dark green but also shades of salmon, orange, rust, brick red, cinnamon, and even pink. Some aloes bear clean, smooth, fleshy leaves without spines or other armature; others are pimpled, mottled, or freckled; and some are tangled, spiny, and menacing. The aloe beds merge into other plantings of species from hot, dry climates, many of them adapting to extreme temperatures in ways not unlike those of the aloes. Agaves, for instance, have been interplanted among the aloes, from which they are botanically distinct but with which they share similar adaptations. *Agave bracteosa* from northeastern Mexico produces long, refined leaves of a muted green and no spines; *A. pattonii* from north central Mexico arranges its sage, spiny leaves in a neat, fastidiously composed rosette.

The emphasis on dry climate plants takes several forms. A South African sand dune displays plants as they might appear in their native habitat, such as *Arctotis*, the African daisy. The California deserts contribute the ocotillo (*Fouquieria dighetti*), blooming with scarlet tubular flowers on the ends of woody stems, the boojum tree (*F. columnaris*), and the slow-growing Joshua tree (*Yucca brevifolia*), healthy but still small after nearly twenty years in this garden. The arboretum displays familiar dry climate plants such as lion's tail (*Leonotis leonuris*), blooming in white or pale orange fuzzy flowers, as well as the rare *Nymania capensis*, a woody shrub whose stringy branches support pale salmon seed pods shaped and hung like Japanese lanterns.

The garden is particularly rich in southern African plants, which include a huge, four-foot specimen of *Aeonium arboretum atropurpureum*, its six-inch rosettes a deep purple darkened almost to black. Also notable is a yellow-flowering bird of paradise (*Strelitzia reginae*), though in all candor it appeared somewhat stunted. The arboretum cultivates many curiosities, such as the ropy stems of *Pedilanthus macrocarpus* that radiate from a central point, bear no leaves, and release only a few fuchsia-colored, claw-shaped flowers in autumn. The Mexican *Senecio praecox* goes dormant in the fall, but in late winter bright yellow daisies cover the fifteen-foot-high tree.

Although not part of the arboretum's public areas, it is important to mention the valuable work being done here on South African bulbs and on orchids. Of a collection of over 30,000 potted bulbs derived from nearly 1,000 species, most are rare, and about two hundred of these bulb species are critically endangered. This collection is kept under lock, key, and shade cloth to protect them from unauthorized pollenization by insects. These flowering bulbs come from a climate similar to that of southern California and bloom mostly in winter or spring. The bulb houses are open only during an annual open house held during the flowering season; viewing is highly recommended.

Many of the bulb species are being tested for their adaptability to home gardens in southern California, where such South African bulbs as freesia, *Sparaxis*, *Babiana*, *Homeria*, and species gladiolus have become or are becoming increasingly well known. Some of the flowers of lesser-known bulb species prove to be simply astonishing: *Moraea villosa*, for instance, produces a three-petaled, white flower marked with gold and green patches, marvelous to see.

Under the direction of Dr. Harold Koopowitz, the arboretum also maintains a cryogenic gene bank to preserve seeds of endangered orchids. The pace of tropical deforestation accelerates with each passing year, threatening 10,000 of the 25,000 orchid species—the world's largest plant family. The UC Irvine Gene Bank packs and stores seeds at temperatures below freezing, where they remain viable for centuries and can be grown when species no longer exist in the wild. That it is a last-ditch strategy makes it all the more crucial.

Needless to say, a cryogenic storage facility does not lend itself to public viewing, but the arboretum contains many other things to see. The site overlooks the San Joaquin Freshwater Marsh Reserve, upper Newport Bay, and the Irvine campus. Lawns wind along the arboretum's eastern and southern perimeters to a stand of _Washingtonia robusta_, other palms, and surrounding beds containing subtropical trees and shrubs. The floss silk tree, coral trees, oleander, New Zealand flax, and beds of geraniums, black-eyed susans, and daylilies surround seating that invites visitors to enjoy a fine view from this distinctive arboretum.

(The University of California, Irvine, Arboretum is located off Campus Dr. just south of Jamboree; look for signs at Campus Dr. Metered parking; free admission; open Monday through Friday from 8:30 a.m. to 3:30 p.m.; closed Saturdays, Sundays, and federal holidays. For information, telephone 714-856-5833.)

SOUTH
COAST
BOTANIC
GARDEN

I t seems clear that eventually it will become necessary to do more than simply conserve natural areas that are as yet undamaged. An environmental ethic must in time apply to land and water everywhere rather than to those few sacred spots that are anointed wildernesses or natural wonders. The day will come when we will have to do more than stop polluting; we will have to repair damage already done.

The South Coast Botanic Garden may provide some lessons about the difficulties and the rewards of restoring the earth. The garden is the third tenant of this site on the lee side of the Palos Verdes Peninsula. An offshore island that remained attached to the continent, the peninsula juts out into the ocean and towers above the metropolitan plain. From 1929 to 1956, an open pit mine produced a million tons of diatomite. Operating a sanitary landfill from 1957 to 1965, Los Angeles County refilled the pit with 3.5 million tons of trash. Restoration and planting began in 1961, and today 200,000 plants representing 2,000 species inhabit the 87-acre site, which is far from being completely planted.

In a sense this garden represents an experiment whose successes and failures are ongoing and whose true result and value may not be known for decades. The plants grow in three feet of soil above one hundred feet of subsurface trash. The trash decays, complicating cultivation by settling, giving off methane gas, and heating the soil from below, which can cook plant roots. However, the site's benefits—a sizable property, protected from ocean winds, largely free of frost, with a fine view— balance these difficulties, as does enthusiastic community support.

Several gardens cluster around the administration and horticultural buildings near the entrance. A small grove of mature coral trees (*Erythrina caffra*), underplanted with kalanchoe and confetti-colored lantana, sets an almost festive tone. Under a simple structure draped with shade cloth, a shade garden displays cycads, philodendrons, *Chamaedorea* palms, fuchsias, and hanging staghorn and other ferns. A bank of ginger screens the garden from specialized plots containing vegetables and herbs, flowers, and a splendid row of weeping bottlebrush trees (_Callistemon viminalis_ "Red cascade") festooned with pendulous, vivid scarlet blooms.

The coastal climate permits the flower garden to bloom all year. In December, its raised beds contained lavender ageratum, dark zinfandel-red carnations, orange Iceland poppies, gaillardia, petunias, pansies, late hollyhocks, red and blue salvia, and lavender. Most spectacularly, multiple, ten-foot canes of a tree dahlia (_Dahlia imperialis_) leaned under the weight of dozens of lavender blossoms. Beyond the flower garden, rectangular beds of contemporary roses extend to a white gazebo.

With that abruptness that can be so effective in gardens, just beyond the roses a desert garden displays mature cacti, agaves, and aloes, but the collection is especially strong in upright euphorbias. The garden also contains several _Opuntia_ cacti, such as _O. linguiformis_, a Texas species named for its tongue-shaped, three-foot leaves. Many opuntias, neat but spiny with golden or gray needles on olive flesh, make an exceptionally aesthetic impression.

From the dry garden, past several coral trees and a grove of flowering fruit trees, the path reaches a "blue" perennial garden. The blue garden illustrates what Vita Sackville-West would call "color planning." An exercise in rhyming and timing, color planning requires a gardener not only to obtain complementary colors but to do so simultaneously. Even though this collection stretched the definition of "blue" to include lavender and deep purple, the flowers bloomed enthusiastically even in early December: powder blue rosemary; two species of blue hibiscus; the royal purple princess flower; and the dark purple, tubular blooms of _Iochroma cyaneum_ and its relative, _I. grandiflora_ "Logees." _Lycianthus rantonnei_ "Royal robe" wore hundreds of one-inch dark purple flowers, each with a golden dot in the center.

The route through the South Coast Botanic Garden follows a great circle; an asphalt pedestrian road gives access to the entire property except for a lake and stream in the center. (Water features are easily approached by well-marked detours.) After a grove of coast redwoods, another small flower garden, and an orchard of young fruit trees and magnolias, an "English garden" appears. One rather doubts that many English gardens have proteas (e.g., _Banksia marcescens_), _Dombeya cayeuxii_, scarlet bougainvillea "San Diego Red," or East African canary bird bush (_Crotalaria agatiflora_), with its claw-shaped, pale chartreuse flowers and handsome foliage on a sprawling shrub. This "typical English garden" falls somewhat short of that advertised claim; a Japanese torii, bonsai, and bamboo beds across a path scarcely harm an illusion that had little chance to form in the first place. Despite the design confusion, this area merits a visit, as it contains some fine plants and even a few rarities, such as the Florida yellow trumpet (*Stenolobium stans*).

After the English garden, the path becomes distinctly a back road; from here on, you are literally on your own. It is a large property, and no criticism is intended by stating that this botanical garden remains unfinished. Like all gardens it is a work in progress, and periodically a whiff of methane recalls the distinct difficulties posed by the site's history. Although there are many plants to see along the way, the tour through a botanic garden now changes its character into a ramble or even a hike. Labels, legs, and spirits now tend to give out; making the entire circuit involves a good, long walk.

Those whom this full disclosure does not discourage will encounter areas of palms and pines, a slope with a tangle of dry and desert plants that has great possibilities, and plantings of eucalyptus and ginkgo. Down the middle of the garden, below the pine area, an artificial stream fosters bog and water plants, more a nature and wildlife preserve than a botanic garden. As the road returns to the starting point, it passes through a ficus grove representing more than twenty species, many of which seem to share characteristic gray bark, red new growth, aggressive surface roots, strongly midribbed leaves, and fruits in odd places (see, e.g., the rare sycamore fig, *Ficus sycomorus*, with hundreds of tiny figs on trunk and branches).

Throughout the garden, located high above the city, fine views north and west open up at many points. This garden is notable for its work in restoring an ecologically ravaged site, for the intense involvement of volunteers and horticultural societies in its creation and maintenance, and for its specialized displays and wide variety of plants.

(The South Coast Botanic Garden, 26300 Crenshaw Blvd., Palos Verdes Peninsula; open daily from 9:00 a.m. to 5:00 p.m.; $3.00 adult admission. Books, plants, and gifts are for sale; for information, telephone 213-377-0468.)

Two
Long Beach
Adobes

The City of Long Beach contains two historic adobes and surrounding estates, both donated by branches of the Bixby
family, one of the city's oldest. The estates were formerly
occupied by Don Abel Stearns and Don Juan Temple, Americans who acquired property in California during Mexican times by
marrying into local landed families. The adobes eventually became
Bixby family homes for several generations until suburbanization after
World War II ended the ranching era. The gardens of both Rancho Los
Alamitos and Rancho Los Cerritos also reflect the involvement of some
eminent southern California landscapers.

RANCHO LOS ALAMITOS dates from a 1784 Spanish land grant
of over 156,000 acres to Manuel Nieto, a part of which Don Abel Stearns
later purchased in the early 1840s as a summer home for his bride, Arcadia Bandini. Although Abel and Arcadia probably had a garden when
they lived in the adobe, John and Susan Bixby found only a single pepper and eucalyptus tree when they arrived in the 1870s. Susan Bixby
planted what are now the largest trees on the property, a massive pair
of Moreton Bay figs next to the house. John and Susan's daughter-in-
law, Florence Green Bixby, added most of the other trees and landscaping
after 1922, engaging several landscaping professionals to develop the
residential gardens while the house acted as the headquarters for the
ranching and farming that continued here until 1952. Perhaps the best
known of these designers was the firm of Florence Yoch and Lucile
Council, who designed a gazebo, a small rose garden, and an oleander
walkway where a self-guided tour of five acres of gardens begins.

Covered by a Lady Banks' rose, a gazebo forms the transition to a
small sunken rose garden, where a curved seating area, Olive Tree Terrace, is lined with a half-circle of olives planted to screen a view of the
wells that sprouted in Long Beach after oil was discovered in Signal Hill

in 1921. (A skyline of derricks may have spoiled the view, but as the Bixby family still owned substantial acreage, the oil boom considerably increased the value of their holdings and helped finance improvements at Rancho Los Alamitos and its gardens.) From the rose garden, another axis, parallel to Geranium Walk but several steps lower, extends under an allée of oleanders trained as twenty-five-foot trees.

Typical of Yoch and Council's designs, this romantic oleander walkway changes direction as it concludes near garden statuary and Italian cypresses. A few sandstone steps lead to a view of the adobe's front lawn under its twin Moreton Bay figs. The adobe, though much changed since it was built in 1806, is considered the oldest domestic structure in southern California. Two dozen Canary Island palms line a drive curving around the lawn, behind which is a tennis court surrounded by gardens on three sides. A "Friendly Garden" received cuttings and plants that friends gave as gifts to Mrs. Bixby. Dating from 1921, an elevated tennis court is surrounded by grape and wisteria vines and appointed with Adirondack chairs for linesmen and spectators.

Behind the court a jacaranda walk shades a rose-covered trellis and potted *Agave attenuata* before leading to a large cactus garden, begun in 1924 with the assistance of the eminent creator of the desert garden at the Huntington Botanical Gardens, William Hertrich. A self-guided tour sketches the collection: massive, treelike *Opuntia* cactus; neat beds of succulents such as *Aeonium arboreum* "Swartkop"; and a large coast live oak shading aloes, jade plants, and *Cereus peruvianus monstrosa*.

The estate's most charming garden lies north of the house, opening onto an outsized patio. The family used the patio for dancing and formal entertaining, its glaring cement expanse no doubt softened by potted plants and outdoor furniture. Hedging follows paved paths leading away from the house to an octagonal "Spanish fountain" next to a pergola under a California pepper tree. A tropical "wonga-wonga vine" (*Pandorea pandorana*) engulfs the pergola, immersing its seating area in deep shade. One can easily imagine this "old garden" hosting parties or family gatherings during hot summers or when autumnal Santa Ana winds blow. The beds are lush with subtropical bananas, callas, agapanthus, bird of paradise, bamboo, and viburnum; an imposing Italian stone pine towers behind. (Rancho Los Alamitos, 6400 Bixby Hill Rd., Long Beach, is entered from Palo Verde Ave.; visitors check in at a guarded gate. Open Wednesday through Sunday, 1:00 p.m. to 5:00 p.m.; free admission; docents give house and building tours; maps and information assist a self-guided tour of the grounds. Telephone 213-431-3541.)

Rancho Los Alamitos

It would seem that gardens interested many members of the large Bixby family. Susanna Bixby Bryant later founded the Rancho Santa Ana Botanic Garden on a family property in Orange County as a memorial to her father, John Bixby. (In the early 1950s, that institution moved to Claremont: see "Inland and Desert Areas.") Another branch of the Bixby family occupied a second Long Beach adobe, where they engaged Ralph D. Cornell to redesign the garden surrounding RANCHO LOS CERRITOS. Although much changed since Jonathan "Don Juan" Temple built it in 1844, this beautifully restored residence is considered an excellent example of the Monterey-style adobe in southern California.

When the cattle industry declined in the 1860s, Temple sold his 27,000-acre ranch to Flint, Bixby and Co. Jotham Bixby, a brother of one of the company principals, managed the property, raising sheep for wool; _Adobe Days_ (1925), the memoir of Jotham's niece, Sarah Bixby Smith, portrays Rancho Los Cerritos life at this time. After 1881, the property fell into ruin until 1929, when Llewellyn Bixby purchased and renovated the house and, in consultation with Cornell, the grounds. In 1955, the City of Long Beach purchased the 4.9-acre property, which is operated as a library, museum, and historic site.

The dwelling surrounds an inner courtyard, two low wings extending from the two-story main house whose elegant sun room forms the third side of a courtyard of white walls, olive wood trim, and rusty red tile roofs. The early California plantings surround a herringbone brick terrace, sandstone goldfish pond, boxwood hedges, and a small lawn. Besides an orange tree against a southwestern exposure, the courtyard contains tree bird of paradise, a king palm, two clumps of European fan palm, and beds for lantana, hawthorne, jade plant, and agapanthus: a simple, unpretentious garden whose strong architectural features and symmetrical design require nothing more elaborate. The Bixbys came from Maine and carefully guarded their New England heritage, while remaining open to the romance and the facts of California; various rooms of the house are restored to early California and Victorian period use, showing both the working and the leisure lives of workers, artisans, and owners.

A larger garden behind the house contains plants installed about 1850 by Don Juan Temple. A *Jasmine officinale,* for instance, climbs a balcony overlooking the back garden. The garden contains roses, fruit trees (a Nagami kumquat and other citrus, and a pomegranate planted by Temple), an ancient crepe myrtle, flowering shrubs (such as *Cestrum aurantiacum,* with small, golden orange trumpet flowers) and beds of heliconia, camellias, and azaleas. Tall trees—some very old and large—screen the rear perimeter: besides a row of black locusts (*Robinia pseudoacacia*), there is a Brazilian cockspur coral tree (*Erythrina crista-galli*), a small Guatemala holly (*Olmediella betschlerana*), an enormous *Ginkgo biloba,* and a vast Moreton Bay fig planted around 1880.

A pair of Italian cypresses (*Cupressus sempervirens*) planted by Don Juan Temple dominate the back garden. The rare true species, not the columnar selection that has become so widespread and artlessly planted along property lines, they grow upright with exposed trunks and spreading branches. Through the rear garden's spacious lawns, bricked paths follow the perimeter and curve from the veranda out to a lath gazebo. When they restored the garden, Ralph D. Cornell and Llewellyn Bixby sought to preserve not only its fine old trees but also these paths. The brick of which they are composed dates from the early nineteenth century, shipped as ballast around the Horn and used by Temple to build the house. The foot-worn bricks and old trees create a garden that is generous but subdued, mature but not overgrown. Although not without its rare plants, it is a family garden rather than a showplace. (Rancho Los Cerritos, 4600 Virginia Rd., Long Beach; free admission; open Wednesday through Sunday, 1:00 p.m. to 5:00 p.m.; closed Monday, Tuesday, and city holidays.)

FULLERTON
ARBORETUM

The Fullerton Arboretum displays plants that have already proven their value for southern California or that may prove to have a horticultural use in this area. The arboretum is young: initial planting was completed and the garden was officially opened in 1979. California State University, Fullerton, provided twenty-five acres for the arboretum; also on the property is a historic Fullerton house, restored during 1973-1975.

Entering the Fullerton Arboretum, one encounters a small waterfall emptying into a still stream that flows into an area devoted to evergreens—deodar, junipers, and pines—and interplanted with flowering plants. Daylilies and bearded iris line the stream, and the path leads past dawn redwoods before reaching "the only man-made bog in southern California." Protected by shade cloth, irrigated by purified water, and filled with a soil of quartz sand and peat moss, the bog grows *Sarracenia* species, carnivorous "pitcher plants" adapted to trap and consume insects for nitrogen that is unavailable in acidic bog soil.

A conifer area includes several *Araucaria* species, including two young New Caledonian pines (*A. columnaris*), and exotic evergreens such as the Mexican *Pinus pseudostropus* and pungently fragrant Australian cypresses, such as the white cypress pine, *Callitris columellaris*. The evergreen collection is considered one of the best in southern California, with many rarities such as the fine blue weeping Kashmir cypress (*Cupressus cashmeriana*) and the slow-growing Himalayan white pine (*Pinus wallichiana*).

A stand of bamboo near the creek signals a shift from the evergreens to the tropics; here the creek widens to a duck pond, surrounded by palms, two elephant ear species amid water plants (the bright chartreuse *Alocasia odora* and the dark purple-stemmed *Xanthosoma violaceum* from the West Indies), a small cycad collection, and a ficus grove: the rubber plant (*Ficus elastica*); the deciduous *F. palmata* from India, considered a form of the edible fig, *F. carica*; and the Socotra fig (*F. socotrana*), a rare species adapted to dry conditions. This tropical area also contains many plants familiar as house plants or as sources of tropical fruit: hybrid bananas (*Musa paradisiaca*), *Schefflera*, variegated Chinese banyan (*F. microcarpa alba variegata*), and the Madagascar dragon tree (*Dracaena marginata*) that grows to forty feet in its habitat but is found on office credenzas everywhere.

Having circled past the end of the stream and through a grove of coral trees, the path leads through a dry garden that contains many curiosities, such as the sprawling Chilean *Acacia cavenia*, armed with vicious spikes and covered with tiny sage leaves. Across the path a giant Mukumari (*Cordia abyssinica*), an African timber tree, blooms in autumnal clouds of white flowers even as the previous year's black seeds still hang on the tree.

Among the arboretum's horticulturally most valuable displays is its "dry palm grove," which collects *Washingtonia* fan palms, *Trachycarpus fortuneii*, *Brahea edulis*, the pindo palm (*Butia capitata*), *Livistona robinsoniana* from the Philippines, and several date palm and *Brahea* species. The dry palm grove grows next to Heritage House, the restored house and medical offices of George Crook Clark, the first doctor in Fullerton and Orange County's first coroner. Dating from 1894 and moved here from its original site in downtown Fullerton, the house is in the Eastlake style, with a picket fence and yard continuing a lawn, small rose garden, and fruit trees.

These last two elements designate the remaining specialties of the Fullerton Arboretum. From the rear of Dr. Clark's house, an elegant if rustic arbor, covered with wisteria, leads into a grove of citrus and avocado, two commercially grown species demanding almost identical climates which contributed greatly to Orange County's history. The path ends at a gazebo amid a rose garden near the arboretum's rare fruit orchard, a project of the California Rare Fruit Growers. Besides pomegranate, apple, quince, persimmon, and apricot varieties suited to relatively warm Orange County winters, the grove specializes in exotic fruit varieties for local gardeners desiring to create an edible landscape of tropical or rare fruits: sapote, lychee, kiwi, black mulberry (*Morus nigra*), bananas, yellow strawberry guava, loquat, longan (*Dimocarpus longan*), and cherimoya.

The arboretum also contains a large desert section displaying yuccas, *Opuntia* cactus, euphorbias, and an imposing *Agave picta*, its seven-foot, striped leaves tangling in young offshoot plants emerging around its base. Chaparral Hill displays California species native to low-elevation hillsides. Community gardens fill a considerable portion of the property. The arboretum is well known in the area for its plant sales held several times during the year. The arboretum's twenty-five acres include a variety of species, many rarities, and some history and practical horticulture as well.

(Fullerton Arboretum, Associated Rd. and Yorba Linda Blvd., is located in the northeast corner of California State University, Fullerton. Free admission and parking; open 8:00 a.m. to 4:45 p.m. daily; closed major holidays. A map and self-guided tour brochure are available at the entrance. The arboretum has a bookshop and plant sales; tours are conducted at 2:00 p.m. on Sundays; group tours by prior arrangement. Heritage House tours are Sundays, 2:00 p.m. to 4:00 p.m., $1.00 per adult. Telephone 714-773-3579.)

SOUTH COAST
AND
ORANGE COUNTY
BRIEFLY NOTED

In the flat country of coastal Long Beach, the California State University campus offers the EARL BURNS MILLER JAPANESE GARDEN. A gated entry door between a pair of stone lions presents the first view of the 1.3-acre garden and its irregularly shaped lake. The walled garden has been sunk among berms created by soil excavated to make the pond, creating an illusion of many changes of level as the path circulates along a perimeter screen of liquidambar, birch, podocarpus, and flowering pear. Several weeping willows overlook the pond, as do azaleas, camellias, heavenly bamboo, and small pines horizontally pruned into the snow-cloud shape. A stylized beach of black river stones slopes into the pond, where swirling schools of creamy white, orange, and golden koi will approach to be fed, their suction cup mouths exerting gentle pressure on palms and fingers offering bits of food.

Two small waterfalls drain down steep, fern-lined watercourses into the pond. Snow lamps, a miniature stone pagoda, a stone plaque of the meditating Buddha, a bamboo tube fountain dripping into a stone basin, and a zigzag footbridge appear along the path. The placement of rocks as stepping-stones, as "islands" in a gravel Zen garden, as defining features of the pond, shoreline, and waterfalls, and as solid landscape volumes balancing the green shrubbery is especially careful throughout. The rocks—some as large as boulders—are a reddish or pink beige, giving the garden a kind of inanimate, mineral unity. The Earl Burns Miller and Loraine H. Miller Foundation donated the garden in 1980 in memory of Earl Burns Miller. It was designed by local landscape architect Edward R. Lovell. (Enter California State University, Long Beach, at State University Dr. from Bellflower Blvd.; turn left at Earl Warren Dr. and park in Lot D across from the garden. Free admission; open Tuesdays through Thursdays 9:00 a.m. to 4:00 p.m., Sundays noon to 4:00 p.m.; closed holidays. For group tours and information, telephone 213-985-8885.)

At the EL DORADO NATURE CENTER not far away, a head-quarters building presents educational displays on natural history, the pond ecosystem, and the center's role as an animal refuge. A one-mile nature trail around a duck-filled lake and through the large property points out weeping willows, native California sycamores, chaparral, and oaks, redwoods, native shrubs, eucalyptus, and natural features. A grove of white alders is probably the most scenic stop on the informative, self-guided tour. With only a few plants labeled, this is not primarily a garden site. The emphasis is on nature, even if what is presented is so dammed, graded, and otherwise highly modified by exotic plants and an artificial lake that the site could scarcely resemble what it looked like before the adjacent river was confined to a concrete channel and high tension power poles were installed. Its value therefore is primarily as a metropolitan animal and bird refuge—judging from the chorus of bird calls it is succeeding admirably—and for children as a first glimpse of nature. (El Dorado Nature Center, 7550 E. Spring St., Long Beach; $3.00 per car admission; trails open 8:00 a.m. to 5:00 p.m. Tuesday through Sunday. Telephone 213-421-9431, ext. 3415.)

Noted sculptor Isamu Noguchi's concept at THE CALIFORNIA SCENARIO is straightforward and executed with quality materials. Among assemblages bearing blunt titles like "Water Use," "Energy Fountain," and "Land Use," water, stone, and plants represent the regions of California: redwood forest, desert, river, Sierra.

What undercuts Noguchi's meritorious efforts considerably, however, is the fact that no trouble has been taken to help the public find and appreciate this 1.6-acre sculpture garden. Concealed behind an office tower, nearly inaccessible from the street, hemmed in by monolithic parking structures and visually infringed by catalog quality lamps, The California Scenario remains something of a missed opportunity. It illustrates how any work of landscape design inevitably depends on its surroundings. One should not have to ask where the art is; it should appear everywhere, instead of being reverently jailed in its own little preserve. A fragment of a disorienting, pedestrian-hostile shopping zone, The California Scenario may be approached by the intrepid at 711 Anton St., Costa Mesa. (Across from Westin South Coast Plaza Hotel, between the Central Bank Tower and Great Western Savings.)

In Orange County, the latest phases of California society mingle with some of its earliest. At MISSION SAN JUAN CAPISTRANO, founded by Father Junipero Serra in 1776, ruins of some of the oldest mission structures still stand. Ten acres of grounds contain two garden

Inner patio, Mission San Juan Capistrano

plazas. The first, asymmetrical and surrounded by arcaded padres' quarters, soldiers' barracks, and mission walls, encloses a fountain in the Moorish style dating from the 1920s, when the gardens were restored under Father St. John O'Sullivan's direction.

Most imposing are the massive arches of a ruined stone church begun in 1797 and destroyed by an 1812 earthquake six years after completion. Focusing the perspectives of the plaza garden, the still impressive ruin supports brilliant bougainvillea vines. Even in late December, a great aloe mound, poinsettia, and several dozen bird of paradise shrubs make this a colorful winter garden, as do many other plants associated with the mission style: yucca, *Agave attenuata*, citrus, cacti, plumbago and *Tecomaria capensis* vines, oleanders, and the ubiquitous California pepper trees.

A passage leads through the padres' quarters into a larger "inner patio," arcaded on four sides and plotted symmetrically around a "fountain of the four evangelists" dating from 1929. Unlike the entry plaza's bare earth, here a lawn, the arcade's rhythms, and the plan's symmetrical proportions create a more hospitable, sheltered mood, even though both plazas draw on the vocabulary of mission-style trees and shrubs: jacarandas, queen palms, strawberry trees, Canary Island palms, a large cape chestnut tree, and olives. Along the west arcade is a large "Baja garden" of cactus and desert plants, and beyond the wall at the property's western edge is a large rose garden, a small pond, and a bird and plant sanctuary in which a variety of native and introduced vegetables, fruits, berries, and herbal plants grow, many labeled. (Mission San Juan Capistrano, Ortega Highway and Camino Capistrano, San Juan Capistrano; open daily all year 7:30 a.m. to 5:00 p.m.; $2.00 per adult purchases admission, a map, and self-guided tour of buildings and grounds; for information, telephone 714-493-1424.)

III
Inland
and
Desert Areas

Rancho
Santa Ana
Botanic
Garden

P art of the interest in the origins of public gardens arises from the networks of family, personal, and professional relationships that history reveals. With its links to the Bixbys of Long Beach, to Henry Huntington, and to horticulturists and scientists such as Theodore Payne, W. L. Jepson, Philip Munz, and even Charles Sprague Sargent at the Arnold Arboretum, the story of the Rancho Santa Ana Botanic Garden offers a particularly good example of how public gardens begin in these networks and survive by exploiting them. If botanic and other public gardens may satisfy a desire for social status held by those who found and fund them, they also serve impersonal ideals of education and science. As the network surrounding Sarah Bixby Bryant and the Rancho Santa Ana Botanic Garden illustrates, botany and horticulture are activities in which civilized and intelligent people take an interest.

Just inside the Los Angeles County line, the lovely college town of Claremont offers the state's best botanic garden devoted to California native plants. The reasons for its preeminence go back to its founding, in another county, early in this century. As a child, Susanna Bixby Bryant knew the Bixby family's adobe at Rancho Los Alamitos in Long Beach (see South Coast and Orange County, "Two Long Beach Adobes"). She later became the owner of the 6,000-acre Rancho Santa Ana in Orange County and managed the property and its several hundred acres of citrus trees. (Her husband was surgical director for the Southern Pacific Railroad and Henry Huntington's personal physician.)

Bryant became acquainted with Theodore Payne, who operated a Los Angeles nursery specializing in California native plants and helped popularize them around the world. After consulting Payne and other interested parties, Bryant began to build a botanic garden on 165 acres at her Santa Ana Canyon ranch in 1926. There she intended to concentrate as many of the thousands of California native species as could be

Rancho Santa Ana Botanic Garden, a desert oasis in Claremont

grown. She was also interested in organizing and staffing the collection for use by botanists and other scientists. The experts she consulted impressed on her that at the time no such botanic garden existed in California.

As work proceeded, Bryant began to acquire a botanical library and to plan for the garden's long-term administration and growth by establishing an endowment, forming a board of trustees, and engaging a scientific director. In 1928, the garden's first public announcement referred to it as commemorating Susanna Bixby Bryant's father, John W. Bixby.

In the 1930s, Bryant made the garden financially independent by endowing a financial trust and transferring the property to the trustees. Public visiting days began in 1933. In the 1940s, the garden survived the restrictions of the Second World War, a damaging fire in 1943, and the founder's unexpected death in 1946, but it became clear that Susanna Bixby Bryant had successfully established an institution that would survive her. She had also seen to its scientific integrity by hiring as its botanist the eminent Philip Munz, who succeeded her as director and who later published the standard _A California Flora_ (1959) and several popular books on California wildflowers during the 1960s.

Munz oversaw the next great event in the garden's history. The garden's remoteness in an unpopulated part of Orange County, isolation from the scientific community, and its enclosure by private land jeopardized its scientific goals and accessibility to the public. In 1950, the decision was made to move the garden and affiliate with the Claremont Colleges, which supported the move by providing more than eighty acres. Planting began in 1951. Today the botanic garden staff constitutes the graduate department of botany for the Claremont Graduate School. Its scientists carry on research at the site, which besides laboratories contains offices, a library, classrooms, an herbarium comprising over one million specimens, and a publications program that includes _Aliso_, a scholarly journal of botany. (This historical account is largely based on Lee W. Lenz, "Rancho Santa Ana Botanic Garden: The First Fifty Years, 1927-1977," in _Aliso_ [1977].)

Since 1950, the Rancho Santa Ana Botanic Garden has also acted as the botanic garden for Claremont's six independent but affiliated colleges in a way resembling the arrangement at European universities, distinct from the colleges yet affiliated with them. Attempting to include as many California native species as possible, the garden's inclusiveness serves scientific, research, and educational functions. Students can study living plants, and a researcher needing to view a plant under a microscope or to perform a chemical test can collect a living sample from the

1,500 species grown in the garden. The Rancho Santa Ana Botanic Garden also pursues its founder's goals of preserving native California plants and encouraging their use in home gardens. As a tour of the grounds reveals, by no means has science entirely displaced aesthetic concerns, and the garden's newest areas will display ornamental plants.

As recently as the 1880s—when Pomona College was founded—a band of Gabrielino Indians lived on Indian Hill. Today that low mesa (el. 1,250 ft.) contains the administration and laboratory buildings and intensively cultivated demonstration plantings from a plan by C. Jacques Hahn with the assistance of Charles Hoffman. The rear forty acres, less

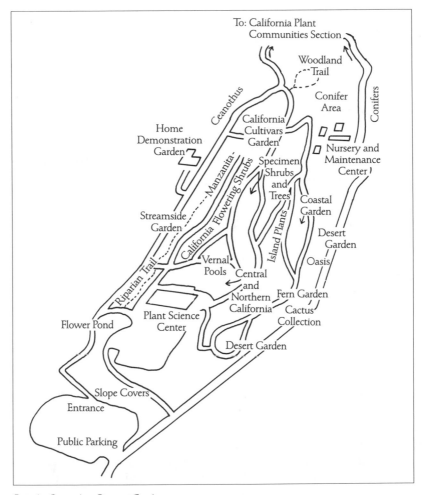

Rancho Santa Ana Botanic Garden

highly developed, follow an ecologically oriented plan of California plant communities based on work by Munz and David D. Keck.

From the entrance, a path slopes gently up the mesa past a stream simulating a riparian habitat. In southern California, such streams run through all soils and ecologies and nourish what trees will grow in its dry climate. Along the path grow western ash (_Fraxinus velutina_), willow (_Salix lasiolepis_), and bigleaf maple (_Acer macrophyllum_). Around a pond, the only native California water lily species, _Nuphar polysepala_, sprouts yellow flowers among a mass of tropical, arrow-shaped leaves. The path curves past the three redwood species, two natives—the coast redwood (_Sequoia sempervirens_) and the Sierra redwood or Big Tree (_Sequoiadendron giganteum_)—and their Chinese cousin, the dawn redwood (_Metasequoia glyptostroboides_), thought to be extinct until discovered alive in the 1940s.

As the path reaches the top of the mesa, administration and scientific buildings become visible, as do some of the garden's horticultural themes. Instead of being concentrated in a single meadow, for instance, patches of wildflowers scatter through the shrubs and trees. Wildflower species have been selected for strong color, and most bloom from midwinter to late spring. They include "Farewell to Spring" (_Clarkia amoena_), sending out rose and salmon pink flower spikes; the California poppy (_Eschscholzia californica_), with its orange flowers and blue-green foliage; "globe gilia" (_Gillia capitata_), with small, dark blue-violet flowers; and the dark lavender salvia "Allen Chickering" (_Salvia clevelandii x. S. leucophylla_), a hybrid honoring a San Francisco attorney who was a childhood friend of Susanna Bixby Bryant. As chairman of the first board of trustees, Chickering helped to ensure this garden's successful establishment.

These and other wildflowers appear throughout the mesa's specialized plantings. In a home demonstration garden, wooden pavilions support _Fremontodendron_ "California Glory," neatly espaliered to contrast with its usual shapelessness, and the California Dutchman's pipe vine (_Aristolochia californica_), a curiosity with its bizarre, mottled cream-and-purple pipe-shaped flowers with a stem and bowl. In surrounding beds grow the dark rose, tubular flowers of coral bells (_Heuchera elegans x. H. sanguinea_); the superb monkey flower, a hybrid _Mimulus aurantiacus_ producing memorable dark mahogany-purple flowers with a yellow orange throat, and the showy Matilija poppy (_Romneya coulteri_), whose white crepe-textured flowers have bright yellow centers. A new, two-acre California Cultivars Garden will expand and elaborate the theme of the existing demonstration garden, containing pavilions with informational displays amid ornamental flowers and shrubs selected or hybridized from wild native species for use in home gardens.

The intense cultivation on the mesa shifts to a more naturally planted landscape to the north and west in a forty-acre "California Plant Communities Section." Here the planting is organized into ecological communities such as "island chaparral," which contains island bush poppy (*Dendromecon harfordii*) in bloom with clear yellow flowers; the finely cut foliage of Catalina ironwood (*Lyonothamnus floribundus*); summer holly (*Comarostaphylis diversifolia*), related to the manzanita as revealed in its white, small flowers; and island mallow (*Malacothamnus clementinus*), an endangered island species with white and pale pink flowers on green, herbaceous leaves.

Other plant communities represented include coastal chaparral, coastal sage, and the woodland communities of the foothills, of piñon and juniper, and of the Joshua tree. In the latter area, the slow-growing specimens of a grove of Joshua trees (*Yucca brevifolia*) attain something like their natural height and branching shape. Perhaps nearly as famous a botanical symbol of California's desert areas as the redwoods are of its coasts or mountains, the Joshua trees stand amid pale orange monkey flowers, the silver-sage foliage of the high desert shrub *Eurotia lanado*, and *Arctostaphylos drupasia*. The latter species bears the largest flower of any manzanita, maturing to produce sticky berries adhering to passing people or animals, an adaptation that spreads the species into new territory.

Twenty-five feet below the mesa's eastern side, a grove of coast live oaks native to the site grows throughout several ecologically themed areas. A coastal sand dune displays alkali heath (*Frankenia salina*) native from Baja to central California; dune manzanita (*Arctostaphylos pumila*) from Monterey Bay coastal dunes; and the magenta-flowered sea fig (*Carpobrotus aequilaterus*), whose thick, juicy leaves will look familiar to every California gardener and to anyone who drives the freeways, as one of several ice plant species.

To the south, a palm oasis simulates the unique desert environment where springs, streams, or underground water no more than twenty feet below the surface provide enough moisture for the only California native palm species, *Washingtonia filifera*. Here about fifteen palms grow as they would in a native habitat, thick trunks shagged with dead fronds. Nearby, western sycamores and cottonwoods (*Populus fremontii*) surround a pond edged with wire grass (*Juncus acutus*).

The palm oasis merges into a desert garden with cactus (look for an exceptional purple beavertail, _Opuntia basilaris famosa_, its bristling paddles a striking shade of dark lavender and mauve); purple trumpet flowers of the desert willow (_Chilopsis linearis_); and the yellow blooms of blue palo verde (_Cercidium floridum_), its green bark capable of photosynthesizing even when the tree drops its leaves in hot weather. As a distinct contrast, a lush fern garden lies directly across from the desert garden at the foot of the mesa, where a trickling, naturalistic cascade feeds a small pond. Redtwig dogwood (_Cornus stolonifera_) and salal (_Gaultheria shallon_) flank the tiny cascade, and ferns include California's only epiphytic plant, _Polypodium scouleri_, the California holly fern (_Polystichum californicum_), the sword fern (_P. munitum_), and the _Woodwardia fimbriata_, the latter two ferns seen commonly in the redwood forest.

Here paths climb back up the mesa or wind along its foot back to the entrance, completing a circular tour. No discussion of the Rancho Santa Ana Botanic Garden would be complete without mentioning its fine trees. Throughout the property but especially on top of the mesa are many fine oaks, coast redwoods, sycamores, and especially the Torrey pines. Dwarfed and contorted in their cool, dry native coastal San Diego County and Santa Rosa Island habitats, in this quite different climate the Torrey pines grow straight and tall with healthy, gray-green needles.

Nor should this botanic garden's site, at least on a clear day, be underestimated. The mesa gains fine northern views of the towering San Gabriel mountains, which this far inland reach elevations of 9,000 and 10,000 feet. The Rancho Santa Ana Botanic Garden's comprehensive scope serves the visitor seeking to view attractive plants in the manner of a museum visit, the practical landscaper interested in plants for a home garden, the ecologist, the botany student, and the professional research scientist. The garden both preserves native species and spreads them through selections and hybrids. And it heightens ecological understanding, a function that perhaps unintentionally places it in the center of contemporary social and political life.

(Rancho Santa Ana Botanic Garden is located at 1500 N. College Ave., north of Foothill Blvd. and east of Indian Hill Blvd., in Claremont. Free admission; open 8:00 a.m. to 5:00 p.m. daily, closed on New Year's Day, the Fourth of July, Thanksgiving Day, and Christmas Day; for information, telephone 714-625-8767. A free map is available at the entrance. For information about tours, lectures and classes, plant sales, and other programs and facilities, telephone the education department at 714-626-1917.

THE
LIVING
DESERT
RESERVE

A zoological and botanical garden that also presents historical, anthropological, and scientific themes, the Living Desert Reserve emphasizes the diverse adaptations that plants, birds and animals, Indian society, and modern development have made in order to survive in extreme desert conditions. Although small display areas and a retail nursery highlight home uses for desert plants, most of the reserve is organized to educate visitors about the desert environment.

Defined as an area receiving less than ten inches of annual rainfall, deserts ordinarily sustain intensely hot summers, and some have cold winters as well. What little rain does come may fall in downpours that evaporate or run off the soil instead of soaking in. Desert plants have evolved several strategies to survive drought and heat. Euphorbias and cacti, two families separated botanically and geographically, store water similarly in roots, enlarged stems, and leaves. An exhibit explains the phenomenon, called convergent evolution, illustrating with a few of the 7,300 euphorbia species distributed throughout the world and 2,000 cactus species confined to the Western Hemisphere. Despite their lack of botanical kinship, some euphorbias and cacti appear superficially to be close cousins.

An excellent history display—the informational plaques are well prepared throughout the reserve—focuses on the routes that exploration, mining, railroads, and aqueducts followed through the southern desert. It proposes three events that made Coachella Valley development inevitable. Transportation (the Southern Pacific Railroad arrived in 1877), water (the Coachella Canal opened in 1949), and relief from summer heat (inexpensive refrigeration became available in the 1960s) fostered the boom the valley continues to experience.

Throughout its property, the reserve features zoological displays: a walk-through aviary; an endangered desert tortoise pit; bird cages with owls, vultures, and eagles; displays of snakes, bats, and insects; and areas devoted to native coyotes, desert bighorn sheep, and kit foxes as well as to exotic Arabian oryx, gazelles, and Grevy's zebras, to name only a few of the sixty animal species displayed. Under a _Washingtonia filifera_ palm oasis, there is even a pond exhibiting the desert pupfish, a rare desert species able to survive wide variations in temperature and salinity. Besides being an accredited zoo, the reserve maintains six miles of nature trails fanning out from the botanical garden into the desert preserve that occupies most of the 1,200-acre property.

The extensively planted botanical parts of the reserve organize desert plants according to ten North American desert regions. The Sonoran arboretum, for instance, includes desert trees such as palo verde (_Cercidium_ species), screwbean and honeypod mesquites (_Prosopis pubescens_ and _P. juliflora_), and ironwood (_Olneya tesota_). It is enclosed by an Indian ethnic garden demonstrating how local Cahuilla tribes boiled flowers of _Agave deserti_ for stews, derived soap from the roots of _Yucca schidigera_ (perhaps anticipating the shampoos and other cosmetic products derived today from _Simmondsia chinensis_, the jojoba), and used _Washingtonia filifera_ palm fronds for baskets, footwear, and home building. (The area contains a Cahuilla _kish_ dwelling made of palm fronds.)

The Joshua tree (_Yucca brevifolia_) distinguishes the Mojave region of California and Nevada, the "high" desert in the rain shadow of the southern Sierras at an elevation of 2,000 to 5,000 feet. The Upper Colorado desert, where the Living Desert Reserve is located, is the Sonoran Desert's driest region. Here grows the Santa Rosa sage (_Salvia eremostachya_), a species of limited habitat, whose tiny, tubular, sky-blue flowers bloom in late winter. Nearby is a globe mallow (_Sphaeralcea ambigua_) collection, its one-inch single flowers blooming in early March in unusual shades of pale apricot. East of the Colorado River in northern Mexico and in Arizona, the Yuman desert contains several distinctive plants, including perhaps most recognizably, the giant saguaro (_Carnegiea gigantea_), the largest cactus in the United States and second largest in the world.

Nearby, a small area serves as a reminder of how desert species tempt those desiring to name plants after things they seem to resemble. The _Opuntia_ genus alone offers the following examples: the beavertail (_O. basilaris_); the grizzlybear (_O. erinacea ursina_); the bunnyears (_O. microdasys_); the pancake pear (_O. chlorotica_); and the cow's tongue (_O. linguiformis_). (The final botanical name suggests that sometimes taxonomers also find it convenient to adopt an obvious metaphor.) The other _Opuntias_, the cholla cactus, seem almost as alluring to the analogizers, with the teddy

The Living Desert Reserve, Palm Desert

bear cholla (*O. bigelovia*), Eve's pin (*O. subulata*), and the staghorn (*O. acanthocarpa*), its spiny, tubular stems branching to resemble antlers slightly.

Boasting the cardon (*Pachycereus pringlei*), the world's largest cactus, the Baja California desert region is also notable for its palms. The most widely planted palm in southern California, the gangly *Washingtonia robusta*, originates in Baja. The reserve has created a Baja palm oasis comprising *robustas*; their California relative, *W. filifera*; and a rare Baja species, the blue fan palm (*Brahea armata*). All three fan palms will withstand heat and some frost and are heavily armed with hooks along the stems of their fronds. Yet they grow together in only one place, Cataviña in north central Baja, a habitat replicated at the reserve. Only the exceptional *Brahea armata*, however, sends out exceptional six- and eight-foot blooming stalks of creamy flowers, drooping by the hundreds well below its unusual, silver-blue fronds.

The reserve's botanical collection contains over 1,500 different plant species, many more than can be described here. Desert heat dominates the Coachella Valley for at least six months a year (the reserve is closed for part of the summer), and people unused to these conditions must take precautions (drinking fountains are located throughout the gardens, though not on the nature trails) or schedule visits between the late fall and early spring. The Living Desert Reserve, which already has an extensive collection of desert plants and animals, has new areas planned to elaborate its unusual presentation of how life persists in extreme circumstances.

(The Living Desert Reserve, 47-900 Portola Ave., Palm Desert, is located 1.5 miles south of Highway 111. $5.00 adult admission; open 9:00 a.m. to 5:00 p.m. daily, except during the summer; telephone 619-346-5694 for summer hours and for information. Besides a gift and book shop, retail nursery, education center, and picnic area, the reserve offers guided tours, live animal programs, children's programs, lectures, and special events during fall, winter, and spring.)

MOORTEN'S "DESERTLAND" BOTANICAL GARDEN

The cactus attracts admirers with an appetite for novelty. Its armament, crafty adaptations to harsh conditions, distinctive patterns of flesh and spines, and dazzling blossoms—a moment of floral profligacy in these otherwise austere plants —explain a part of the attraction. The cactus also seems to elicit imaginative metaphors that call attention to how a cactus, cartoonlike, might resemble a weapon, an animal, a biblical event, or sports equipment. The cactus strikes a chord in those who seek to read human experience in the lives, shapes, and defense mechanisms of plants, prickly inhabitants of a hostile world. Yet the cactus also must be among the most ambivalent of plants, its detailed surfaces and juicy, vivid flowers attracting attention even as its quills and hooks warn off those desiring an acquaintance that is too close, too careless, or too quick.

Cactus and other desert plants find a unique setting in Moorten's Botanical Garden. Novelties abound as the path meanders through the 2.5-acre walled garden organized geographically: the world's tallest cactus, the columnar "Cardon" (*Pachycereus pringlei*), growing to eighty feet in Baja California; the "wax plant" (*Euphorbia pedalanthus*), sending out thornless, tubular stems by the dozen, as tall as six feet; what is said to be the world's tallest Spanish bayonet (*Yucca mohavensis*); or the "tennis racquet cactus," an *Opuntia* species so called for its flat, circular, paddle-shaped leaves.

Each desert region represented has its marker species: Baja California's elephant tree (*Bursera microphylla*); the Mojave's Joshua tree; Arizona's giant saguaro; and so on through the Colorado, Yuman, Texas, Mexican, and Central American desert regions. Many plants are labeled informally, with hand-painted lettering on bits of cactus wood or a miner's wooden shingle. Whimsical commentary underscores the down-home ambience; a rusted-out covered wagon is tagged "the first mobile home."

Despite the prickly plants and unforgiving desert environment, the feeling here is good-natured. Since Patricia and the late "Cactus Slim"

Moorten started the garden at their home in 1938, over half a century of collecting has produced a desert jungle of 3,000 varieties of thickly planted cactus and other desert dwellers. The path leads past ocotillos, several dozen varieties of barrel cactus, a palo verde grove, and an agave collection to "the world's first cactarium," a quonset hut filled with rare cactus, most in small pots, largely unlabeled. The cactarium contains many tiny, pincushion _Mammillaria_ varieties, African succulents and euphorbias, and a South American "creeping cactus," whose spiny tubes snake through the raised beds for fifteen feet. Here the rhythmic patterns and enticing colors of cactus flesh and quills speak eloquently about the arrows of desire this singular plant family lets fly.

Proceeding up a small rise and across a miniature water feature— Little Tahquitz Falls and Little Lake Cahuilla, named for actual places nearby—the path skirts a green lawn leading to the Moorten family residence and passes a "prehistoric garden" with dinosaur footprint fossils from Utah and Texas under a palm oasis. As symbolized by translucent cubes of Mexican onyx and other mineral and geological clues, "Cactus Slim" Moorten prospected in the 1930s before starting this garden. In an area of what later became Joshua Tree National Monument, he built Moorten's Mill in 1934, a five-stamp mill used "to process gold ore from his three claims in the Cottonwood area."

Moorten later landscaped the homes of notable people as Palm Springs came into fashion. Active voices in the Coachella Valley on behalf of the desert and its values, family members continue to operate this private botanical garden. Unlike so much else in this resort, Moorten Botanical Garden is unpretentious and informal. Instead of seeking to be something it is not—a tendency never more glaring than in the golf course lawns and condo lakes of this driest of all North American deserts—Moorten Botanical Garden has a strong local feeling, rooted in the arid soil and climate. Although many plants are exotics—it does not restrict itself to native species—the garden nonetheless experiments within the strictures of the desert, rather than defiantly seeking to transform it into some other environment. That, it would seem, is the necessary wisdom born of heat, drought, and sand.

(Moorten's "Desertland" Botanical Garden, 1701 South Palm Canyon Dr., Palm Springs. Adult admission, $1.50; open Monday through Saturday 9:00 a.m. to 4:30 p.m., Sundays 10:00 a.m. to 4:00 p.m. A nursery sells desert plants. Telephone 619-327-6555. Palm canyons nearby may also be visited; see "Briefly Noted.")

KIMBERLY CREST
HOUSE
AND
GARDENS

Overlooking the city of Redlands and north across the valley to Cajon Pass, Kimberly Crest House and Gardens offers a glimpse of the Edwardian splendor in which easterners "wintered" in citrus country at the turn of the century. The property is generously scaled yet elegantly proportioned, with sweeping flower beds, tall trees, and lawns, staircases, and terraces sloping up to a turreted mansion in the French style at the crest of the hill. Built in 1897, the two-and-one-half story *château éclectique*—green roof, olive gray stucco with cream trim, balconies with Gothic carvings, Victorian grillwork atop the roof peak, and iron turret finials—surveys the property's grand *Washingtonia robusta* palms, deodar cedars, Montezuma cypress, southern magnolia, jacaranda, and eucalyptus.

Edwin Bergstrom, a relative of the Kimberly family that purchased the estate in 1907, designed the garden in the Italian manner. (Bergstrom conducted an active architectural practice in Los Angeles for several decades, designing the Pasadena Civic Auditorium, among many other buildings. Edward Huntsman-Trout also performed landscape work for Mrs. J. A. Kimberly in 1929.) The garden is structured by a series of balustraded staircases, covered with creeping fig, that climb a slope of terraced lawns. Flanking the terraces, the curves of twin crescent pergolas echo those of the turreted mansion, and stone finials in garden structures match carved woodwork inside the house. Although evidently authentic to the period, traditional urns containing the olive and cream stripes and hazardous thorns of *Agave americana marginata* strike a contemporary—or perhaps *moderne*—note, curiously bold amid balustrades, brackets, a lily pond with a "Sons of Poseidon" fountain, and similar emblems of gentility.

The house is entered from its southern side, where before circling to a porte cochere a long drive passes a second, informal pond and waterfall

Skyline trees and terraces at Kimberly Crest, Redlands

before a screen of *Phyllostachys aurea* bamboo, philodendrons, and camellias. House tours highlight furnishings preserved as Louis Tiffany decorated it in 1908. A daughter of the Kimberly family lived in the house until 1979, leaving its French-influenced decor, with many Tiffany touches, essentially unchanged and beautifully maintained. Although some restoration has been necessary, the garden also has survived largely intact, with eighty-year-old clumps of cycad and Mediterranean fan palms, a small citrus grove, a heart-shaped rose garden, and exotic trees and shrubs throughout the property. Adjoining thirty-acre Prospect Park, this small estate has great style and distinction.

(The entrance drive to Kimberly Crest is an extension of Alvarado Street as it crosses Highland Ave. south of downtown Redlands; guided house tours, $2.00 per person, are given Sundays and Thursdays 1:00 p.m. to 4:00 p.m. For information, telephone 714-792-2111, or write Kimberly Crest House & Gardens, P.O. Box 206, Redlands, CA 92373.)

University of California, Riverside, Botanical Garden

Located far inland, at an elevation of 1,100 to 1,450 feet, the UC Riverside Botanical Garden experiences hot summers and meager rainfall. With an average rainfall of 10.65 inches annually, the property lies just outside what would technically be considered a desert. Irrigation and the garden's site in the heart of the citrus belt permit the cultivation of plants ranging from arid desert and South African regions to tropical ficus and palms. Set in uneven terrain on the eastern boundary of the university campus, the thirty-seven-acre garden's canyons, flat highlands, and boulder-strewn, exposed hillsides have encouraged considerable variety in the plantings since they began in 1963.

A hillside desert garden near the entrance contains rare agaves, yuccas, and related species such as the Mexican *Beschorneria yuccoides*, whose hot pink bloom stalks rise above blue-green, thornless leaf spears. The desert garden also contains several *Opuntia* cactus species and desert trees such as the willow (*Chilopsis linearis*), *Washingtonia filifera* and *Brahea armata* palms, and the blue palo verde (*Cercidium floridum*).

Continuing along a southern hillside exposure, the path enters a southern African area dominated during the winter by dozens of blooming aloes: the yellow and orange of *Aloe microstigma*; hot coral of *A. keithii* on grape-purple stems above sage and maroon leaves; and orange torches of the tall *A. marlothii*, buzzing with bees. As its botanical name suggests, the arboreal "Kokerboom" (*A. dichotoma*) branches from a thick trunk into stems clothed in bark that looks smooth as buff-colored skin, each one bearing a star of pale green foliage spears at its growth tips. Other winter-flowering succulents include *Kalanchoe fedtschenkoi* (with mauve, pale apricot, and pink leaves and blooms) and South African *Mesembryanthemum* ground covers.

Paths through the northern, more highly developed part of the UC Riverside Botanical Garden follow the Y-shaped contours of two canyons that converge just inside the entrance. Atop a hill above one of the canyons, just past a flowering peach (*Prunus x blireiana*)—in March a spectacle of bright rose and purple and singing with bees—a flat upland contains a number of specialized areas, including a rose garden, an extensive iris collection of more than 150 varieties, and an herb garden. Most impressive is a geodesic dome built of red cedar and covered with wooden lath, without doubt one of the best uses yet devised for Buckminster Fuller's ingenious design. Paradoxically using triangles to create a sphere, the geodesic method permits a high, open shelter, unobstructed by beams, columns, or other support. The lath strips emphasize the dome's geometry, casting striated shadows on a display of cycads, canna lilies, camellias, angel's trumpet, poinsettias, the tiny, pale violet flowers of *Wigandia caracasana*, and other flowering and tropical plants that comprise one of this botanical garden's most satisfying areas.

From this flat hilltop, several paths venture into rustic areas, winding up and down hilly country through collections organized geographically (Australia, Latin America, Africa, and the Sierra foothills) and according to plant families (conifers, junipers, cypress, pines, palms, grasses, citrus, and ficus). Most notable is a ficus collection assembled by Dr. Ira J. Condit, a ficus authority on the UC Riverside faculty. The extensive display includes the Himalayan *Ficus auriculata*, the Colombian *F. archeri*, the Javan *F. involucrata*, the Mexican *F. petiolaris* (its leaf stems tinged rose), the sea fig of the western Pacific (*F. superba*), and the tropical African *F. natalensis*. The figs merge into the palms, interspersed with bamboos for tropical effect, which are in turn adjoined by stands of conifers, pines, and junipers, the latter sparsely planted on a promontory affording views of the northern part of the botanical garden, the UC Riverside campus, and the surrounding valley and mountains.

Descending through cypresses and chamaecypresses, the path reaches low-lying Alder Canyon. Lined with white alders (*Alnus rhombifolia*) bearing distinctive "eye" trunk scars left by fallen branches, Alder Canyon also contains California native species such as incense cedar (*Calocedrus decurrens*), California walnut (*Juglans californica*), California sycamore (*Platanus racemosa*), big-leaf maple (*Acer macrophyllum*), and Oregon ash (*Fraxinus latifolia*). The canyon—whose trees are among the garden's earliest plantings—contains deciduous trees requiring the cold temperatures of a canyon bottom through which air from higher elevations drains during the winter. The shade they cast and the canyon's steep sides also permit camellias, azaleas, the late-winter-blooming saucer magnolia (*Magnolia x soulangiana*), and Australian tree ferns to survive Riverside's hot summers. A collection of Chinese trees clusters at the bottom of the canyon near the entrance.

(UC Riverside Botanical Garden, Riverside, is located at the eastern edge of campus; open daily 8:00 a.m. to 5:00 p.m., except New Year's Day, Independence Day, Thanksgiving, and Christmas. Free admission and parking. Telephone 714-787-4650.)

INLAND
AND
DESERT AREAS
BRIEFLY NOTED

As Pacific Coast Highway whirls through a tunnel and leaves the beach behind, it becomes the Santa Monica Freeway, the "Christopher Columbus Transcontinental Highway," and Interstate 10. Curving past the distant Hollywood Hills, it sinks and rises imperceptibly between banks and ramps whose proportions highway planners gradually perfected over several decades. The engineers altered large parts of California to meet the demands of high-speed automobile travel. Although designed for safety and convenience, the monumental concrete system not infrequently takes on a kind of futuristic beauty. The state's highways also benefit from skillful landscaping, their familiar contoured gradients planted as green shoulders of ivy and ice plant, swaying eucalyptus and fresh acacia, tall palms and redwoods. Tying the state together not only as transportation but also as a visual unit, the designs of the freeway system—a statewide earthwork—doubtless have a greater influence on the California landscape as it is daily perceived than any other single source. (David Brodsly's *L.A. Freeway: An Appreciative Essay* [1981] explores this and many other ways of looking at the system.)

The Santa Monica Freeway glides toward downtown under fronds of stately Canary Island and *Washingtonia* palms that distinguish the streets throughout older districts of Los Angeles. Lately, within sight of the freeway, once-fashionable suburbs poise once more to become well located, as transportation takes on the proportions of a social problem (the term reserved for those problems society cannot solve) and distance from the city center begins to affect decisions about where to live. East of downtown, Interstate 10 takes on a new name, the San Bernardino Freeway, and a new character, straight as the railroad track that occupies the median strip as it slices through frayed suburbs carpeting the San Gabriel Valley floor. From the beach past downtown and into the inland valleys, the climate, the topography, and the mood gradually change.

Instead of an immense ocean, a great mountain range fills the inland view. Summers are hotter, winter nights are colder, and early morning cloud layers thinner and less persistent. Somewhere inland the distance from the ocean becomes greater than the distance to the desert, and at that uncertain point one begins to leave Los Angeles behind. Riverside and San Bernardino now rank as the state's fastest-growing counties, representing the latest episodes in the classic California fable of rapid change: build first and ask questions later. For decades this region has hopefully called itself the Inland Empire, but sudden, massive growth has rendered that sort of hope no longer necessary, or indeed possible.

There are many interesting places, however, that headlong development has not yet effaced. Overlooking a large lake surrounded by cypress and other large trees, a sizable rose garden in Riverside's FAIRMONT PARK dates from the 1920s and was renovated in 1986. The formal plan sets out modern shrub roses in beds edged with curbs stenciled with the names of rose varieties. *Washingtonia* and queen palms sway above the roses in a 180-acre park with wide lawns, plentiful trees, and Evans Lake, designed in 1911 by the Olmsted brothers (sons of the celebrated landscape architect, Frederick Law Olmsted). (Fairmont Park Rose Garden, Redwood and Dexter Dr., Riverside.)

In 1870, the U.S. Department of Agriculture received a shipment of budded citrus trees from a Presbyterian missionary in Bahia, Brazil, where sixty years earlier a "Selecta" orange had mutated into a large, winter-ripening, seedless orange with a strong flavor. In Riverside, Luther Tibbets read USDA descriptions of the new orange and sent for two trees. Planted in his front yard in December 1873, watered (according to citrus belt legend) by his wife Eliza with her dirty dishwater, and bearing their first fruit in 1878, these plants became the "parent trees" of an industry that would transform Riverside and other citrus belt towns into prosperous, comfortable places. In 1903, one parent tree was transplanted to the Mission Inn in downtown Riverside, where it died in 1922. The other RIVERSIDE PARENT ORANGE TREE, also transplanted, fared better, surviving to this day in a triangular plot, fenced and protected by smudge pots, honoring Eliza Tibbets and "the most valuable fruit introduction yet made" by the USDA. (Arlington and Magnolia aves., Riverside.)

Urbanization has not quite obliterated commercial plantings in the citrus belt; some superb vistas remain of orchards interspersed with rows of *Washingtonia robusta* palms stretching from Interstate 10 near San Bernardino north to the foothills. It is one of the shortcomings of contemporary ecological and environmental ideals that working landscapes, created by human beings and realizing a valuable way of life, are not thought to be fit subjects for preservation. Ideal citrus climates are perfect for people, too. It will not be long before the grandeur of citrus orchards, from San Diego's Pala Valley to San Bernardino to Ventura County, will be gone forever, effacing a landscape whose qualities the historian Kevin Starr has described (in *Inventing the Dream: California Through the Progressive Era*) as "beauty and civility. . . luxuriance and orderly repose."

Rarely have commerce, nature, and art merged more eloquently than in the citrus groves. Like the growers cultivating the vineyards of central and northern California, the citrus industry that fostered this remarkably aesthetic landscape also created for itself a full-blown myth. Those myths survived because they offered more than a mere marketing ploy; besides selling fruit, they also suggested a new, desirable way to live. Like grapes and citrus, the date industry bequeathed an exceptional working landscape to the Coachella Valley. (On the working landscape, see Anthony Hiss, *The Experience of Place* [1990].) Planted from 1911 to 1922, the oldest groves in Indian Wells and Indio have enormous palms, gridded for commercial efficiency. Their shade, height, greenery, and precision form the antithesis of desert horizontality, treelessness, sandy aridity, and the sense of all plants—all life—being at the complete mercy of nature.

The small domes at the entrance to JENSEN'S DATE AND CITRUS GARDENS symbolize the myth—Arabia, camels, oases—on which the local date industry seeks to trade. In essence simply another roadside attraction under a date grove, Jensen's displays date and citrus hybrids, locally developed varieties, and curiosities such as the Hawaiian pomelo (the world's largest citrus, weighing up to six pounds each) or a "combination" citrus, budded in 1935 with fourteen varieties. The garden also tells the story of the date in the United States. After the USDA imported North African date offshoots in 1890 and established a Date Experimental Station in Mecca, California (creative imaginations had already been busy), in 1904, the Coachella Valley date industry grew to produce 90 percent of the American date crop.

Unusual citrus varieties grown here come from all over the world, and Jensen's contains many other flowering shrubs, exotic trees, and a few grandiose, menacing cacti. There are many labels, which even when somewhat irrelevant (e.g., a "Coachella Valley 1968 Crop Report") are mostly in good shape. This is hardly a polished horticultural performance; it offers instead a picturesque but informative desuetude, an erudite hoot. (Jensen's Date and Citrus Gardens, 80-653 Highway 111, Indio. Open 9:00 a.m. to 5:00 p.m. daily. Telephone 619-347-3897.)

Although beyond the scope of this book as a natural area rather than a garden, just south of Palm Springs a number of PALM CANYONS containing groves of California's only native palm, *Washingtonia filifera*, are open for visits. These exceptional palm groves along streams are highly recommended. Most are on land owned by the Agua Caliente Band of Cahuilla Indians, who charge an admission fee. Enter the reservation by proceeding south on South Palm Canyon, and follow signs to Murray, Andreas, or Palm Canyon, the latter named being the largest canyon, watered by a winter stream under hundreds of native palms. A fourth canyon, Tahquitz, may require a special permit available from the Tribal Council Office (telephone 619-325-5673).

Quite different from the desert are the forested slopes of the San Bernardino Mountains that tower above the city by that name. Climbing from the valley floor to "The Rim of the World," it is fascinating to watch native plants change with the elevation from chaparral through oak, incense cedar, big-cone spruce, and finally to the ponderosa pine. Near Lake Arrowhead, the HEAPS PEAK ARBORETUM offers a short but well-organized tour of alpine tree and plant species. Officially opened in 1984, the arboretum originated in efforts by the Lake Arrowhead Women's Club and local elementary school students to reforest after a 1922 forest fire. Plantings continued from 1928 until World War II. Many trees survived despite minimal attention and another fire in 1956. In 1982, the Mountain Chapter of the San Bernardino County Museum Association, with the cooperation of the U.S. Forest Service, developed the site as an arboretum.

The area is mixed native oak (*Quercus kelloggii*), pine, and meadow (with large areas of western brackenfern and wildflowers), through which an easy, mostly level, well-maintained three-quarter-mile path meanders. An interpretive brochure, a map, and displays introduce the history, habitat, and characteristics of incense cedar, white fir, sugar, Coulter and Jeffrey pine, and many other species. Plantings continue, the latest being saplings of the marvelous quaking aspen (*Populus tremuloides*), whose heart-shaped leaves shimmer in the slightest breeze. A grove of sequoia redwoods, planted in 1930 and thriving in this alpine site (elev. 5,996 ft.) that resembles its Sierra Nevada habitat, is particularly impressive.

At one point the tour pauses to peer north through the trees as the mountain range loses elevation and the green forest evaporates into the arid Mojave Desert. Across Rim of the World Drive, there are southern views down to San Bernardino and, smog permitting, into the Los Angeles basin. The comparison shows the contrast between coastal and desert ecologies and emphasizes the fragility of the mountains, a green island in the air above hotter, drier climates below. At Heaps Peak Arboretum, the interpretive materials are well prepared, a forest ranger is on duty (at least on summer weekends), new facilities are under construction, and plantings continue. Good work has been done here over many generations, and contemporary residents are building on that foundation. One gets the refreshing feeling of an arboretum on its way up. A small but agreeable surprise, the arboretum is an asset to the area which local residents can feel proud of. (Heaps Peak Arboretum, Highway 18 about two miles east of Skyforest; free admission. For information, telephone the Rim of the World Interpretive Association, 714-337-3408.)

Farther west, down into the basin, and just inside the Los Angeles County line, the Claremont Colleges contain work by two noted landscape architects. Edward Huntsman-Trout's involvement with SCRIPPS COLLEGE—landscaping the original campus in 1927, the east campus in 1958, and the 11th Street entrance in 1965—produced a distinguished design that has been called the work for which he is most likely to be remembered. The gently sloping campus has been terraced along a pedestrian axis, from which garden courtyards extend between campus buildings. At the northeast corner, an interesting symmetrical courtyard sets four old olives in swept earthen beds edged by twisted cement pavers, with a fountain and a vine-covered pergola on three sides. Rows of olives, sycamores, and elms line paths leading to college buildings set in eucalyptus, oaks, deodar, and other large trees. The campus is listed on the National Register of Historic Places.

A graduate of the college that gave him his first professional job as supervising landscape architect, Ralph D. Cornell's work at POMONA COLLEGE is held in similar high regard. A large quadrangle of trees, flower beds, and lawn extends west from Bridges Auditorium to the Carnegie Building on College Avenue. The plan contains some subtle symmetries—twin coast redwoods at the west end of the lawn, across from a pair of blue fan palms flanking the entrance to the Carnegie Building and mimicking the columns of its portico—that relieve the main quadrangle's grand scale. A gem of a walled courtyard to the south, Cornell's Harwood Garden (1921) fits snugly between "Little Bridges" and Sumner halls, with benches along rows of young sycamores and vines shrouding courtyard walls and college buildings. (Scripps and Pomona Colleges are located in Claremont, north of Interstate 10 and a few blocks east of Indian Hill Blvd.)

IV
Los Angeles
West

THE
J. PAUL GETTY
MUSEUM
GARDENS

The sudden rumble of Roman paving stones slows automobiles as they climb a steep hill past a guardhouse into a leafy canyon, along fern-edged ponds by a glistening spring, and under native sycamores in green lawns. After negotiating a stairwell rising from a distinctly un-Roman underground parking structure, visitors pass along a portico commanding a prospect down the canyon just traversed to the Pacific Ocean. After a few last stairs, a colonnade framing a symmetrical, first-century Roman garden and villa comes into view, completing the sequence of surprises that greet visitors to the J. Paul Getty Museum.

Having spent the better part of half a century acquiring antiquities and classical art, J. Paul Getty determined to design a setting that would best complement his collection. He once remarked, "What could be more logical than to display it in a classical building where it might originally have been seen?" Getty decided to re-create the Villa de Papiri, an immense residence inundated when Vesuvius erupted in A.D. 79. The villa was located near Herculaneum, one of several settlements along the Bay of Naples, whose fashionable affluence Cicero scorned as "a crater of luxury." The area enjoyed a rich, volcanic soil, yielding four crops a year and supporting splendid gardens, until the volcano overwhelmed Herculaneum beneath a muddy torrent that hardened into crystalline rock. Later lava flows sealed its doom until an eighteenth-century well digger accidentally struck an upper tier of seats in the city's theater.

Sporadic excavation followed until Swiss architect Karl Weber's discovery of the Villa de Papiri proved its immense importance. Tunneling through tufa rock fifty feet beneath the surface and battling seeping water, noxious gas, and hostile colleagues, Weber retrieved ninety pieces of sculpture, including the largest cache of ancient bronze statuary ever discovered. He also unearthed the first complete ancient library, whose

The main peristyle garden, J. Paul Getty Museum

scrolls gave the villa of "papiri" its name. And before closing the explora-
tory shafts, he prepared a plan of the villa and its immense peristyle.

Weber's plan, Pliny's _Natural History_ and other ancient writings, and
recent archaeological digs exploring the gardens of Pompeii enabled the
Getty Museum to create a garden following classical design principles
and containing plants known in antiquity. (Wilhelmina Jashemski's _The
Gardens of Pompeii_ [1979] recounts how archaeologists identified plants
known to Roman horticulture by methods ranging from close study of
villa murals to plaster-filled root cavities. The gardens were designed by
Dennis Kurutz and Emmet Wemple.) Even small domestic Roman
gardens ordinarily grew in a peristyle, a court enclosed by a colonnade.
On surrounding walls, a Roman home owner could contract with painters
"by the yard" to produce something not unlike a modern trompe l'ocil
mural, a landscape window of painted garden scenes, flowery swags,
or imaginary vistas. Those few ancient murals that survived the Vesu-
vian deluge, excavation, and the depredations of time, tourists, and connoisseurs provided yet another source for making a Roman garden.

From the portico, Getty Museum visitors may proceed through the
garden or follow the colonnades forming the two long sides of the rectangular peristyle. On colonnade walls, murals portray a bright bird,
lounging lizard, or whimsical insect on alternating panels of garlands
and "oscilla" (plaster masks that in a real garden would "oscillate") suspended from an architrave. Wheat, apples, pine cones, grapes, apples,
and pomegranates comprise one garland pattern. The other contains
flowers the Romans grew—coronaria, roses, violas, candytuft, the _clu-
siana_ "candystripe" tulip, and the poet's narcissus. (As if for the sake of
comparison, living specimens bloom nearby in peristyle garden beds.)
Varro, an ancient agricultural writer, advised Roman farmers to seek two
goals: profit and pleasure. The museum's two mural patterns neatly
mark the spectrum of Roman gardens—and perhaps of all gardens—
ranging between the poles of utility (plants harvested for food, medicine,
clothing, or shelter) and pleasure (ornamental cultivation for interest,
comfort, or beauty).

Several other features link the main peristyle to its prototypes. A long
blue pool reflects the Roman taste for water features. In antiquity, basins,
fountains, and cascades helped cool and humidify summer gardens and
water the plants. The Romans even dined around a water triclinium, a
pool on which servants floated tiny vessels shaped as birds or boats bearing morsels of food. And having stocked their garden ponds, affluent
Romans delighted in training fish to take food from their hands. (Cic-

ero decried such devotees as "fishpond addicts," upon whom eels exerted a particularly strong, almost sinister attraction. The orator L. Licinius Crassus, for instance, decked out his pet moray eel with earrings and necklaces; Quintus Hortensius shed tears when a beloved eel died.)

Only reliable, abundant water could have made such indulgences possible. It was supplied by miles of concrete aqueducts and dozens of reservoirs, a far-flung system that was the engineering marvel of the age and essential to its gardens. The Roman art of topiary depended on this technology as it required regular watering as much as meticulous pruning. In the museum's main peristyle, the elaborate topiary creates a symmetrical "mirror" garden, with each sharp-edged hedge pattern and large plant (European fan palms, pomegranates, and oleanders) on one side of the central pool corresponding to a twin plant or pattern on the other.

Nearly a mile of boxwood hedging, mounded ivy, and the umbrella shapes of trimmed bay laurel trees (*Laurus nobilis*) illustrate the techniques Romans applied to any plant they could clip into a hedge, cone, obelisk, or other geometrical volume. Of the six species Roman writers mention most frequently, all except the acanthus accept some kind of topiary treatment. Significantly, all six—ivy, clipped box, laurel, myrtle, acanthus, and rosemary—are evergreen, warming up a garden (at least visually) in winter and cooling it in summer. Although these half-dozen species dominate the Getty Museum's main peristyle, it saves room for smaller plants whose color and detail relieve the enormous garden's formal precision. In season, the beds bloom with anemones, madonna lilies, daffodils, bearded irises, and a spring-blooming rose of antiquity, *Rosa gallica*. The relative prominence of flowers makes one of this garden's few concessions to modern taste for floral display. Although appreciated, flowers formed a distinctly secondary order of importance in Roman gardens, which would have more strongly subordinated the flowering plants grown in the main peristyle to an evergreen structure.

True landscape architects, the ancient Romans leveled mountains and carved out building sites that clung to promontories to gain the most coveted view, to see and be seen. Given the Roman formal garden's reliance on sophisticated engineering, it is less surprising to learn that the museum's main peristyle rests on that modern necessity, the underground parking structure. Except for a few tubbed specimens, the plants occupy only about eighteen inches of soil, growing in what is actually an enormous container garden holding hundreds of plants.

As a roof garden, its weight must not compromise the building's structural integrity, yet the soil must remain dense enough to anchor the

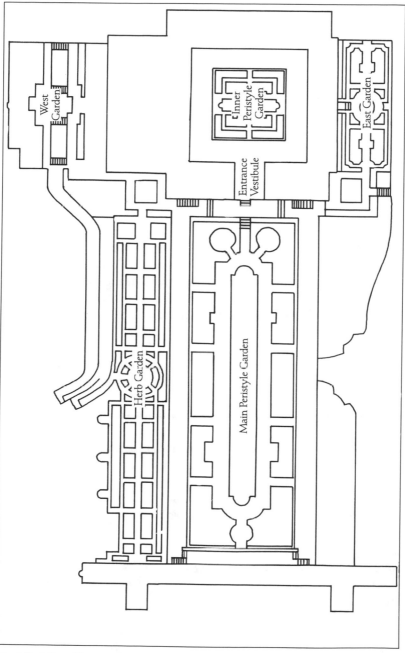

The J. Paul Getty Museum Gardens

plants. So the gardeners add cinders and pumice—volcanic matter not unlike the peach pit-sized "lapilli" that Vesuvius rained down upon Pompeii nineteen centuries ago. Blended with sand and an organic soil mix, the volcanic matter aerates and absorbs moisture while remaining lighter than ordinary soil. It also points up a small historical irony: the very material that destroyed ancient gardens near Vesuvius helps this modern Roman garden thrive.

Mixing profit and pleasure, no Roman garden was ever very far from a vineyard. Of the nine elements of the best kind of farm, Cato ranked vineyards highest. High economic return undoubtedly explained some of this esteem, but Romans valued grapevines for fragrance when in bloom, for summer shade, and for the variety of their berries. The vine's paradoxical associations suggest some of its mystery. Its sapling formed the centurion's rod of office, yet contradicting that aura of discipline and authority was the cult of Bacchus, god of wine, pleasure, and disorderly conduct, who was often pictured wearing a cloak of ruby grapes or crowned by grape leaves. The Getty Museum's main peristyle, with grapevines coiling around twin arbors flanking its central pool, acknowledges the vine's importance in Roman life and symbolically links Mediterranean civilization with the grapes and wine produced throughout California.

At the villa entrance, a short flight of marble stairs opens into a small foyer leading to the villa's ground floor galleries. The foyer's ceiling mural, based on a Pompeiian example, depicts the view beneath a fanciful grape arbor, with assorted Dionysian paraphernalia—a quiver of Cupid's darts, drinking horns, masks, tambourines, panpipes—dispersed among sinuous vines supporting plenty of fat, ripe grape clusters. Like the peristyle murals, it joins plants living in the garden to the museum's art and symbolizes a great Roman household's abundance and hospitality.

The gardens also invite comparisons between living plants and the museum's art and architecture. According to the Roman architectural writer Vitruvius, for instance, *Acanthus mollis* inspired Greek sculptor Callimachus to incorporate its deep-cut leaves into his design for the capital of the Corinthian column, the most ornate of the three Greek architectural orders. The acanthus grows throughout the main peristyle, where you may compare its dark, lustrous leaves with the Corinthian columns supporting porticoes in the colonnade.

Many of the museum's European paintings also contain horticultural themes or details, sometimes rhyming with garden plants outdoors. Oleander flowers and foliage, for instance, grace Winterhalter's portrait of Princess Leonilla of Sayn-Wittgenstein-Sayn, suggesting the warm, sensuous south and emphasizing the exotic beauty of a princess reclining at her ease. The museum's collection contains two fine eighteenth-century studies by Jan Van Huysum, a master of European floral still-life painting. The Romans themselves would have recognized the blue species irises whether they saw them in van Gogh's painting in the gallery or in the museum garden.

Through the foyer, the villa arranges itself around a smaller version of the main peristyle garden that likewise contains a pool, garden statuary, and mainly evergreen plants. An open gallery leads to the busy west garden, where the museum restaurant offers refreshment. Its outdoor seating in a colonnade provides the setting for a further series of mural panels showing small date palms, severely trimmed and fenced in by a kind of lattice barrier.

To the south, a gate opens onto the museum's agricultural garden. A large Italian stone pine marks a ramp inclining between two pomegranates into fragrant beds of herbs, flowers, and vegetables. Smaller and more formally planted than that which would have supplied a Roman villa of this size, it surveys the plants grown in a classical agricultural garden as well as some flowering plants known in antiquity. The true, unhybridized magenta of the crown-pink (_Lychnis coronaria_) and intense fragrances of ancient herbs and vegetables thrive beneath a grove of olive trees. This other great botanical symbol of Mediterranean life presides over the garden from a sunny, terraced slope.

Besides enlivening a spicy cuisine, herbal plants in Roman times had many other uses, both ritual and practical. At weddings, the ancients adorned the bride and groom with rosemary, but without apparent irony, they also placed it in the hands of the dead. Romans linked major garden plants to a deity: ivy to Bacchus, laurel to Apollo, myrtle to Venus. They also thought that gods and goddesses, as well as deceased family members, dwelled in household gardens. Some trees were sacred and were worshiped. The Roman domestic garden, besides bringing nature into the home, opened portals of religious imagination into the supernatural world.

For all its importance as a source of food and a place of labor, the Roman garden also connoted ease and contemplation. At the Getty Museum, a small meditation garden east of the villa suggests the value some Romans placed on private leisure despite—or because of—their violent, competitive, status-seeking society. Although the plane tree the Romans knew, _Platanus orientalis_, does not grow in this climate, specimens of the London plane (*P. acerifolia*) shade this meditation garden. Roman praise of the plane makes it the ideal tree for a garden of repose. Ovid, for instance, who wrote poetry in his garden, spoke of "the genial plane." Its associations with learning have caused the species to be named "the scholar's tree," perhaps because Plato set the dialogue between Socrates and Phaedrus beneath its shade.

Like scholars seeking truth, the plane tree has also enjoyed a special relationship with wine. The poet Horace bid a friend not to vex his mind with eternal, hopeless problems but to recline and imbibe convivially "beneath the lofty plane tree." Pliny the Elder recorded an odd horticultural favor accorded to the species. While engaged in a court case, Hortensius begged his colleague Cicero to change the order of their speeches so he could leave for his country house on the urgent errand of pouring wine on a favorite plane tree. (Hortensius, it must be admitted, cut a studied, dandyish figure; if other men let their toga fall where they might, Hortensius artfully knotted and draped the folds before a mirror and once sued a passerby for the tort of accidentally brushing against him and spoiling the "set" of his toga.)

For all its intimate, humane proportions and shady trees, an *aedicula* makes this meditation garden Roman. The ancients placed these small fountains in a wall niche ornamented with mosaic work, shells, and shiny bits of glass. Water, issuing from a statue or mask or flowing down a tiny staircase, added an agreeable music. In the Getty Museum's tranquil garden with few flowers and no through traffic, the aedicula adds accents of color and sound to accompany meditation without distracting it. Amid the splendor of the museum's building and its works of art, this modest garden reminds us that some Romans pursued the simple life. A few desired, as the Stoic Seneca put it, "the small garden that does not arouse hunger but satisfies it."

The ancient Romans gained lasting notoriety for achievements they performed well, or easily: conquest, civil engineering, religious persecution, loose-fitting menswear. The paradox of their civilization is that while signs of intelligence abound, they coexist with a startlingly high threshold of socially approved cruelty and moral blindness. Yet for some Romans a life at home—and sometimes only the hope of it—balanced the frenzy of war, politics, bloody spectacle, and other efforts to make the world safe for the Middle Ages. To be sure, as Cicero remarked, even the attention lavished on the villas could degenerate into a kind of craziness. Yet the Getty Museum's Roman gardens remind us that daily living of ease and integration balanced imperial marauding and acquisition.

They symbolize the importance in Roman life of husbandry in farm, orchard, and vineyard, and of the garden as a place where daily work and pleasures merge.

The Getty Museum may also serve as an emblem of a second Mediterranean culture, rising on the shore of another ocean. The Coliseum and Forum in Los Angeles nod—feebly, it must be admitted—at those of ancient Rome. The two cities also share a similar climate and an open-air way of life, with bathing ritual and physical culture; architecture blending indoor and outdoor living; the monumental but essential roads and aqueducts; and a ferocious appetite for material consumption and public display, at once driving the cities' achievements but in some ways undercutting the well-being of their residents.

The Getty Museum has encouraged the cultural aspirations of Los Angeles, even if a few strained comparisons to nearby theme parks initially stirred up some of the city's primordial insecurities. The museum's crisp-edged marble, striking colors, and gleaming tiles may well portray Roman life with an imaginative immediacy and even a kind of truth that is lacking in a weed-choked ruin of chipped columns or collapsing roofs. Like Alma-Tadema's *Spring* in its galleries, the museum tries to capture the spirit of the thing at noon, with the Roman sun at its height, eschewing mere authenticity if reduced to a crumbling shadow of its former self.

Even in its brief life, however, the museum has observed some subtle changes. Colors have mellowed a shade; use has muted the marble floors' high polish; the structure having literally settled into its site, hairline cracks creep picturesquely up the painted walls and crawl across the ceilings. Most crucial to the ripening classical illusion, however, the gardens and plantings have matured. Ivy clings to columns or hangs between trellis uprights in handsome swags. Gardeners elaborate the topiary hedging and retire species too rank or too timid in favor of those compatible with the coastal climate. And the canyon plantings grow on, shading and nurturing the Roman mood with the ancient renewal of green growth.

You can only see this sort of garden here. Even the attempts at classical gardens in the Pompeiian ruins suffer from anachronism and the lack of sound horticultural knowledge about what actually grew there in ancient times. For all its apparent vigor, a garden remains among the most ephemeral of the fine arts. It begins to decline a day or two after it ceases to be cared for, and nature regains the upper hand over art with surprising speed and decision. The Getty Museum's founder, besides having the vision to bring this garden into being, also left the means to maintain it. J. Paul Getty did not live to see his classical gardens. But by planting these vines and flowers, shrubs and trees, as an early Roman poet had it, "to shade another generation," he left the future in his debt.

(The J. Paul Getty Museum, 17985 Pacific Coast Highway [between Sunset Blvd. and Topanga Canyon Blvd., just east of Coastline Dr.], Malibu. Open Tuesday through Sunday 10:00 a.m. to 5:00 p.m.; closed Mondays and New Year's Day, Independence Day, Thanksgiving, and Christmas Day. Admission is free, but visitors must obtain a parking reservation, arrive by taxi or RTD bus [request a museum pass from the driver], or be dropped off and picked up; walk-in visitors are not admitted. For reservations, telephone 213-458-2003 at least a week in advance. The museum contains a bookstore and restaurant, offers tours of the gardens and of its antiquities, European paintings, and decorative arts, and presents lectures and classes in the arts and humanities.)

VIRGINIA
ROBINSON
GARDENS

The Virginia Robinson Gardens offers a rare glimpse of estate gardening and living in Beverly Hills. After several owners and decades of false starts (livestock ranching, lima bean farming, and oil drilling), in 1907 the Rodeo Land and Water Co. subdivided Beverly Hills according to the plan of landscape architect Wilbur David Cook, Jr. Following a pattern similar to those in places as diverse as Monterey and Pasadena, the developers made their city fashionable by building a resort, the Beverly Hills Hotel. (Civic lore maintains that only after Douglas Fairbanks, Sr., and Mary Pickford established a hunting lodge, Pickfair, within the city did Beverly Hills finally become the well-heeled enclave that it remains today.) Still distinguished by its intact city plan and exceptional street trees, Beverly Hills incorporated in 1914.

Settlement and incorporation occurred after Harry and Virginia Robinson had discovered a knoll in the virtually empty subdivision, purchased fifteen acres, and built a 6,000-square-foot house in 1911, one of the first in the city. Harry, the son of the founder of the J. W. Robinson's department store, lived in the house until his death in 1934. Intelligent, lively, interested in horticulture and stylish entertaining, and wealthy enough to indulge those interests, Virginia enjoyed a long, active life on the estate (later reduced to its present 6.5 acres) until her own death in 1977, forty-one days before her hundredth birthday. Mrs. Robinson bequeathed the property and a substantial endowment to Los Angeles County, which administers it through its Department of Arboreta and Botanic Gardens.

The property comprises a saddle of land from the bottom of a knoll to the east, cresting and crossing over the top, and sloping down again to the west. Its varying elevations, exposures, and microclimates have been skillfully exploited to create a range of effects. Visitors enter at a cypress court, a lawn panel forming an axis that extends from the house, between twin rows of Italian cypresses, and along a swimming pool, before terminating at a guest house. Flanking the lawn under the cypresses, horticulturist John Copeland has created a mixed border of purple Mexican salvia, delphiniums, lavender, blue-violet floral domes of *Trachelium caeruleum*, creamy yellow *Nicotiana*, and on the east wall, purple *Iochroma lanceolatum* and climbing roses. Formal in tone, the cypresses, walls, architectural terraces, balustrades, and urns that ornament the house comprise the most highly finished part of the garden.

Mr. and Mrs. Robinson built mortared brick paths, staircases, terraces, and water features on the hillsides below the knoll. To the west, exposed to the hottest sun, they planted a grove of southern magnolias, now tall and providing filtered shade along with a large deodar, a mock orange (*Pittosporum undulatum*), a pineapple guava, and a Montezuma cypress. The canopy shelters camellias and azaleas (Mrs. Robinson's favorites), ferns (Mr. Robinson's interest), and callas, clivia, hydrangea, bergenia, and rust-red Chinese lantern (*Abutilon*). Below the shade garden, a staircase descends to "the musical patio," a terrace and fountain next to a hibiscus with a thick trunk like a small tree. It typifies specimens throughout the property, which have had up to eighty years to mature.

The pool, cypress court, and house at Virginia Robinson Gardens

A staircase descends farther to terraces planted with dwarf citrus before climbing back toward the house past a bank of ferns, fragrant, golden-flowered kahili ginger, _Fuchsia arborescens,_ and a Himalayan _Talauma hodgsonii,_ grown to great size on this nearly frost-free site. Although there is a servants' wing and dormitory, the main house has only a single story and two bedrooms. It is distinguished by a spacious entry hall that leads from the front door into the cypress court and by a superb, open-air dining loggia that commands a view of the property's most dramatic area, a palm grove down the knoll to the east.

The area was originally planted as an exotic fruit orchard. But by the early 1930s, the fruit trees' lack of success prompted Mrs. Robinson to consult landscape architect Charles Gibbs Adams, who created a palm grove that is now considered the largest stand of king palms (_Archontophoenix cunninghamiana_) outside their native Australia. It proves again how mass planting underscores the impact of palms. Other palms (two _Washingtonia filifera, Howea forsteriana, Chamaerops humilis, Caryota urens, Rhapis excelsa_) appear, and the tropical leaves of tree bird of paradise counterpoint all the palmy fans and fringe. The preeminent king palms, however, form a vegetative ceiling so shady that only the ti plant (_Cordyline terminalis_), clivia, and (supported by the trees) staghorn ferns and _Monstera deliciosa_ can survive. It creates that most delightful paradox, a cool jungle.

The king palms, covering 2.5 acres, so alter the climate that deep within the grove, _Ficus rubiginosa_ trees revert to their tropical habit: sprouting aerial roots, they send these appendages down from branches twenty or thirty feet to plunge through still, humid air and into moist earth. To have inspired such behavior in the dry California climate is quite rare and indicates how unusual this palm grove microclimate has become. Sixty years after planting, the king palms are now very tall. The original two hundred specimens have gone to seed, creating children and grandchildren of the original plantation so that some two thousand king palms of all sizes fill up every possible space.

The path emerges from the palm grove into the sunlight of another bricked terrace, the "palm court," giving a view of a sunny, open area planted with ginger and bananas. A small rectangular pond set in the terrace contains water lilies, pickerel weed (_Pontederia cordata_), and umbrella plant (_Cyperus alternifolius_), their roots submerged in the water, and elsewhere an inset square of rhapis palms. The path proceeds past a small aviary (Mrs. Robinson kept bluebirds and blue parrots), across a fine tennis court (surrounded by green vines and a magnificent magenta bougainvillea), to a crescent-shaped rose garden next to a guest house designed in 1924 by William Richards with columns, friezes, and Palladian windows. The guest house overlooks the lawn and cypress court where the tour began.

Wealth and social status are in some respects isolating. On the subject of her wealth, late in life Mrs. Robinson was quoted as saying that "maybe things would have been different if I'd worked. I never knew a woman who did." There is nonetheless something to be said for the concept of splendid isolation as realized at Virginia Robinson Gardens. Even Beverly Hills, of course, cannot remain untouched by time; all about the hillsides are being scraped and rebuilt with squatty palaces that seem premised on the sort of Veblenesque anxieties that even the greatest house could scarcely assuage. Virginia Robinson Gardens, by contrast, demonstrates a feeling for the art of living. Besides being a connoisseur of rare plants, Virginia Robinson possessed a wide horticultural sensibility, at ease with formality yet also interested in tropical drama, calm lawns and classical balustrades as well as jungle passions. Her garden reveals artistry and virtuosity, erudition and feeling, and great beauty.

(Virginia Robinson Gardens, Beverly Hills, is open for guided tours by reservation only, Tuesday through Friday. Adult admission is $3.00. For reservations, directions, and information, telephone 213-276-5367.)

University of California, Los Angeles, Campus Landscaping

Around a core of ten buildings completed by the early 1930s, the University of California, Los Angeles (UCLA), has grown steadily since the Second World War, the pace quickening in recent years. The oldest, core buildings, such as Powell Hall or the especially fine Royce Hall, cluster along an east-west axis. Although later construction diverged from their Italian Romanesque style, it remained influential enough to make red brick seem to pervade the campus. The regents decided to abandon the Romanesque style in 1947, however, and through the 1970s, the failure of architectural vision ranged between prefab academic warehouses insouciantly chucked up and the health center's pharaonic pile.

Fortunately, from 1937 to 1972, noted landscape architect Ralph D. Cornell supervised the UCLA landscaping. University President Robert Gordon Sproul is said to have hired him after seeing Pomona College, Cornell's first commission. As UCLA grew, Cornell played a key role in preserving traditional parts of the campus, in reinforcing for campus unity, in keeping a human scale by using courts and open space, and in planting to hide a multitude of architectural sins. (On the north side of Knudsen Hall, for instance, landscaping literally masks mistakes, as creeping fig and espaliered laurel fig make foliar friezes to disguise blank, featureless walls.) More than establishing any single idiom—he saw his task in units, concentrating on distinctly designed areas—Cornell set a standard of quality. (Current campus landscaping follows his unitary approach by letting projects one by one, transforming Cornell's governing design principle into an administrative technique.) The landscaping by Cornell and his successors humanizes this busy, confusing university, horticulturally orienting and guiding people through and around a large, crowded campus.

Cornell also helped give the UCLA campus a kind of center, where axes cross at a flagpole between Haines and Kinsey halls in Dickson Plaza. (A free map—available at parking kiosks at campus entrances—is essential.) At the flagpole, several key landscaping elements emerge. First, while in some sense a luxury item, wide lawns give a needed openness to a campus that attracts 60,000 people daily when classes are in session and that continues to shoehorn new structures between its already closely spaced buildings.

Second, the axial plan is quite visible here. From Murphy Hall, past Royce and Powell, down Janss Steps, between the men's and women's gyms runs a main east-west axis, from drive, through lawn, down steps, to brick and mortared pavement. (Another east-west axis, Bruin Walk, shapes the undergraduate day by extending from College Library past the student union to dormitories across the valley.) Westwood Plaza divides the campus in half, north to south, and provides entry from Westwood Village and Bel Air. A pedestrian axis begins at the health center to the south, proceeds north along a courtyard of science and mathematics buildings, takes a dogleg before continuing north through the old campus, and terminates at the Franklin Murphy Sculpture Garden.

Rodin among the jacarandas: the Franklin Murphy Sculpture Garden, UCLA

Third, by alternating symmetry, free-form design, and distinct horticultural styles, landscapers have changed context and mood in courtyards, staircases, bridges, and walkways. The flagpole, for instance, overlooks Dickson Plaza's twin sunken lawns, crossed diagonally by paths whose brick paving and stairs impose a perfectly regular pattern on each grassy quad. In *Conspicuous California Plants*, Cornell declared that even among California's beautiful native species, few trees could surpass the sycamore's picturesque beauty and charm. "Always a rugged tree of striking individuality in its form and branching structure, this sycamore is an arresting accent in the landscape." So he used them here, their leaning trunks and maculate bark working against the pie slices of flat lawn, free-form organicism countervailing mortared, geometrical symmetry.

Fourth, perhaps UCLA's distinguishing landscaping element places large, specimen trees in groves and allées that complement the axial plan. Statuesque eucalyptus line Westwood Plaza, for example, and London plane trees flank Bruin Walk as it climbs past Kerckhoff Hall. At the flagpole, two such axial allées meet: a row of carob trees stretches from Schoenberg north to Bunche Hall, intersected by a double row of stately, brooding rusty-leaf figs (*Ficus rubiginosa*), their green and gold foliage and massive gray trunks extending from Murphy Hall and the School of Law, through Dickson Plaza, and into a lawn between Powell and Royce halls.

Throughout the campus, landscapers have achieved distinct effects by filling in nooks and crannies created by the axial grid. North of the flagpole towers Bunche Hall's purple slab, fenestrated like a wall-eyed waffle iron. The smaller unit of the complex contains four floors of classrooms and offices enclosing a courtyard beneath a metal grid that admits rain but shields the courtyard garden from wind and direct sun. In this shade garden, one of few areas on campus using palms, chamaedorea, caryota, European fan palms, and tropical shade plants fill in the understory. The dominant species, however, are *Archontophoenix alexandrae* and especially *Howea forsteriana*, under these prime conditions growing four stories tall and rarely found larger or more beautiful. Different heights present interesting views of this enclosed vertical courtyard garden, which can be seen from the ground, up four stories, to the ceiling.

Bunche Hall overlooks the Franklin Murphy Sculpture Garden, created by Cornell and by a former UCLA chancellor for whom it is named. They conceived of placing statuary outdoors in natural surroundings, accessible to all who pass through each day or linger only once. Tall trees—Canary Island pine, sycamores, spotted gum, and coast redwoods—screen the five-acre garden from surrounding buildings, and it remains distinct from the rest of campus in several ways. Here the paths curve and interweave, abandoning the axial plan and ceasing to function merely as the shortest distance between two points. The level undulates, with berms, hillocks, and a large saucer-shaped basin, itself something of a sculptural earthwork. Under a jacaranda canopy, the sculpture garden concentrates over seventy twentieth-century sculptures, in many periods and styles: works by Jacques Lipchitz, Barbara Hepworth, Jean Arp, Miró, Henry Moore, Robert Graham, Calder, Matisse, Noguchi, Alexander Archipenko, Anthony Caro, the obligatory Rodin, and many others.

The ideal time to visit is in May and June, when the jacarandas burst into showers of blue-lavender blooms the color of a gas flame. So intensely hued they are almost shocking, the trumpet flowers litter the lawn below the trees and harmonize with drifts of agapanthus in a sublime spectacle. Such effects typify the horticultural literacy that was a hallmark of Cornell's career. The sculpture garden's majestic allée of *Erythrina caffra*, grown into a superb canopy along MacGowan Hall, likewise illustrates Cornell's foresight and artistry and his acumen for putting the right plant in the right place. All parts of the sculpture garden are skillfully lit at night, making it especially evocative of a foggy evening. With age and limbing up, the tiny shrubs installed in the late 1960s have grown up to become sculpture rivaling those of the artists—a resemblance that concealed lamps, pointed through the coral trees' bare trunks into the dark night sky, brilliantly illuminate.

The plantings in a sunken horticultural moat around the University Research Library and courtyards north and east of Royce Hall deserve a look for their integration with nearby structures, diverse plant choices, and large specimens. Southwest of Royce Hall, a balustraded terrace above Janss Steps commands a view of the western campus—gymnasiums, playing fields, Pauley Pavilion, and undergraduate dormitories, physical culture carefully segregated from intellectual pursuits—and of the villas clinging to Bel Air's wooded slopes. To the south lie several landmarks: the spires—like episcopal miters—of Kerckhoff Hall, UCLA's only Gothic structure; the paradoxical "inverted fountain," flowing down into a drain rather than jetting upward; and the Placement and Career Planning Center. Although one of architect Frank Gehry's most subdued and contextually considerate designs, the latter is landscaped with an odd didacticism, forcing pedestrians off the sidewalk, putting them in peril, and complicating the way for drivers: it seems to warn the undergraduates to pay attention as they step off the protected academic sidewalk into the dangerous streets of the real world.

UCLA's plan observes the dubious schism between the sciences and humanities. At the center of the south campus lies a large science quadrangle planted with magnolia, a rare tulipwood (_Harpullia pendula_), cape chestnut, _Brachychiton bidwillii_, Senegal date palm, and farthest south, a row of laurel fig, here permitted to grow in a more natural shape. As is the case throughout the campus, the quadrangle emphasizes large trees: Canary Island pine, ficus, podocarpus, and especially eucalyptus are used repeatedly. Generally, UCLA is a green campus, with annuals and flowering plants appearing only incidentally, although there are many exceptions. It is best to visit when classes are not in session—during weekends, summers, or breaks between quarters. An active program generally keeps trees and shrubs well labeled. (Not every specimen bears a label, but the trick is to keep looking. Since trees and shrubs are usually planted in groups of two to twenty, if a plant bears no label, scrutinize others of the same species nearby and a label will nearly always appear.) The labeling heightens the sense that the entire campus is a botanical garden, admirably integrated into the lives of the people who use it.

(UCLA, 405 Hilgard Ave., is located in the Westwood district of Los Angeles; by automobile, use entrances at Westholme and Hilgard, Wyton and Hilgard, or Sunset Blvd. and Westwood Plaza; $4.00 for campus parking, which is difficult to obtain on weekdays if classes are in session. Parking kiosks at campus entrances distribute free campus maps. For information, telephone the UCLA Visitor's Center at 213-206-8147.)

UNIVERSITY OF CALIFORNIA, LOS ANGELES: MILDRED E. MATHIAS BOTANICAL GARDEN

Although the main UCLA campus covers 411 acres, it is the smallest of the eight University of California branches. The expansion of UCLA has occurred at the expense of the botanical garden, which had thirty-one acres when it began in 1930. Today its very existence, on a remaining eight acres not far from the teenaged trendiness of Westwood Village, tends to come as a surprise. To honor its director from 1956 to 1974, an eminent botanist of Central and South American plants and author of the excellent popular reference work for California horticulture, *Flowering Plants in the Landscape*, it was renamed the Mildred E. Mathias Botanical Garden in 1979.

The botanical garden contains about 4,000 species in 225 families growing in a site ordinarily free of frost whose hilly topography and deep canyon create several microclimates. They include a cool, shaded creek and bog area, an exposed desert collection, and other situations for palms, cycads, ficus, aloes, Australian genera (*Eucalyptus, Leptospermum, Melaleuca, Acacia,* and *Callistemon*), and California native plants.

The garden is entered either at its lowest elevation (at Le Conte and Hilgard aves.) or at its highest (off Tiverton Ave. near the UCLA Medical Center). The view from the Tiverton entrance discloses the botanical garden's exceptional trees. These include a huge Torrey pine (*Pinus torreyana*); magnificent twin flooded gums (*Eucalyptus grandis*), well over 100 feet tall with smooth, white bark, joined by a spotted gum (*E. maculata*), nearly as large and distinguished by its mottled bark; the "ribbon" or "Mindanao gum" (*E. deglupta*), a rare non-Australian, tropical eucalyptus native to New Guinea and the Philippines, whose dusty purple bark flakes away in orange strips to reveal olive or bright green new bark; an enormous Arizona cypress (*Cupressus glabra*) near the Hilgard entrance; and superb dawn redwoods, planted in the canyon bottom in 1948 and reputed to be the tallest in the United States.

Lined by paths, crossed by footbridges, and landscaped tropically, an artificially irrigated series of ponds and streams curve through the canyon. It supports aquatic and subtropical plants such as ginger, elephant ears, aspidistra, banana, rhapis and chamaedorea palms, bamboo, philodendron, and ferns of many varieties. It also contains flowering camellias, bird of paradise, cymbidium orchids, clivia, callas, azaleas, and agapanthus.

The botanical garden's most distinctive feature, however, remains its trees, notable not only for their diverse origins but also in many cases for their rarity and flowers. They include the evergreen *Deutzia pulchra*; *Talauma hodgsonii*, from the tropical Himalayas; the "Bourbon Dombeya" (*Dombeya punctata*), from Mauritius; the "monkey-hand tree" (*Chiranthodendron pentadactylon*), named for the digital shape of its rose flowers; a South African pine relative, the "Sapreehout" (*Widdringtonia schwarzii*); the Malayan "Dammar pine" (*Agathis alba*); the Brazilian "silk cotton tree" (*Bombax cyathophorum*); and the unusual *Melaleuca styphelioides*, named "prickly paper-bark" for its beige bark that shaves off like paper-thin layers of a crisp croissant. Many trees grow on the high elevations along the garden's western perimeter, as do small collections of cycads, succulents, and similar species near the Tiverton entrance.

The garden's northeast corner contains a desert collection with aloes, cacti, and succulents. Beyond an oddly placed coast redwood appears a small collection of shrubs from the world's five Mediterranean climate regions: California, central Chile, southern Australia, the South African Cape region, and lands around the Mediterranean Sea. The display focuses on plant communities—chaparral in California, matorral in Spain and Chile, maquis in France, macchia in Italy, fynbos in South Africa, and kwongan in Australia—illustrating the phenomenon of convergence, wherein botanically unrelated chaparral species nevertheless develop similar adaptive traits: "sclerophylly" (small, thick, leathery evergreen leaves), extensive or deep root systems, and adaptations to survive periodic fires.

UCLA's botanical garden offers seclusion at the edge of a busy campus near an even busier office and commercial district. It also cultivates an impressive array of plant species in its relatively small plot and displays them in a manner that keeps aesthetic interest in mind.

(Mildred E. Mathias Botanical Garden, UCLA, at Hilgard and LeConte aves., Los Angeles; open 8:00 a.m. to 5:00 p.m. weekdays and until 4:00 p.m. on weekends; closed holidays; free admission.)

THE UCLA
HANNAH CARTER
JAPANESE GARDEN

One of the most carefully assembled of California's many Japanese gardens and located in an exclusive residential district, the UCLA Hannah Carter Japanese Garden looks to the heart of Japanese garden tradition as "a garden that reminds one of Kyoto." On a sloping site next to their Bel Air house, Mr. and Mrs. Gordon Guiberson created the garden in 1961, with Nagao Sakurai acting as landscape architect. (A Tokyo University professor and supervisor of the Imperial Palace Gardens, Sakurai designed some 160 gardens, including those in San Mateo's Central Park, Micke Grove Park near Stockton, and portions of the Japanese Garden in Golden Gate Park.) Kazuo Nakamura of Kyoto is credited with design and construction; after rain damage in 1969, Koichi Kawana performed reconstruction and restoration work.

The Guibersons were interested in authentic materials and craftsmanship, and to this end they had the garden's gate, teahouse, family shrine, and bridges built in Japan and reassembled here. Likewise, they imported water basins, large symbolic rocks, and antique stone carvings from Japan. (Of particular note, a thousand-year-old Buddha Stone near the entry, the oldest carved stone in the garden, shows the Buddha in sixteen seated positions of worship.) Many garden features follow design precedents from Kyoto gardens, such as the main gate (after the Ichida estate in the Nanzen-ji district) and bamboo fence (after one at the Katsura Detached Palace built for Prince Hachijo no Miyo Toshihito in the seventeenth century, considered a summit of Japanese landscape art). Construction incorporated locally quarried stone, although aside from coast live oaks native to the site, the garden primarily uses plants grown in Japan. Edward W. Carter, chairman of the University of California Regents, donated the garden to UCLA in 1965.

The garden fills a natural amphitheater sloping down a canyon face to a small pond in a level area. The exposed slope, covered with plants pruned to a small scale, seems to enlarge the two-acre site. The garden explores the tension between its level parts (the pond area and platforms around a family shrine, teahouse, and moon-viewing and bonsai display terraces) and the hillside's incline (dramatized by the waterfall and streams that hurtle down its almost dizzying grade). Paths that crisscross and hairpin up the slope may express the tension best, ascending the slope but smoothing out its steep pitch.

The garden's irregular stone paths have a slippery surface, so one finds oneself constantly having to secure one's footing. When attention must be paid to each step, one slows down to note the variety of stones embedded as patterns in the paths. Granite, sandstone, white and black polished river stones, pebble composition in concrete, loose gravel, and many other pavings shift and change, though one repeated motif embeds a footprint of three polished river stones every few feet. Every planting bed is edged in stone, and stonework also composes the terraces, streams, and waterfalls prominent throughout this garden.

The slippery, almost unsafe paving also points to the opposite of stone, the living plants, a link governed by how the gardener influences the pace. Glancing down while walking introduces both a focus on physical safety and an element of visual discontinuity. As each downward look to precarious stepping-stones or slippery paving interrupts views into the garden, it places each new perspective into a sequence and inside a kind of frame. As Kenzo Tange explains in _Katsura_ (1972), "Gardeners do everything they can do to see that their landscape will stand up under the close scrutiny of a person circumscribed in this fashion. After walking from stone to stone for a time, one usually comes to a place where one looks up in surprise at an unexpected vista. There is an attempt in the placing of the stones to emphasize these changes in the landscape; they serve not merely as pavement but as a guide for the viewer."

The garden's artifice also appears in the selection and maintenance of the plants. The relatively few flowering plants—camellias, magnolias, azaleas, and rhododendrons—bloom over several months so as not to distract from foliar textures of needle and leaf. Some plants can be "read" in terms of Japanese garden design, for instance, the cascade-screening pines near the waterfall. Most plants in the heart of the garden, especially those extending up the slope, are kept small by severe pruning, with azaleas or box sheared into spheres and Japanese black

Pagoda, pond, and pines: UCLA Hannah Carter Japanese Garden

pines trimmed horizontally into the twiggy, snow-collecting planes. Surrounding the garden, a screen of bamboo and pittosporum limbed up into tall, straight-trunked trees emphasizes the amphitheatrical site. The center of the garden, open to the sun and inhabited by small plants, contrasts with the peripheral curtain of boscage and the slope's solid earthen barrier.

The sense of enclosure provided by these visual barriers has an aural equivalent, with rushing, falling, or dripping water heard in every corner of this garden. The sound of water and the visual screen exclude distractions from beyond the garden as the pavement's subtle anxieties and minutely tended plants guide attention toward what is close at hand. To approach the abstract meaning of the Japanese garden means attending to its sensory details, one by one, so as to see and hear rhymes and contrasts, to discern similarities and opposites. To be in the Japanese garden is to allow oneself to be led by perceptions, encouraged by small difficulties.

Only at the garden's highest point, a small "family shrine" or *hokura* (an unpainted cryptomeria pavilion housing a gilt Buddha), does the view extend into Bel Air's vast greenery as a pink mansion floats in vegetation across the canyon. The view follows the sound of rushing water down the slope to a moon-viewing pavilion and to a small bonsai display. Although the bonsai is an art of extremity, careful pruning nearly everywhere constrains any sense of profusion except in that corner that forms the site's second garden, not Japanese at all. Snuggled into a smaller gorge behind the teahouse, the Hawaiian Garden's dense ferns, palms, and other subtropical plants flank a waterfall draining from another face of the slope. A hillside of lacy, chartreuse ferns proliferates under native oaks, large *Howea forsteriana*, and miniature Chamaedorea palms. Solids contrasting with lacy fringe, the undivided leaves of subtropicals (bromeliads, philodendron, tree bird of paradise) counterpoint the ferns' fragile textures.

The Japanese garden is open by reservation only, so few people visit at any given moment. This fortuity emphasizes the solitude that many observers feel the Japanese garden elicits and perfects. One occasionally yields to the skepticism that the Japanese garden, in the phrase of poet Mona van Duyn, arranges trivialities to look significant. All too often in California one encounters glib, symbolic readings of plants and features in ostensibly Japanese gardens of dubious provenance. Such spots seem less to honor an ancient style than to post dire warnings against the dangers of lifting cultural achievements out of their proper context. The quality of the UCLA Japanese garden dispels such doubts, however, by suggesting ways this landscape tradition appeals to intellectual perception.

(The UCLA Hannah Carter Japanese Garden, located near the Westwood campus, is open by reservation only, Tuesdays 10:00 a.m. to 1:00 p.m. and Wednesdays noon to 3:00 p.m. Free admission; for reservations and directions to the garden, telephone the UCLA Visitor's Center at 213-825-4574.)

FOUR
LOS ANGELES
CITY PARKS

Although it has the nation's second largest population and administers what is supposedly its largest municipal park, Los Angeles has never quite accepted the necessity of providing usable park space and horticultural amenities. The city has nothing even remotely comparable to Golden Gate Park or to Balboa Park, much less to the public gardens of the world's major cities, to whose company Los Angeles constantly seeks entry—the catchphrase "world-class" has become a kind of civic mantra—even as it remains ignorant of the price of admission. When most residents had a front and back garden, a scarcity of parks might have mattered less. But if historical lack of necessity could explain the origin of this municipal refusal to provide public amenities, by now it is a cultural and political refusal. In the 1990s, most people rent in crowded neighborhoods, and the tacit goal of local government is to refashion the city into Manhattan with palm trees, to save Los Angeles by destroying it.

Hence it is disappointing to see the city squander what few park resources it already has, as witness the disaster that has befallen the once fashionable MacArthur Park. FERNDELL, a tiny but picturesque water and fern garden in Griffith Park, for years seemed headed toward the same fate. But an eternity of renovation was completed in 1990, and the dell once more evokes the otherworldliness that in the mid-sixties caused the Byrds to be photographed there for their first album—through a fish-eye lens. Sycamores, coast redwoods, and alders shelter groves of tree ferns, elephant ears, ginger, and other shade plants growing along the ponds and tiny waterfalls of a small stream. Said to contain over one hundred fern species, making it California's largest public fern garden, Ferndell began in 1912 when a city park superintendent, Frank Shearer, transformed the 4.5-acre canyon. Its siting between two streets, one a heavily traveled route into Griffith Park, is unfortunate. But the rippling water and patchy sunlight overcome such difficulties, and soon the vegetation will recover for the dell its picturesque profusion that the trim terracing of renovation has only temporarily placed in abeyance. (Ferndell, enter at Ferndell Dr. from Los Feliz Blvd.)

ELYSIAN PARK was the site of the city's first arboretum, begun in 1893. Despite the arboretum's failure, the Pasadena Freeway, Dodger Stadium, the Los Angeles Police Academy, a reservoir, and other encroachments, seventy species survive from the earliest plantings of 37,000 trees. These include what is reputed to be the only _Baphia chrysophylla_ in the United States, the country's first cape chestnut (_Calodendrum capense_), and the oldest _Brachychiton populneus_ in California. Rough terrain leaves much of the park's 575 acres unusable, but renewed tree planting by volunteers recently has created many improvements. In what remains from the old arboretum (Stadium Way from Scott Ave. to Academy Rd.), a double row of Canary Island palms and many fine trees overlook lawns that hosted sixties love-ins: still pleasant, if something less than Elysium. (Elysian Park, the easiest entry is from the north, Stadium Way from Riverside Dr.)

A subliminally familiar locale, or more accurately, location, ECHO PARK appeared on the silver screen during the silent movie era as a backdrop to the antics of Harold Lloyd, Chaplin, and Laurel and Hardy. Designed by the first city park superintendent, Joseph Henry Tomlinson, Echo Park is said to resemble a park in Tomlinson's native Derbyshire. Its lake, dating from 1893, offers boats for rent, an island reached by a footbridge, a large fountain, and a mat of sacred lotus (_Nelumbo nucifera_) in its northwestern inlet, in summer a fragrant, blooming salad and something of a symbol for the district. Echo Park contains many flowering trees (e.g., cape chestnut by the boat house), but stands of Canary Island, _Washingtonia robusta_, and _W. filifera_ palms create its distinctive ambience. Its horticultural details do not really merit close scrutiny; the park makes its best impression from a distance or driving by. (Echo Park, Glendale Blvd., north of the Hollywood Freeway.)

Its proximity to museums, a large university, and adjacent sports megaliths makes the survival of the seven-acre EXPOSITION PARK ROSE GARDEN seem almost miraculous. In 1986, for instance, a proposal by the Coliseum Commission planned to replace it with a multistory, 1,200-space parking garage. News headlines reported the rose garden to have been "spared" when a rare public outcry convinced the commission to impose its pharaonic solutions elsewhere. First planted before World War I, with over 200 rose varieties and many thousands of plants, the garden is one of the country's largest, attracting a million visitors annually to see it bloom from April through December.

The rose garden is surrounded on three sides by museums whose facades illustrate the sequence of shifting cultural values in twentieth-century Los Angeles, from beaux arts domes to Gehry glitz. The well-maintained, symmetrical rose garden nearly resolves the surrounding architectural confusion, however, as four quadrants of rose beds in lawns, each containing a whitewashed summer house, surround a circular fountain. A low brick wall separates the rose garden, which is sunk several feet below grade, from surrounding pedestrian thoroughfares. A border of trees and flowering shrubs reinforces a sense of enclosure. Four corner plantings provide a picturesque background for the roses' clouds of color and fragrance. The northwest corner, a subtropical composition of several palm species, Australian tree ferns, dracaena, and tree bird of paradise, is particularly noteworthy.

Los Angeles thinks big but has never had much patience in investing in traditional urban amenities. The powers that be view such things, suspicious because difficult to define and potentially expensive, as restraints on development and population growth—the twin gods always busy creating the problems they promise to solve. The Exposition Park Rose Garden, one of the city's few such amenities, remains intact for now. (Exposition Park Rose Garden, Exposition Blvd. between Figueroa and Vermont.)

There really is a seacoast of Bohemia. It begins with the high-powered leisure of Malibu, quickly culminates in the physical culture of Venice, and then follows a varied coastline of surfers and Zen capitalists south and east before terminating in the art colony of Laguna Beach. A rare seaside public garden, the ADAMSON HOME AND MALIBU LAGOON MUSEUM, lies between Pacific Coast Highway and the ocean. Overlooking an arm of the Malibu Lagoon, the grounds remain fairly rustic, a rough lawn set with prominent old trees (the distinctive silhouette of a large bunya bunya marks the property on the skyline). Among the statuesque trees, colorful details appear everywhere: in hot blue pride of Madeira bloom spikes against a green lath house; in a rose garden; and in hibiscus, fuchsia, and scarlet *Tecomaria capensis* around the Adamson house.

Although he would later become known for his art deco architecture, Stiles Clements designed this Spanish colonial dwelling in 1929 for descendants of the Rindge family whose property derived from the Malibu Spanish land grant. Attention to quality distinguishes the two-story house: the unusual, multilayered red-tiled roof; a flagstone entry courtyard under large pepper, jacaranda, and olive trees; facing the sea on two sides of the house, patios and terraces (each with an outdoor fireplace) paved with terra-cotta tiles inset with blue botanical designs; wood carvings, metal lanterns and other grillework, and ornamental fenestration; and particularly the decorative ceramic tile applied to windows, doors, and patios.

A product of Malibu Potteries (active 1926-1932), the tile has its finest moment in an eight-pointed "star fountain" whose blue, orange, mustard, yellow, and black geometrical patterns strike a Moorish note. Set in a lawn among European fan palms, the fountain overlooks surfers riding the waves toward the Malibu Pier. Although the grounds contain over 100 different plant species (a gift shop sells a plant list and map), the house, its terraces and tiled fountains, and the exceptional site distinguish this public garden as much as its plants. On clear days the view extends south along Santa Monica Bay to Palos Verdes. (Adamson House and Malibu Lagoon Museum, 23200 Pacific Coast Highway, Malibu; group tours Tuesdays by reservation, 213-456-8432; house and museum open Wednesdays through Sundays 10:00 a.m. to 2:00 p.m., grounds open during daylight hours.)

On Sunset Boulevard just up the hill from Pacific Coast Highway, the SELF-REALIZATION FELLOWSHIP LAKE SHRINE occupies an unusual, ten-acre site created in 1927 when developers hydraulically graded hills to obtain soil for a nearby building site. Ironically, the despoliation created a large, spring-fed lake nearly surrounded by cliffs that form a dramatic amphitheater. In 1949, the grounds were donated to the Self-Realization Fellowship, whose spiritual leader, Paramahansa Yogananda, supervised the landscaping by fellowship monks.

A path—filled not with crunchy, noisy gravel, lest pedestrians disturb ongoing meditation, but with whisper-quiet, footstep-muffling sawdust and bark—circles the lake, passing assorted garden and religious features. A tiny, immaculate desert garden begins the tour before the path slopes up to a view of the lake. The garden's main features are tall *Washingtonia robusta* palms, the gilded domes of the crenellated white and blue Golden Lotus Archway beautifully set in a grove of tree bird of paradise, a windmill (used as a chapel), and the lake.

Near the lake, the landscaping is lushly subtropical (with palms, bananas, ferns, bougainvillea, and long-necked, wispy *Cyperus papyrus*); pine, pittosporum, eucalyptus, acacia, and Hollywood juniper densely cover the steep cliffs above. Near the path are tidy borders and hedges and lots of color; lantana, agapanthus, geranium, iris, and wax begonias strike almost a domestic note amid a raft of ecumenical otherworldliness. (Religious quotations line the path, which ultimately arrives—past a rose garden and arbor covered in *Distictis buccinatoria*—at the Court of Religions containing symbols of five world religions, symbolizing the unity of humanity and common faith.) The lake shrine and gardens realize how natural beauty reflects an appreciation of life and the ideal of a friendly, benign world. (Self-Realization Fellowship Lake Shrine, 17190 Sunset Blvd., Pacific Palisades; free admission; open Tuesday through Saturday 9:00 a.m. to 4:45 p.m., Sunday 12:30 to 4:45 p.m.; closed Mondays, holidays, and occasionally on Saturdays. Telephone 213-454-4114.)

Two coastal districts west of Los Angeles have books about their park and street trees. Grace L. Heintz wrote _Trees of Pacific Palisades_ and a new edition of George T. Hasting's _Trees of Santa Monica_. The books list trees street by street and in parks, schools, and horticulturally interesting sites, and they contain information about and photographs of several hundred. Though mainly of local interest, these two books make fine appreciations of and contributions to these favored communities.

With the plants one sees every day in Los Angeles—olives, Hollywood junipers, bird of paradise, clipped _Ficus microcarpa_, and lawns—the symmetrical, minimalistic composition and immaculate maintenance of the LOS ANGELES TEMPLE, CHURCH OF JESUS CHRIST OF LATTER DAY SAINTS, nonetheless create a theatrical grandeur. The familiar, gangly _Washingtonia robusta_ can scarcely be said to have been better used anywhere else. Their fronded topknots on absurdly tall trunks match the temple's monumental scale and emphasize its Oz-like facade and tower. The grounds, which are open to the public, contain ponds, fountains, rose beds, and trees. But the southern facade, twin allées of olive trees sloping up to an almost Tibetan terrace and the gleaming temple, is the view to be relished, if nothing else for its acres of manicured, kelly green lawn, a blessing in this part of town. (Santa Monica Blvd. at Overland, Los Angeles.)

If Wilshire Boulevard is a linear downtown, BEVERLY GARDENS PARK is a linear park, extending along the north side of Santa Monica and Wilshire boulevards the width of Beverly Hills. Designed by Ralph D. Cornell and dedicated in 1931, the park divides the city's exclusive residential neighborhood from its commercial district, in both cases among the priciest real estate in the world. But a line must be drawn, as Rayner Banham aptly stated (in _Los Angeles: The Architecture of Four Ecologies_), to defend residential illusions against the facts that make them possible.

Beverly Gardens Park is best seen on the move: walking, jogging, or driving by. For most of its length no more than a residential lot in width, the park is unified by a canopy of eucalyptus and Chinese elms over a gravel path and punctuated by an occasional pergola or fountain, exotic large plants, and a series of specialized gardens and mass plantings. From east to west, these include a good collection of mature palms between Hillcrest and Palm drives, a rose garden between Maple and Elm, and the fine trees and lawn in a square between Crescent and Rodeo. Unforgettably splendid municipal tree plantings line streets curving north, such as on Canon and Beverly drives, for example, where mature, carefully trimmed Canary Island palms alternate with _Washingtonia robustas_.

Three churches, lushly planted, vary the sequence only slightly, and separating them between Camden and Bedford drives, a compact desert garden has room enough for *Agave picta*, dracaenas, opuntia cactus, yuccas, and aloes. Providing clouds of lavender and white blooms in late spring, drifts of agapanthus appear between Roxbury and Linden before the park takes a dogleg at Wilshire and its prominent fountain, lit with colored lights at night. The city funds seasonal displays and quality maintenance, making this park an exceptional urban amenity. Not to overlook the considerable horticultural variety to be seen on foot, Beverly Gardens Park remains a pleasure to drive by, perhaps especially when stuck in traffic.

The large properties above Sunset Boulevard and their owners' ample fortunes offered opportunities to A. E. Hanson, Edward Huntsman-Trout, Florence Yoch, and other talented landscapers during the twenties and thirties, when fortunes in the oil, transportation, real estate, and film industries made instant landscape grandeur possible and necessary. Even though the property is now much reduced in size and otherwise changed, GREYSTONE PARK is still worth a visit.

"The entrance was barred by a wrought-iron gate with a flying Cupid in the middle. There were busts on light pillars and a stone seat

A formal terrace high above the city at Greystone Park, Beverly Hills

with crouching griffins at each end. There was an oblong pool with stone water lilies in it and a big stone bullfrog sitting on one of the leaves. Still further a rose colonnade led to a thing like an altar, hedged in at both sides, yet not so completely but that the sun lay in an arabesque along the steps of the altar. And far over to the left there was a wild garden." In _Farewell My Lovely_, Chandler's Philip Marlowe might have been describing Greystone in its heyday. Long enough to encourage Marlowe's melancholy musings on the corruption of wealth, its entry drive winds leisurely past mature deodar cedars before depositing visitors in a courtyard of the mansion. While neither house nor entry drive are open to the public, the City of Beverly Hills operates the estate's 18.5 acres as a municipal park.

Early in its life, the house and its over 400 acres were considered the greatest estate in Los Angeles. Greystone was the fifty-five-room, 46,054-square-foot residence of Edward Laurence Doheny, Jr., designed by Gordon Kaufmann in 1927. The gray Arizona stone-and-slate-roofed mansion has a rustic Tudor style, oddly enclosed by subtropical vegetation. If less elaborate today than in the twenties (when it contained a cascade, pools, and fountains), its grounds remain impressive. Formal terraces of Indiana limestone, sunken gardens, balustrades, staircases, and several water features are planted architecturally with eugenia, box, and yew in hedges and small allées. But for the house, one could term the gardens Italianate. Created by Paul Thiene with A. E. Kuehl as principal designer, they stylishly climb a steep foothill to present exceptional views from downtown Los Angeles to Century City and out to Palos Verdes, an almost surreal expanse. (Greystone Park, 905 Loma Vista Dr., Beverly Hills; open daily 10:00 a.m. to 5:00 p.m.)

Over the hill in the San Fernando Valley, since purchasing the ORCUTT RANCH HORTICULTURE CENTER in 1966, the City of Los Angeles has created an unusual park around the residence of William and Mary Orcutt. Originally their country home, the property grew into the 200-acre Rancho Sombra del Roble (Ranch of the Shaded Oak), as Mr. Orcutt, a pioneering oil company geologist and engineer, prospered. A small rose garden, a whitewashed trellis, and a religious shrine in a river rock grotto adjoin the Spanish revival house, designed in 1920 by C. G. Knipe. Besides ancient, massive oaks (one estimated to be 700 years old measures 32 feet in circumference), the property contains impressive trees of many species shading flower gardens, bamboo groves, and a riparian area with tropical plants. But the property's most exceptional feature is sixteen acres of producing citrus groves, whose golden grapefruit hang tantalizingly on beautiful trees that scent the air. Let doubters beware: the pungent fragrance testifies to the sweetness of life not long ago in the citrus groves. (Orcutt Ranch Horticultural Center, 23600 Roscoe Blvd., Los Angeles. Free admission; open 7:00 a.m. to 5:00 p.m. Historical tours 2:00 to 5:00 p.m., last Sunday of every month. Telephone 818-346-7449.)

Located in an expansive flood control *cum* recreation area behind Sepulveda Dam, the beautifully maintained DONALD C. TILLMAN JAPANESE GARDEN anomalously shares space with a silver-gray, high-tech water reclamation plant, whose humming machinery provides a constant susurrus. In flat terrain, designer Koichi Kawana set a large lake in rolling topography, partially screened by coast redwoods, bamboo, and a high wall. Precisely trimmed mounds of variegated pittosporum, azaleas, ferns, *Cycas revoluta*, and undulating dichondra lawns provide a setting for miniaturized black pines set in the lake's islands and for wisteria, willows, alders, flowering plums, and magnolias.

The design observes many Japanese garden conventions: an irregular "zigzag" or *yatsuhashi* bridge, a polished river stone beach, granite pagodas and *Kasuga* and *Yukimi* lamps, rustic arbors, and a teahouse. The lake attracts stately white herons—perhaps the garden's most evocative feature— and other picturesque waterfowl. A *karesansui* (dry garden) composes gravel in *samon* patterns to symbolize ocean waves and presents stone arrangements such as the traditional *sanson* (three Buddha) motif. The 6.5-acre garden adapts the *Chisen-Kaiyushiki*—water garden with promenade—style, an eighteenth- and nineteenth-century mode that gave rise to stroll gardens with lawns and vistas. Acknowledging its unusual co-tenant, the garden's waterfall, stream, and lake show three modes of reclaimed water: falling and vertical, flowing and horizontal, and at rest. (Tillman Japanese Garden, 6100 Woodley Ave., Van Nuys; guided tours by appointment only; for tour reservations, telephone 818-989-8166.)

In Sun Valley, the THEODORE PAYNE FOUNDATION carries on the work of the landscaper and nurseryman who helped popularize California native plants within the state and around the world. Besides sales of seeds and plants at a large nursery on the site, the property contains small display areas of plants and a hillside devoted to spring wildflowers. The foundation is a major resource for those interested in obtaining California native plants. (10459 Tuxford St., Sun Valley; open Tuesday through Saturday 8:30 a.m. to 4:30 p.m.; free admission; telephone 213-768-1802.)

V
Los Angeles East

Renaissance grandeur at the Huntington Botanical Gardens

HUNTINGTON
BOTANICAL
GARDENS

I n the nineteenth century, two Huntingtons came to California and made it big. An uncle and nephew became renowned—and in some quarters reviled—in the railroad business. With the gold rush going full blast, Collis P. Huntington arrived in 1849 and sold supplies to the miners from his dry goods store in Sacramento. As one of the Big Four, he invested in the Central Pacific, the western length of the transcontinental railway. By the time Huntington, Hopkins, Stanford, and Crocker sent a Southern Pacific branch line into Los Angeles in 1876, they had acquired immense wealth and power in California. In 1872, Collis hired his nephew, Henry E. Huntington, to help him run the railroads. Twenty years later, after a sojourn at "San Marino," J. deBarth Shorb's estate near Pasadena, Henry settled in San Francisco as vice-president of Southern Pacific.

When Collis Huntington died in 1900, he bequeathed half his fortune to his wife, Arabella, and half to Henry. Frozen out of the presidency of the Southern Pacific, Henry sold his stock and came south to invest in a real estate-mass transit synergy that would double his fortune within ten years and determine the sprawling shape that metropolitan Los Angeles would assume. Purchasing undeveloped acreage and linking it to downtown Los Angeles by an efficient rail system, Huntington could sell the properties at considerably increased prices once they were served by his Pacific Electric "red cars."

Within ten years of incorporation in 1901, the Pacific Electric comprised the world's largest electrical transit system, more than 1,150 miles of track connecting Los Angeles to points as far away as San Bernardino, Riverside, and Newport Beach. Setting the stage for the region's explosive growth, Huntington's system had an influence on southern California that remained unequaled until the next transport system: the freeways, whose routes often followed those of the red cars. Traffic having long since exceeded the freeways' capacity, it now appears that Los Angeles County, venturing back to the future, will reassemble a commuter rail system not unlike the one it dismantled after World War II.

Huntington sold the Pacific Electric in 1910 and retired to devote himself to creating a monument to art and culture. Perhaps the zeal with which Huntington acquired pictures, books, and plants provides a sense of continuity between his former life in business and his new role as a connoisseur. Otherwise, it is remarkable that Huntington should late in life shift gears so decisively to art and culture, building a monument to timeless beauty that seems almost a critique of ad hoc enterprise.

In 1903, Huntington had purchased the 600-acre Shorb estate that he had visited briefly in 1892. There he built a grand house designed by Myron Hunt and hired William Hertrich, a young botanist and landscaper, to convert the raw ranch into an estate, lavishly cultivated with as many exotic plants as would grow in San Marino. Thorough and adventurous, Hertrich successfully enlisted his employer's interest in seeking out and testing the suitability of plants not known in the area. Hertrich's industry, imagination, and flair during his tenure as superintendent from 1904 to 1947 earned the garden a reputation for the variety and rarity of its plants. (Hertrich recalled his career in a charming memoir, *The Huntington Botanical Gardens, 1905-1949: Personal Recollections of William Hertrich* [1949].) To this day, its horticulturists continually try new species against the vagaries of the San Marino climate, a key element in the interest and exhilaration that the Huntington Botanical Gardens create for visitors.

Huntington's remarkable self-transformation produced a monument to himself, to the southern California region, and to the ideals of culture, horticulture, and cultivation. The botanical equivalent of Huntington's art and book collections were the full-sized trees—including over 600 live oaks—transplanted to San Marino from properties he owned throughout Los Angeles. (Huntington's railroad connections enabled him to bring in specimen trees from as far away as San Francisco.) In this way, he and Hertrich installed a mature landscape within a few years and inaugurated a tradition of fine trees that still distinguishes the Huntington Gardens.

In 1913, Henry Huntington married Arabella Huntington, the widow and heiress of his uncle, Collis. Having thus reunited the family fortune, Huntington turned away from business to culture, seeking the expertise of several cultural businessmen. Engaging the famous rare book dealers George D. Smith and Dr. A. S. W. Rosenbach, he acquired whole

libraries of rare books and other literary and historical materials. To fill
his art gallery, he purchased from English broker Sir Joseph Duveen,
through whose good offices Gainsborough's _The Blue Boy_, Reynolds's
Sarah Siddons as the Tragic Muse, Constable's _View on the Stour near Dedham_,
and many other eighteenth- and nineteenth-century English pictures
found their way to San Marino. With an avidity amounting almost to
aesthetic plunder, Huntington quickly acquired a coherent collection of
high connoisseurship, reminiscent of the Wallace Collection in London
or the Frick Museum in New York.

In 1919, Arabella and Henry Huntington executed a deed of trust
incorporating the Huntington Library, Art Collections, and Botanical
Gardens and transferring more than 200 acres, their home, and collections to a nonprofit educational trust. Arabella died in 1924, Henry in
1927. As the Huntingtons had desired, Hertrich supervised the conver-
sion of the estate to receive the public. Besides the Huntington's house,
now the art gallery, a separate library contains several million books, let-

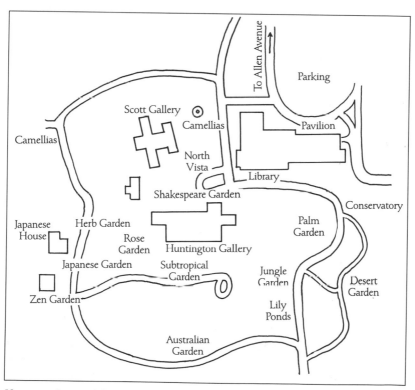

Huntington Botanical Gardens

ters, maps, and rare documents in British, American, and California history and literature (though open for use only to qualified scholars, the library's public gallery displays some of its most interesting holdings). Opened in 1984, the Virginia Steele Scott Gallery displays three centuries of American art. The gardens display some 14,000 different species and cultivars on 130 acres.

Experiencing the Huntington Botanical Gardens means moving through a sequence of horticulturally distinct areas organized according to one of several principles: national styles (English, Italian, and Japanese); botanical specialties (cactus, camellia, rose, palm); theme gardens (Shakespeare and herb gardens); and ecological collections (jungle, subtropical, Australian). Some areas merge into one another gradually and logically, while others make abrupt, dramatic transitions. Flowing more or less continuously around the art gallery, an opulent lawn—the feature that makes the gardens seem "English," at least before its exotic details emerge—links many of the gardens as a visually orienting feature.

In the North Vista, for instance, the lawn becomes a rectangular panel stretching axially between a palm allée. Overlooked by parallel rows of late Renaissance garden statuary, a large stone fountain terminates the axis, lifting the eye to the sheer face of the San Gabriel mountains in the distance. To the west, eleven evenly spaced *Livistona decipiens* fan palms divide the lawn from oak woodland shading azaleas and camellias (one of two camellia collections, together containing 1,700 cultivars). The eastern edge reveals a broken line of only four *Livistonas*, exceptional for their moderate size, smooth trunks, and pendulous fronds that shine in the sun in shades of olive, silver, and gold. Surprisingly, the allée's imperfect symmetry seems to emphasize the North Vista's Italianate grandeur. A view from the fountain back to the art gallery silhouettes coast live oaks and *Caryota urens* palms against the mansion's columns and tiled roof.

Near the art gallery entrance, a circular garden suggests the attention to detail found throughout the gardens. Next to the familiar plant, *Acanthus mollis*, for instance, will appear its rarely seen cousin, *A. spinossiums*; a universal cultivar, such as bright orange *Clivia miniata*, is found near a new and unusual pale yellow variety. Experiments with variegation create foliar color rhymes: variegated ivy spilling from an urn calls attention to golden spots of "the leopard plant" (*Ligularia tussilaquivea aureomaculata*). In its boldest step, this planting interweaves the bananalike foliage of tree bird of paradise with the rugged trunks and green leaves of the coast live oak, subtropical with temperate, exotic with native.

Across from this circular garden another view frames several characteristic features. The tortuous branches of a magnificent mesa oak (*Quercus
engelmannii*), at two hundred years of age the estate's largest and oldest
tree, spread into an umbrella form requiring the support of clamps and
guy wires. In the distance, across wide lawns, a pair of English oaks (*Q.
robur*)—unexpectedly majestic in a climate that could scarcely be less like
England's—mark the transition from English turf and trees to a palm
collection, comprising about seventy-five species. In southern California's more benign microclimates, up to 500 palm species may be grown
outdoors, but here palms must withstand merciless summer heat and
predictable frosts on winter nights. Palms interested Hertrich, and the
horticulturists have continued to experiment with new ones, discovering that tender Hawaiian *Pritchardia* and Central American *Chamaedorea*
palms will survive if protected by trees in the jungle garden.

In irregularly curving beds set in wiry St. Augustine grass, tall palms
(*Sabal mexicana, Jubea chilensis,* and *Phoenix dactylifera*) shade miniature
Chamaedorea, Rhapis, and pygmy date palms and underplanted purple-
leaved canna and *Justicia brandegeana* "Chartreuse." With faultless logic,
the palm garden diverges into the two directions palms themselves follow. *Washingtonia filifera, W. robusta,* and *Phoenix canariensis* appear in the
desert garden across a drive, and tropical palms (the Colombian *Ceroxylon quindiuense* and the handsome, clean-trunked, *Trachycarpus martianus*
from Burma) thrive in the jungle garden's protection from sun, wind,
and frost.

Although it can only approximate equatorial conditions in a climate
that is rainless much of the year and experiences winter frosts, the jungle
garden does capture something of a tropical forest's layered composition.
Both giving and taking a good deal of shade, *Ficus thonningii, F. watkin-
siana, F. columnaris,* the Chinese wingnut (*Pterocarya stenoptera*), and giant
bamboo (*Dendrocalamus asper*) form a jungle canopy. Australian tree ferns
and bananas fill the understory, and shade plants near the ground
include the huge-leaved *Philodendron* "*evansii,*" the wide fans of *Pritchardia
beccariana* palms, bromeliads (*Aechmea* are especially well represented),
ginger, cycads, cymbidium orchids, and tropical rhododendrons (e.g.,
Rhododendron aurigeranum, blooming golden yellow in May). Epiphytes
(staghorn ferns and epiphyllum cactus) and vines (the Laotian chestnut
vine, *Tetrastigma voinieranum,* and *Monstera deliciosa*) emphasize the jungle
effect, clambering up the dominant ficus trees towering up to 100 feet.
Wispy foliage of Mexican weeping bamboo (*Otatea acuminata aztecorum*)
leans elegantly from its jungle garden redoubt into sunlight, a luxuriant
screen between lawn and forest.

The jungle garden canopy parts to bathe a waterfall in sun as it rushes down a cleft lined with elephant's ear, ferns, bamboo, cycads, horsetail, and bird of paradise before draining into lily ponds set in the more level land below. East of this water garden, the lawn extends past bamboo and magnolia to a driveway marking an almost shocking transition into a desert garden. It contains one of the world's largest outdoor cactus and agave collections, and over 5,000 xeriphytic species inhabit a wonderland of spines, spikes, and spires.

As he set about developing the estate, Huntington solicited suggestions from Hertrich about what use might be made of a large plot of thin, sandy soil occupying a prominent position along the drive up to his mansion. Years earlier while supervising Southern Pacific Railroad construction in the desert Southwest, Huntington had a close, painful encounter with a cactus that dissuaded him from taking any further interest in such hostile, heavily armed plants. Hence it seemed unlikely that he should entertain Hertrich's notion that the site would support a collection of cacti and assorted desert plants. Huntington nonetheless agreed to the project, if in a tentative fashion, by committing half an acre to Hertrich's scheme.

Something about the desert garden must have excited his collector's instinct, for as the number and rarity of the plants increased, so did the resources Huntington was prepared to make available. Only a year after the garden began in 1907, Huntington dispatched a three-month expedition to Arizona, New Mexico, and Texas, where Hertrich literally collected cacti by the carload, returning with three railroad cars of plants. A 1912 expedition to Mexico returned with two more carloads of desert plants, expanding the desert garden to five acres. It has since grown to about twelve acres crowded with specimens obtained by collection or exchanges with botanical gardens and fanciers around the world. Huntington was later honored by a cactus named for him, *Cereus huntingtonianus,* which grows in the garden he established.

The desert garden begins near the visitors' entrance, where a drive descends between the palm garden and a bank of succulents and aloes. As the twenty-five-foot tree aloes (*Aloe bainesii*) suggest, the desert garden does not lack trees. The floss silk tree, western sycamores, and coast live oaks throw considerable shade, as do desert palms (*Brahea, Washingtonia,* and *Phoenix* species), euphorbias, and several yuccas. Some of the largest cacti, tons of prickly flesh above woody trunks, also cast dense shade, such as a fifteen-foot Mexican *Polaskia chende* bearing pale rose and yellow blossoms in late spring.

Desert Garden, Huntington Botanical Gardens

   As always, the agaves produce bizarre shapes and colors, particularly the tangled, six-foot spears of *Agave picta*, olive green edged with creamy yellow, one of nature's most creative color schemes. But perhaps the desert garden's most amazing plants are its *Puyas*, about 100 species native to the South American Andes and considered the most primitive bromeliads. Blooming in late spring, *Puyas* appeal to those with an eye for color. *Puya alpestris* flowers have a metallic, green-blue cast, each tubular flower sprouting tangerine pollen-bearing anthers and a tufted, apple green stigma, an unforgettable color combination. Salmon pink branches of *P. spathacea* support dark aquamarine and maroon flowers. *P. coerulea violacea* may be the most bizarre of all; atop six-foot rose stalks, gold-green, powdery stamens emerge from tightly rolled tubular flowers so purple they are nearly black. Here, as in many other blooming plants, the desert garden seems to confirm the suspicion that there is no such thing as a color not found in nature.
   Although the desert garden displays many other fine flowers and a variety of succulent ground covers, it is best known for the bewildering shapes, colors, and textures of its cacti: miniature mountain ranges of gray, three-inch *Mammillaria geminispina* tufts; patches of pale green, spoon-

like leaves of *Opuntia microdavys,* bearing waxy yellow flowers; and a load-
ing dock of dozens of golden barrel cactus (*Echinocactus grusonii*), truly the
size of barrels, three feet in diameter and as tall. A rockery created in 1927
with tons of Arizona lava rock displays sixty *Mammillaria* species, a Dis-
neyesque landscape of fuzzy, dwarfish pincushions making miniature
haste slowly over lava hill and sandy dale. Elsewhere spiny, prostrate tubes
of Argentinian *Trichocereus thelogonus* snake by the dozen over jagged rocks,
while ridges of *Cereus chalybaeus "beysiegelii"* undulate like crazy corduroy. The massed cacti present a landscape surreal and hallucinatory but
also jokey and cartoonish. "A landscape may be beautiful, charming or
sublime, or insignificant and ugly," Bergson said in his essay on laughter;
"it will never be laughable." He must never have visited a cactus garden.

In what must be California's most unusual indoor garden, a dry conservatory protects tender succulents and species that cannot compete with
more vigorous desert plants. This glasshouse (open only from 2:00 p.m.
to 4:00 p.m.) contains 3,000 potted specimens in thirty-five plant families:
bromeliads, *Lithops* (one of nature's visual puns, the so-called living rocks),
cacti, and the mauve, rust, pale green, and flesh-colored leaves of *Cras-
sulaceae* succulents. The potted plants are notable not only for flowers—
such as the three-inch, scarlet trumpet blooms with yellow-white throats
of *Adenium obesum*—but for shapes, patterns, and colors as extreme as the
environments that influenced them, whether the creamy flesh of the
"white ghost" (*Euphorbia lactea*) or the golden, furry spines of *Borzicactus.*
A small area displays Madagascarian plants, mostly *Didieraceae*; among
several outstanding plants is *Uncarina grandidieri,* a ten-foot tree displaying
brilliant yellow flowers with black-purple throats.

At the bottom of the desert garden, the view across a lawn, lake, and
water lilies, with bamboo canes next to tropical pines, makes a jump cut
from desert to meadow, juxtaposing south and north, arid and wet, New
World and Old. Next to a watercourse and lily ponds, some of the Huntington's finest large trees appear against the skyline: *Araucaria cunning-
hamii,* coast and dawn redwoods, the elegant weeping Kashmir cypress
(*Cupressus cashmeriana*), and another memorable weeping evergreen, the
Montezuma cypress (*Taxodium mucronatum*).

Near the jungle garden's cascade is a true curiosity, the ombu (*Phytolacca
dioica*), its multiple trunks sprouting from a hugely enlarged base and trunk.
Called the "lighthouse of the pampas" by the gauchos, in Argentina enormous, solitary specimens act as aids to navigation across a sea of grassland
and make shaded resting places. From the ombu, informal paths meander
up and down the gentle slope of a subtropical garden planted with flower-

ing trees and plants selected for the local climate. During late spring, the lavender-flowering jacarandas prove why so many local residents consider them a favorite tree. Others are less frequently seen, such as the red trumpet flowers on the Peruvian shrub _Delostima lobbii;_ the small rose flowers of vining _Dolichos lignosus "atropurpureus";_ the cloudlike white flowers of "snow in summer" (_Melaleuca linariifolia);_ or the salmon-colored _Hibiscus schizopetalus_ hybrid. Flowering trees include coral trees, cape chestnut, acacia, _Wigandiaurens,_ and _Tipuana tipu._ A mature Italian stone pine (_Pinus pinea_) towers magnificently over the subtropical garden, its branches and needles held high on a slightly leaning forty-foot trunk.

Between stone lions marking a portal through a dense screen of spotted black bamboo (_Phyllostachys nigra punctata_), the path ascends a dense glade of cryptomeria, Japanese maple, and _Rosa chinensis mutabilis._ Climbing under native oak woodland, it reaches a stone-paved terrace displaying trays of bonsaied plants and Japanese "view stones" (_to-yama-ishi_). The terrace opens into a Zen garden, a courtyard within which a slim border of black river stones parallels a pedestrian pavement. Beyond lies a raked gravel ocean, its gray surface furrowed with alternating straight and curved rows, some swirling around rock formations embedded in the gravel to suggest islands in a dry sea. Large black stones, pruned Japanese black pine, and sheared evergreens fill the horizon. The Zen garden invites visitors to perceive abstract forms symbolizing natural features: a ginkgo grove as a forest, raked gravel patterns as flowing water, and tall stones as a waterless cascade.

During the fourteenth- to sixteenth-century Muomachi period, Zen Buddhism influenced a departure from naturalistic Japanese gardens, landscaped to provide a beautiful, impressive setting for prince or shogun. Attached to temples, modestly scaled Zen gardens sought instead to aid that religious contemplation which aspired toward enlightenment. As an intellectual means rather than a material and aesthetic end, Zen gardens emphasized austerity and abstraction, suggesting rather than imitating nature. (It will be noted that a near-abandonment of plants in favor of gravel, rock, and stone typifies Zen gardens; and unlike other Japanese gardens, they are completely dry, even if they constantly signify water, setting boulder archipelagoes in a swirling gravel stream or sea.) Meticulous in execution, the Huntington Zen garden's design seems to reflect the influence of Ryoan-ji in Kyoto, a fifteenth-century temple garden considered the culmination of this refined form.

Down steps to a wooden zigzag bridge that crosses a transitional dry streambed, the path visits a Japanese house replicating a seventeenth-century dwelling. It commands a view of a more familiar Japanese garden, with its crimson *taikobashi* or drum bridge arching over a lily pond, a weeping willow, evergreens, stone lanterns and pagodas appointing a steeply sloping valley, pretty and picturesque by contrast to Zen austerity. More camellias extend to the north, and near the garden's eastern entrance an eighteenth-century Japanese temple bell marks the way toward several other specialized gardens.

The first and largest is the rose garden, bounded by a lath arbor and a cement pergola simulating tree limbs and supporting climbing roses such as the hybrid musk rose "Danae and Cornelia," the Noisette "Champney's Pink Cluster," and "Alister Stella Gray," as well as the showy Brazilian purple trumpet vine (*Clytostoma callistegioides*). Down the middle of the rose garden an axial path proceeds under traditional metal hoops supporting white "Climbing Snowbird" and the exceedingly pale yellow "Paul's Lemon Pillar." Shrub roses parallel the trellis and flank the central axis; All America Rose Selections and all rose varieties are labeled. Two Montezuma cypresses shade the axis where it terminates in a small stone belvedere, an eighteenth-century French "Temple of Love."

Combined with the main collection, roses in the Shakespeare and herb gardens trace a thousand years of rose history. (The main rose garden's periphery presents a rose history walk from the earliest varieties through ancestors of hybrid teas.) San Marino is part of the Pasadena culture area, to which the Huntington contributes by this justly famous rose garden of nearly 2,000 cultivars, a collection that is aesthetically pleasing, distinguished by the sheer number of roses cultivated, and informed by historical principles.

Roses—whose vitamin C-rich hips are used in tea and from which fragrant rose water, oil, and attar are extracted—also appear in the adjacent herb garden, whose slightly raised, formal beds glance back to the late Renaissance vogue for "herbals," or books on herbal remedies, which are collected in the Huntington Library. The extensive plantings are classified as "liquer herbs" (imparting their essences to alcohol more readily than to water), sachet and strewing herbs (to sweeten the doggy, ripe ambience of the medieval household, whose low hygienic standard fostered a high atmosphere), and herbs for cooking, medicine, perfumes, cosmetics, and "tussy mussy." The last group refers to scented flowers and herbs bearing symbolic meanings sent as communiqués between lovers or as messages of peace, war, and victory: all is floral in love and war. The rose signified beauty or love; penstemon, "pleasure without alloy"; and goldenrod, "precaution." While it must be admitted that the sexual organs of plants have an obvious, if rather crude, relevance to a love affair, the system seems also to have had some flaws. To keep all parties alert, some flowers had contradictory meanings, then as now the spice of love being doubt, ambiguity, and breakdown of communication.

Another link between the library and the garden, the Shakespeare garden fills a naturalistic flower meadow arranged along a dry creek bed near the Amanda Scott Gallery of American Art. Its abundant flowers—some accompanied by quotations indicating where Shakespeare mentions them—also act as a reminder that among the many ways the Huntington Botanic Gardens excels, it truly does have flowers in bloom during every month of the year. From January's aloes and pink ball _Dombeya x Cayeuxii_ to late spring cacti to October's floss silk trees, this tradition comes down from the Huntingtons, who used the estate as a winter home and wanted flowers indoors and out. The Huntington's labeling program also sets a standard for botanic gardens; legible, accurate labels identify nearly every specimen. The garden's superb maintenance also cannot be too highly praised; even when expert connoisseurship guides decisions about what to plant, no garden can survive without maintenance being a first priority.

As a general rule, if the Huntington chooses to grow it, the result will be superb. There is no other large garden in California whose breadth and depth of plants, quality of display and maintenance, and aesthetically superb design equals that of the Huntington Botanical Gardens. It fulfills a special function, which is to provide a place for the private and the public imagination. Its beauty seems a kind of miracle, for the sheer diversity of horticultural styles in less competent hands might have dispersed the impact of each one. Yet by subtle transitions and sharp contrasts, the horticultural sequence plays out a kind of high drama, almost like that of a dream. Only a dream would set English turf and oaks against a screen of bamboo or palms. Surrealism might choose to glimpse the Gothic, gargoyle shapes of cactus, aloe, yucca, and agave from a lily pond or under a jungle canopy. Montage might unleash in succession an Italianate allée, a Japanese garden, and collections of medieval herbs, roses, and exotic subtropicals.

Although they are all present, it is not necessary to wheel out the Freudian machinery of wish fulfillment, condensation and compromise of opposites, and the erection of a dream facade. Instead the dream qualities in the Huntington Gardens are vivid color, heightened reality, and the surprises created by rapid shifts of style. Surprising juxtapositions are found, on reflection, to have a submerged logic. Everything seems to have a deepened color, a perfection of shape, or the blend of intensity and effortlessness that characterizes pleasure and play. The exceptional visual quality of these surroundings—the presence of beauty and interest and the absence of ugliness and repetition—means that unlike in the real world, one devotes one's energy to paying attention rather than to tuning out.

Unlike all too many modern cities, visually boring when not actively ugly, here for a few hours one may concentrate on seeing rather than on not seeing. That is the true achievement of these gardens, and it explains why a visit can seem at once perceptually fatiguing and spiritually refreshing. Their splendor challenges a society that denies the value of beautiful physical surroundings and ruthlessly suppresses it as a factor in making its decisions. These gardens realize "The Dream Place"—the phrase is Hertrich's, and he used it to imply that it was Huntington's—to the shame of the real places that we permit to surround us.

(The Huntington Library, Art Galleries, and Botanical Gardens, 1151 Oxford Rd., San Marino; a second entrance is Orlando Rd. at Allen Ave. Admission is free, but there is a suggested contribution of $5.00 per adult. Open Tuesday through Friday 1:00 to 4:30 p.m. and Saturday and Sunday 10:30 a.m. to 4:30 p.m. Closed Mondays and major holidays. For information, telephone 818-405-2141. Garden tours are given daily shortly after the garden opens. Several maps and introductory guides to the gardens are available at small cost in the entry pavilion near the bookstore. Besides the art galleries and library, facilities include a book and gift shop and a restaurant serving teas, lunches, and light refreshments.)

DESCANSO
GARDENS

The centerpiece of Descanso Gardens, the natural fact that called it into being in its creator's imagination, was a thirty-acre grove of native coast live oaks (*Quercus agrifolia*). Their gnarled trunks and branches provide an evergreen, shady canopy, which with the slightly acid soil contributed by the oak leaf litter creates ideal conditions for camellias. First planted in the late 1930s as a self-supporting nursery supplying wholesale plants and flowers, Descanso's 100,000 camellias today form a thicket of small trees twenty feet high and in many places impenetrable.

Camellia season extends from December through March, usually peaking in February. At the height of bloom, the camellia forest's pink, red, white, and particolored blossoms beneath the oaks' vaguely menacing contortions create an unusual, Alice-in-Wonderland atmosphere. On clear February days, the low winter sun slants through the broken canopy—besides the oaks there are coast redwoods, ash, podocarpus, and white birch—making glossy camellia leaves shine and glitter. The camellias grow so closely that their shade leaves bare, slender trunks that catch the dappled light on clean, buff bark, smooth as skin, an effect nearly as fine as the flowers.

Throughout the camellia forest, shade-loving plants flower at other times of the year, such as agapanthus, calla, azalea, clivia, bird of paradise, acanthus, Chinese maple, and even rhododendron, a rarity in southern California. The forest also offers foliage plants such as philodendrons, gold dust plant, *Fatsia japonica*, aspidistras, and junipers. Yet the very conditions that made the splendid camellia forest possible here pose a key problem for this garden, whose dominant species blooms only during the winter. The rest of Descanso Gardens may be viewed as a series of efforts—largely successful—to elaborate itself into a garden possessing year-round horticultural interest. While it will always be best known for its extraordinary camellias, Descanso Gardens' other features give it interest at nearly every time of the year.

A series of garden structures helps to relieve the almost disorienting oak and camellia forest. Recognizing the camellia's Japanese origins, a blue-tiled teahouse, designed by Whitney Smith and Wayne Williams and completed in 1966, overlooks a stream and the enclosing forest. Azalea, bamboo, *Cycas revoluta*, Japanese maples, rhapis palms, and tree ferns furnish the teahouse curtilage. Just behind the teahouse, by forcing special hybrids into dormancy by withholding water after September, Descanso's gardeners coax and bully lilacs into bloom in March and April.

At the garden's southeastern perimeter is the residence of E. Manchester Boddy, then owner of the Los Angeles *Daily News*, who after purchasing Descanso in the late 1930s developed it by planting the camellias. Renamed Hospitality House, it serves as the Descanso Gardens Guild Art Gallery. Its patio offers views into the oak grove as well as a prospect of the imposing San Gabriel mountains across La Cañada valley. Near the house assorted exotic trees—deodar, cryptomeria, Chinese golden rain tree, loquat, pittosporum, European copper beech, bay (*Lauris nobilis*), and the Australian tea tree (*Leptospermum laevigatum*)—suggest the horticultural possibilities of this site and climate beyond the oak and camellia. Just below the house, cymbidium orchids fill a small natural amphitheater, adding another season of color under the oaks in late winter and early spring.

From Hospitality House, a paved drive leads above the camellia forest as rough chaparral slopes up the San Rafael Hills south of the drive. Beyond plantings of agapanthus and bird of paradise, the path reaches Fern Canyon. Hundreds of low-growing sword ferns hug the banks of a streambed where Australian and Tasmanian tree ferns and pendulous fronds of *Asplenium bulbiferum* preside over calla, ginger, and camellias. Seen from a bridge built of smooth river stone, it makes a fine, lush composition.

The southern path leads directly into the camellia forest, which may be entered and explored at many points, though this scarcely seems necessary as the twenty-foot plants nearly close overhead. In this part of the camellia forest are several examples of backyard patios, terraces, shelters, and rock gardens. Of particular note, near a lath structure paved with four brick wings, is a *Michelia doltsopa*, a magnolia relative that blooms in winter with large, creamy blooms having green centers. Benefiting from the oaks' filtered shade, a southern magnolia grows nearby, for comparison's sake.

This part of the forest surrounds a large lawn area on three sides. On the fourth side is a length of the stream that flows through the property. Alive with ducks, the stream marks a transition to another horticultural spectacle for which Descanso has become known, a border of spring bulbs—daffodils, tulips, hyacinths, and similar traditional bulbs not commonly grown in southern California.

Just past the border lies Descanso's four-acre rose garden, with a large section devoted to "roses of yesterday," hybrid perpetual roses from the nineteenth century and earlier species types. A larger area displays hundreds of modern roses, with All American Rose Selections marked and most other varieties labeled as well, planted along curving and circular paths in bare earth. The contrast with the shaded, enclosed oak and camellia forest could not be stronger, and the lack of ground cover makes this large area seem full of glare and emphasizes the bareness of the canes. It might also account for an impression that harsh or garish colors predominate among modern roses, for example, the confused yellow, pink, and rose floribunda "Redgold" (1971) and the hot coral-orange of the grandiflora "Prominent" (1977) or floribunda "Bahia" (1974). The color of blisters, such blooms seem to borrow the chroma of rock videos.

Around the edge of the camellia forest, the garden emphasis lessens, and a nature preservation theme emerges. Next to the roses, Descanso maintains a bird refuge, and a trail leading to California native plants also begins near the rose garden. It ascends to a high part of the property, passing Washingtonia palms, coast redwoods, incense cedar, a Torrey pine grove, several other pines (Knobcone, Coulter, Bishop, and Jeffrey), manzanitas, and California oaks. From the California native plant area, an unpaved chaparral trail follows the southern edge of the camellia forest through rough country and uncultivated vegetation, green and lush in a rainy winter, hot, brown, and parched each summer.

For all its many horticultural features—and these are continually expanding—Descanso remains best known for its exceptional camellias. Timing is important: sometime in February when thousands of camellia flowers pop out under the oaks, Descanso becomes one of the most amazing public gardens in California, a spectacle not to be missed.

(Descanso Gardens, 1418 Descanso Dr., La Canada; adult admission $3.00; open daily 9:00 a.m. to 5:00 p.m.; closed Christmas Day. Free parking. Guided tram tours and walking tours are offered; facilities include a gift shop, Japanese souvenir shop, cafe court, and Japanese teahouse. For information, telephone 818-790-7751.)

LOS ANGELES
STATE AND COUNTY
ARBORETUM

Descanso Gardens, the Huntington Botanical Gardens, and the Los Angeles State and County Arboretum cluster near one another north and east of Los Angeles. Each one comprises well over one hundred acres around a large house and displays exceptional plant collections. Together they make this area one of the state's finest horticultural regions. The idea for creating the arboretum is credited to Dr. Samuel Ayres, professionally a dermatologist but by avocation an enthusiast for flowering trees and plants, who devoted decades to a civic crusade for flowering trees and introduced many new species into Los Angeles. In 1948, the California Arboretum Foundation formed, and Ayres headed a committee that acquired the 127-acre site.

This area was named Santa Anita during Mission times, and after the 1821 Mexican revolution, it became part of a 13,000-acre grant to Hugo Reid, whose reconstructed adobe is one of several historic structures preserved on the property. Title passed in 1875 to Elias "Lucky" Baldwin, who made a fortune in the Comstock Lode, moved south, and invested in horseflesh and agribusiness. (Baldwin later owned 54,000 acres, and his prize-winning stables anticipated today's Santa Anita racetrack across Baldwin Blvd. from the arboretum.) Baldwin began to landscape, dredging a lake, planting many of the oldest trees, and hiring A. A. Bennett in 1881 to design an eclectic Queen Anne-style guest house on the lakeshore. (With the jungle garden across the lake, the Queen Anne Cottage has become an arboretum trademark; Johnny Weissmuller trumpeted through the ropy vegetation in Tarzan films, and more recently, television's *Fantasy Island* featured the cottage. Its botanical variety and relative proximity to the studios account for the arboretum's appearance in over 100 films since its founding.)

The arboretum opened in 1955, with Edward Huntsman-Trout involved in restoring the Reid Adobe and designing the paths around the lake and through the vast property. In 1958, the Arboretum Foundation and *Sunset* magazine opened a "Demonstration Home Garden," the first feature inside the entrance. It offers structures, materials, and plants suitable for home gardens: wooden decks under shade cloth; trellises draped with creepers such as *Thunbergia mysorensis*; sixteen fencing choices, from hand-split cedar grapestake to two-inch lodgepole pine; assorted water features, outdoor patios, and paving options; and shade plants, ground covers, and trees.

North of Ayres Hall, commemorating Dr. Ayres and his wife, Helen, for their leadership in arboretum affairs, a "garden for all seasons" displays vegetables, flowering bulbs, and annuals. The path leads past a begonia greenhouse to a modest structure housing one of the most remarkable indoor plant collections in California. Designated a "tropical greenhouse," its true distinction is a display of orchids selected from a mammoth collection housed elsewhere on the property. Tiny waterfalls and streams humidify an astonishing display of tropical plants: cycads; hanging strands of Spanish moss; bird's nest ferns with five-foot, undivided fronds; and staghorn and maidenhair ferns. An emphasis on colored foliage appears in the peach, rose, and yellow croton; all manner of bromeliads; maroon underleaves and spotted green upper

Palms, a lagoon, and a Queen Anne cottage, Los Angeles State and County Arboretum

leaves of *Calathea insignis*; and rose, purple, and green leaves of the ti plant (*Cordyline terminalis tricolor*).

Tropical vines hang from the building's frame, particularly the extraordinary *Dioscorea macrostachys*. From its enlarged, woody root resembling a tortoise shell emerge spindly stems that range for thirty feet about the greenhouse ceiling. Although flowering tropicals include dark rose plumeria, pale pink anthurium, and delicacies such as *Pleurothallis giesbrechtiana* (bearing minute chartreuse-yellow flowers on six-inch spikes), the orchids' dazzling hues and shapes overwhelm all challengers. Cymbidiums, cattleyas, lady slippers (*Paphiopedilum*), and other orchids make an astonishing spectacle, even though this display comprises only a fraction of the arboretum's 10,000 plants derived from 2,000 orchid species. As a grand finale, a sunken garden fills one end of the greenhouse, the yard-long leaf blades and stalks of giant elephant ears (*Xanthosoma sagittifolium*) emerging from a pit of orchids and other tropical flowers and foliage.

Outdoors once more, the path circles through the arboretum's extensive Australian section, displaying acacias, pittosporum, callistemon, and an exceptional eucalyptus collection. The Australian section also includes several *Melaleuca*, many introduced into California by the arboretum, a grove of *Brachychiton* trees (*B. discolor, B. acerifolius,* and *B. bidwillii*), and curiosities such as the grass tree (*Xanthorrhoea quadrangulata*), bearing slim, grassy spears by the hundreds on a short, six-foot trunk.

The path through the Australian section curves west and south before entering a South African area that is most impressive for its hundreds of aloes, coming into outstanding orange, coral, gold, and crimson bloom in January and February. Adjacent to the African section, the Henry C. Soto Water Conservation Garden comprises educational displays covering regional water sources and supply, irrigation systems, soils, and drought-resistant plants: acanthus, calla, blue hibiscus, and *Ceanothus maritimus*.

Past an enormous lawn and the axial pond and fountain, the path circles around the property's most intensively developed area, containing historic buildings and many specialized gardens. Beyond a screen of bamboo and coast redwoods appears the tangle of vines, palms, and canopy trees of the "Prehistoric and Jungle Garden." This area has views across a lagoon to the Queen Anne Cottage set in a grove of *Washingtonia robusta* fan palms said to be among the tallest in California. The garden's prehistoric theme appears most prominently in an extensive collection of cycads, a plant family dating from the Mesozoic era (66 million to 230 million years ago), and in several fine dawn redwoods, a species dating from the same era. (The redwoods tower above a display presenting biological, geological, and historical time lines, world cycad distribution, the history of primitive dawn redwood and _Ginkgo biloba_ species, and the jungle's composition, value, and threatened disappearance.)

The garden does not quite come together as a jungle; the Washingtonias are a desert, not a jungle, palm, and the canopy trees (dawn redwood, ginkgo, eucalyptus, weeping willow, magnolia, and black walnut) are not jungle species. As the educational display makes clear, jungles are wet, humid, tropical, and equatorial, with temperatures averaging 80 degrees and annual rainfall of 150 to 200 inches. The dry San Gabriel Valley, by contrast, receives less than 10 percent of this annual rainfall, and smudge pots among the cycads testify to Arcadia's freezing temperatures on winter nights.

The jungle garden is thus primarily an evocation of when dinosaurs stalked the earth, an overwhelming mass of not necessarily tropical vegetation ranging from the lagoon's cattails (_Typha latifolia_) to the vining wild grape (_Vitis californica_) that engulfs over one-third of this 3.5 acres. Corridors through the overarching bamboo canes almost shut out the sun, with only the stalwart aspidistra able to grow in densely shaded tunnels. Just before the exit, azaleas and a grove of young _Caryota_ palms share space, for no apparent reason, with coast redwoods.

The recently developed Meadowbrook area offers irises, daffodils, and other spring bulbs under groves of jacarandas, birches, pale lavender-flowering _Paulownia kawakamii_, and Japanese and red maples along a pond filled with Japanese nishikigoi, literally "brocaded carp." The Grace V. Kallam Perennial Garden, designed by Shirley A. Kerins and under development, will contain a rock garden, drought-tolerant plants, and a "rainbow garden" projected to cultivate over 400 species and varieties.

Here the path proceeds through a magnolia collection, a 1.2-acre herb garden, and a small "old-fashioned rose garden," set against a citrus backdrop, with whitewashed arches and pergolas for climbing and pillar rose varieties. Brick paths pass through a display of rarely seen traditional varieties. Across from the rose garden, a path leads through native oaks and past an interesting (if mostly unlabeled) ficus collection, an avocado grove, and a South American section (displaying acacias, a Brazilian _Tabebuia avellanedae_, and crepe myrtles). Eventually the path ascends Tallac Knoll past an array of rare _Bauhinia_ species, from trees to vines, and a similarly impressive area of more than two dozen _Erythrina_ species.

Several *Bombax* species (e.g., *B. valetonii*) appear before the path reaches the top of Tallac Knoll, the arboretum's highest point with a fine view of the San Gabriel mountains. Besides daylilies, hibiscus, society garlic, palms, and subtropicals surrounding a pond that runs in a small creek down to a waterfall below, the knoll contains a superb yellow trumpet tree (*Tabebuia chrysotricha*) that blooms in the spring with papery, bright golden yellow trumpets on bare, twiggy branches.

A path follows the sound of the waterfall down past the Meadowbrook section to rejoin the circular path as it enters a palm and bamboo collection across from the lagoon. Although palms appear throughout the arboretum, this area is especially strong in *Livistona, Phoenix, Sabal,* and *Trachycarpus* palms and contains rarities like the Formosa sugar palm (*Arenga engleri*). The palms grow near the arboretum's historic sites: Hugo Reid's adobe; Indian wickiups behind an impenetrable, ten-foot-high prickly pear cactus hedge; and the Queen Anne-style Santa Anita Depot, a restored nineteenth-century railroad station relocated from its site in nearby Sierra Madre.

A vast property, the arboretum's 4,000 species and more than 35,000 plants will doubtless try the stamina of all but the most dedicated visitor. (Multiple visits, or ruthless selectivity, are recommended.) As some of the less well maintained and labeled areas indicate, its size and vast plant collections appear to exceed available resources. The arboretum is nevertheless one of the area's most popular public gardens, and for the most part it fulfills its educational, horticultural, and botanical roles well. Besides its plants, the arboretum preserves historical sites, acts as a bird refuge, and hosts horticultural exhibits throughout the year. The sheer range of its plant collections is impressive. Its outstanding horticultural and botanical collections comprise a major public garden for this region and for the entire state.

(Los Angeles State and County Arboretum, 301 N. Baldwin Ave., Arcadia. Open daily from 9:00 a.m. to 5:00 p.m.; closed Christmas Day; adult admission $3.00. The arboretum offers a book and plant shop, coffee shop, plant science library, herbarium, and guided tram tours. For information, telephone 818-446-8251.)

EL ALISAL:
CHARLES F. LUMMIS
HOME

H ard by the serpentine, Mr.-Toad's-Wild-Ride Pasadena Freeway near downtown Los Angeles, under the tower of the
Southwestern Museum, and built of river stones that Lummis himself retrieved from the bottom of the Arroyo Seco,
El Alisal is a survivor from another era. The energetic, multifarious personality of Charles Lummis mixed his careers as journalist (he was city
editor of the *Los Angeles Times* for three years); boosterish mythologist
of the Southwest (he wrote ten books on California and the Southwest
and originated the slogan, "See America First"); anthropologist, folk-
lorist, and scholar (he was director of the Los Angeles Public Library for
five years, founded the Southwest Museum, and edited the magazines
Land of Sunshine and *Out West*); early preservationist of the California missions and of the folk culture that survived from Mexican California; and
physical culturist (he walked from Ohio to California in 112 days during 1884 and later battled breakdowns and strokes with physical labor).
Lummis was part Harvard-educated aesthete (the doors of the house
copied Velázquez's *The Queen's Pages*) and part crackpot eccentric.

Lummis's home unites the facets of his personality. Between 1898
and 1910, he built a stone fortress in a grove of the sycamores that fill
much of the Arroyo Seco. Calling it "El Alisal" after the Spanish word
for sycamore, he consciously designed it to integrate the functional utility beloved of traditional America (he had the floors angled and drained
so he could clean the house by hosing it down) and the rustic dignity
he associated with Spanish colonial heritage (thick walls, rough-hewn
beams, and doors with wrought-iron monograms). Although he traipsed
about in corduroy suits and a Spanish sash and hat and managed to per-
suade acquaintances to call him "Don Carlos," his commitment to
regional history, aesthetics, and imagination balanced those affectations.
Located in the historic, arts-oriented suburb of Highland Park and

History and horticulture in Highland Park: The Charles F. Lummis Home

owned by the City of Los Angeles, the property today houses the head-quarters of the Historical Society of Southern California.

If the Lummis home recalls an earlier era, the garden may point the way to a water-conserving future. Displaying drought-resistant plants and water-conservation techniques for home use, it successfully illustrates how these methods can create a satisfying landscape. Following a design by Robert Perry and installed since 1986, paths circulate among the three-acre property's five distinct zones. Near the entry, a yarrow meadow shows how a drought-resistant ground cover—_Achillea millefolium "Rosea"_—can create a traditional effect. Although shaggier than manicured turf, the yarrow resembles a lawn, and besides taking far less water, it needs a high mowing only about four times a year and can take considerable foot traffic. Other ground covers clothe the bare earth that makes many drought-resistant gardens such baleful places. _Ceanothus_, for instance, combines well with the gray-blue spears of _Senecio mandraliscae_ across the path from the yarrow meadow. The hot orange band of California poppy nearby emphasizes the _Ceanothus-Senecio_ composition, with its blue color rhyme and foliar contrast.

Under steep cliffs in the Arroyo Seco between Pasadena and down-town Los Angeles, El Alisal does not experience the hottest summer temperatures. It nonetheless remains subject not only to relentless summer sun but humid spring fogs, winter downpours, and desert heat of autumn Santa Ana winds. The garden's California native zone emphasizes tree species tough enough for this variable climate, particularly the California sycamore, with its fresh foliage, leaning trunk, and maculate bark; the California bay laurel (_Umbellularia californica_), its dark green leaves casting dense shade; Bishop and Torrey pines; the lacy, bright green foliage of the southern California black walnut (_Juglans californica_), and the coast live oak (_Quercus agrifolia_).

Throughout this section are specimens of that honorary California tree, the olive, as native species merge into a third zone, a "regional plant garden," containing exotics from the world's Mediterranean climate regions: eucalyptus, acacia, camphor, strawberry (_Arbutus unedo_), and pepper trees, as well as colorful shrubs or perennials such as the tough but showy Pride of Madeira, purple salvia, Australian bluebell creeper (_Sollya heterophylla_), bougainvillea, and in a shady site in Lummis's patio, the lavender Douglas iris.

Although the fourth zone, a small citrus garden, departs somewhat from the drought-resistant theme—citrus trees require considerable water to get through the hot summer that they need to ripen fruit—

these are traditional, useful, and colorful inhabitants of southern California gardens. Perhaps the fifth zone, a desert garden, compensates for the extra water the citrus demand. The desert garden is composed unusually, with wildflowers planted throughout the agave, "Heart of Flame" (*Bromelia balansae*), *Opuntia* and other cacti, the bright yellow daisies of *Coreopsis gigantea*, and the bird of paradise bush (*Caesalpinia gilliesii*), flowering brilliantly during summers.

With its mix of horticultural demonstration, irrigation and water-saving techniques, and cultural and regional history, El Alisal's architecturally unusual house and accomplished garden offer features nearly as multifaceted as Charles Lummis himself. Attentive to the demands of preservation, history, and local climate and conditions, the Lummis Home convincingly extends the influence of the man who built it.

(El Alisal—Lummis Home, 200 E. Ave. 43, Los Angeles [entrance on Carlota Blvd.]. Admission is free; open Thursday to Sunday, 1:00 p.m. to 4:00 p.m.; telephone 213-222-0546 for information on docent tours, horticultural programs, and historical presentations.)

PASADENA
GARDENS

Horticultural symbol of what may be called the Pasadena culture area, the rose has lent itself to a defining annual event in Pasadena and surrounding communities. The Tournament of Roses, originally a simple matter of Chamber of Commerce boosterism, called attention to the fact that roses could bloom here on New Year's Day. Rooted in the myth of a winterless climate, the tournament has been elaborated over a century into a small-town civic ritual of national proportion. The WRIGLEY MANSION, built in 1911 and headquarters of the Tournament of Roses, survives from an earlier Orange Grove Boulevard before rezoning and demoli-

Wide lawns, tall palms, and roses on New Year's Day: the Wrigley Mansion

tion made way for luxury flats. The mansion's green tiled roof and brackets, balustrades and grilles, and especially the lavish grounds suggest the scale of life along this millionaires' street.

The expansive lawns are beautifully planted with palms, coast redwood, Norfolk Island pine, southern magnolias, eucalyptus, and a large Moreton Bay fig shading a subtropical flower garden. As is fitting, rose beds surround the mansion terrace, an unusual gazebo fountain, and a splendid pergola, tiled and painted a cream color to match the mansion. The pergola rose garden contains labeled All-American Rose Selections surrounded by beds of annuals and flowering plants. (At 391 S. Orange Grove Blvd., Pasadena, the grounds are open all year; the mansion is open to the public for free guided tours Wednesdays from 2:00 p.m. to 4:00 p.m., February 1 to September 1; telephone 818-449-4100.)

Almost directly across Orange Grove Boulevard from the Wrigley Mansion, the AMBASSADOR COLLEGE CAMPUS illustrates how to change the use of a neighborhood without demolishing it in a clean sweep. (Ralph D. Cornell and Edward Huntsman-Trout landscaped the campus in 1951-1953, but it has changed considerably since then.) The campus integrates several blocks of two-story dwellings by means of axial pedestrian streets. Although fencing and access to the homes have been altered, new fountains and plazas where the pedestrian streets cross, masonry, lamps, urns, and terracing have preserved many old plants. Water flows throughout the campus, ranging stylistically from the modernist sheet (in which the Ambassador Auditorium seems to float) to formal pools to streams appointed by Japanese stone lanterns and wooden bridges or emboldened by steep, naturalistically bouldered watercourses.

Benches mark secluded spots, inviting one to marvel at the exceptionally high level of campus maintenance. Extensive beds of annuals and bulbs beneath artfully pruned trees embellish acres of dichondra lawn. To see dichondra, something of a status symbol a generation ago but so difficult to maintain that today it is almost a lost art, seems quite unexpected at this late date. It shows they know and care. So do stately formal gardens on a slope east of the Loma D. Armstrong Academic Center. A watercourse, wooden bridge, abstract sculptural fountains, lawns, and plantings of camellias, azaleas, and Chinese magnolias preclude utter stylistic consistency. But a staircase lined by Italian cypresses, precision-clipped box and *Eugenia paniculata,* and extensive hedging extending from the mansion at the top of the hill suggest Italianate formality with considerable style.

West of the mansion, style turns into panache: here an even more formal garden sinks about ten feet below grade, surrounded by a balustrade and a pergola's columns and grille. In the sunken garden, razor-trimmed hedging and brick paths define small beds of annuals, lawns, and ivy and juniper. They make a symmetrical mirror garden on either side of a rectangular pond headed by an abstract sculptural fountain, perhaps the only false note in this composition. Vertical clipped arborvitae and laurel ficus, crepe myrtle, and twin winter-blooming star magnolia (_Magnolia kobus stellata_) relieve the horizontal geometry of the paths and hedging. When fourteen fountain jets play on the central pond, the effect becomes dynamic, even exuberant, a tour de force in a campus with much to enjoy and appreciate. (Ambassador College, S. Orange Grove Blvd. north of Del Mar Blvd.)

A collector and dealer of Asian art, Grace Nicholson built herself a spacious home and shop in 1924. Deeded to the City of Pasadena in the 1940s, it became the PACIFIC ASIA MUSEUM in 1971, an ideal tenant for the building. Its two-story brown stucco walls and green glazed roof tiles, corners upswept in the Asian style, enclose a Chinese courtyard garden designed by Erikson, Peters, Thomas and Associates in 1979. In 3,000 square feet, paved courtyard stones make way for a koi-filled pond crossed by a zigzag bridge of acid-washed mica sandstone. Limestone rocks in the Tai-hu manner symbolize remote mountains, as twin eighteenth-century Ch'ing dynasty marble lion dogs control access up staircases to the second floor. The garden contains only three trees: _Pittosporum tobira_, the golden rain tree, and _Ginkgo biloba_, since ancient times preserved against extinction in Chinese temple gardens.

Azaleas and mondo grass, with potted Chinese banana, _Ficus benjamina_, and cymbidium orchids, occupy the level nearest the ground. The Yulan magnolia (_M. heptapeta_), the slender lady palm (_Rhapis humilis_), and four symmetrically placed _Podocarpus macrophyllus_ fill in the middle level, with a Chinese wisteria climbing one of four carved stone staircases and twining around its railing and lotus blossom finials. In this city of roses, it is fitting that two Chinese species, the _Rosa banksiae_ "Alba Plena" and the shrubby _R. chinensis_, also grow in the courtyard garden. Two centuries ago, _R. chinensis_ varieties were the first Chinese roses to appear in Europe. Their arrival touched off the revolution in Occidental rose breeding to which Chinese roses contributed their colors and repeat blooming habit.

Parts of the courtyard seem a bit frayed around the edges; some corners store artifacts or forlorn tubbed plants in need of rejuvenation, and more than one black plastic nursery pot has been left artlessly exposed in planting beds. The dead stump of a too-vigorous timber bamboo that threatened the building's plumbing and structural integrity points out the relative absence of this key genus. It is possible that the courtyard appears best from inside the ground floor galleries that surround it. (Pacific Asia Museum, 46 N. Los Robles Ave.; $3.00 adult admission; telephone 818-449-2742.)

The CALIFORNIA INSTITUTE OF TECHNOLOGY contains one of the few public commissions executed by Florence Yoch and Lucile Council, whose work concentrated on residential landscaping in Pasadena and Beverly Hills from the twenties through the early sixties. (James Y. Yoch's *Landscaping the American Dream: The Gardens and Film Sets of Florence Yoch* covers the partnership's gardens, with a good chapter on Yoch's particularly accessible commissions: *Gone With the Wind, Romeo and Juliet,* and other films incorporated her garden set designs.) At Cal Tech, Yoch and Council landscaped the Athenaeum, an Italianate faculty club building designed by Gordon Kaufmann in 1930 located on Hill Avenue between California Boulevard and San Pasqual. Surrounded by staircases and terraces, roofed in terra-cotta tile, and painted a creamy beige with olive trim, the building presents four distinct facades.

Dating from 1930-31, Yoch and Council's landscape plan survives fairly completely. Regularly spaced, mature olive trees, clumps of Senegal date palms, and assorted espaliered and vining plants fill the Hill Street facade's terraces. A service area is concealed by a high wall supporting bird of paradise in terra-cotta pots and a heavy wood double gate, bolted and defended by menacing fleur-de-lis iron daggers across the top. At times the design verges on exact symmetry, as in twin European fan palms, each superintended by a single Senegal date palm, flanking the southern entry. But considered as a whole, the landscaping balances regularity with asymmetry, as sprawling vines (jasmine spilling over a terrace and wisteria climbing drainpipes) counterstate formally spaced olives along Hill Street, a sycamore allée, and closely planted lemon gum eucalyptus lining a drive to the porte cochere.

The building's arcaded central courtyard creates an outdoor dining area shaded by an old olive and a cluster of rhapis palm, with vining and tubbed plants mitigating the rigor of the surrounding colonnade. The courtyard's fourth side opens through a double colonnade to a view along an olive allée. Elsewhere on the small campus, landscaping helps unify much fine early architecture and not so fine post-World War II additions. The olive walk between low-rise dormitories is inspired, dividing at its western end to terminate in a fountain set in a sheet of water that drains into a lily pond in a jacaranda-covered knoll flanked by two wisteria-draped arcades. Many of the same elements—axial walks, olive allées, lawns under eucalyptus, pink India hawthorn, and the lavender of agapanthus, jacaranda, and wisteria recur throughout the campus, which is at its most colorful during April, May, and June.

ROSE HILLS
MEMORIAL
PARK

The "Pageant of Roses" at Rose Hills Memorial Park opened in 1959. An official display garden for the All-American Rose Selections and the American Rose Society, its 3.5 acres today contain 7,000 plants in more than 600 varieties. Besides the latest shrub hybrids, the garden collects climbing, pillar, standard, miniature, and historical roses. Its ancient roses include the "Apothecary's Rose" (*Rosa gallica officinalis*), the "Rose of Castille" (*Rosa damascena semper flourens*) and the parti-colored "Painter's Rose" (*Rosa des peintres centifolia*), resembling this year's model off the hybridizer's assembly line but in fact dating from about 1600. The garden also preserves curiosities like the the Japanese mutant "bamboo rose" (*Rosa multiflora watsoniana*), with leaves like green slivers along twiggy, nearly thornless canes, the Central European "apple rose" (*Rosa pomifera*), a nonblooming species notable for its scent, and "Old Smoothie," a modern hybrid tea bearing reddish-violet flowers on almost thornless stems.

At least since the the time of the Romans, who planted them in their necropolises to supply wreaths for the dead, the rose has had funerary associations. Cemeteries were among the earliest landscaped public gardens in the United States and especially in New England were felt to be suitable for combining the duties of familial piety with the pleasures of nature. Cemeteries were not infrequently conceived as horticultural showplaces, and many nineteenth-century roses survived because they were planted—and reverentially left undisturbed—in a family plot. Perhaps borrowing from this tradition, the Pageant of Roses displays old roses, gathering the familiar but choice "Cécile Brunner" (1881), the pale pink "La France" (the first hybrid tea, created in 1867 when the Lyonnais breeder Guillot crossed Hybrid Perpetual "Mme Victor Verdier" with Tea "Mme Bravy"), and the moss rose "Gloire des Mousseux" (1852). Nineteenth-century varieties accompany early twentieth-century hybrid teas such as the classic single pink "Dainty Bess" (1925), the crimson "Étoile de Hollande" (1919), and the perfectly shaped coral pink "Picture" (1932).

Garden paths range through eighty-five beds, frequently edged by miniature roses or having a centerpiece pillar, climbing, or standard rose. The modern color range extends from the splendid reds of "Trumpeter" and "Interama" to the clear canary yellow of "Sunsprite" (1977) and the nuanced golden white of "Honor" (1980). But innovation does not always represent progress, as shown by such dubious developments as the blotched, freckled "Bon Bon" (1974), the aptly named, neon-influenced tangerine of "Las Vegas," or the woozy, overexcited pink, orange, and coral "New Year" (1987). Near an information kiosk (where a map and list of varieties is available), distressed metal lath shades benches and several beds containing palms, cycads, magnolias, camellias, azaleas, begonias, and evergreens clipped into topiary horses, fish, and other cartoonish animal shapes.

More may not necessarily mean better when it comes to mass rose plantings, and peak bloom season in April and May presents an almost jarring sense of visual busyness. Yet the Pageant of Roses remains a place to breathe deeply, look carefully, and make notes of memorable plants. On a sloping hillside above the Pageant of Roses is a modern "lawn cemetery" of the type generic in southern California—flush graves in grassland, with olive, palm, and evergreen trees along curving lanes. A drive to the top reveals the rough country from which this orderly community was redeemed and—in clear weather—views of Mount Wilson, downtown Los Angeles, and the metropolis. South and east of Workman Mill Road and quite distinct in style, the most traditional part of Rose Hills' 2,500 acres dates from the 1920s, with funerary monuments, a Mediterranean chapel complex, and mature trees.

(The Pageant of Roses, Rose Hills Memorial Park, 3900 S. Workman Mill Rd., Whittier. Free admission; open 8:00 a.m. to sunset. For information, telephone 213-699-0921.)

Los Angeles East Briefly Noted

ounded in 1771 and one of California's most historic missions, MISSION SAN GABRIEL ARCANGEL has fallen on hard times, most recently because of a 1987 earthquake. Although its thick walls are braced and the sanctuary is closed, the grounds remain open. The entry courtyard garden displays considerable winter color, as deep purple princess flower, camellias, pink-ball Dombeya, rosemary, and poinsettias surround a small fountain painted a garish aqua. A second walled dry garden contains a substantial collection of succulent, euphorbia, and cactus species.

Although not without horticultural variety, the mission cemetery garden's primary interest remains historical and symbolic. Next to the old mission sanctuary, a large trellis dominates the cemetery garden, supporting—or supported by—the shaggy, foot-thick trunks and vast branching of grapevines planted in 1910 from cuttings of original vines brought by the Franciscan fathers from Spain. Two olives planted in 1860 symbolize the importance of olive oil to the early mission economy, and a Valencia orange remembers California's first orange grove, planted by Franciscans at Mission San Gabriel from Spanish seedlings. Introduced in mission times, grape, olive, and citrus played key roles in the culture, history, and economic development of California, and in its myth. (Mission San Gabriel Arcangel, 537 W. Mission Dr., San Gabriel; $1.00 adult admission; telephone 818-282-5191, ext. 52.)

The San Gabriel Valley contains several horticulturally noteworthy or curious sites. Glendora once contained the nation's largest bougainvillea planting, which was established in 1901. It is the first and only plant listed in the National Register of Historic Sites. With that special creativity that characterizes the real estate imagination, however, condominiums now bear the name of historic plants they all but destroyed. According to the *Guinness Book of World Records*, the 1.5 million flowers of the world's "largest blossoming plant" bloom from a _Wisteria sinensis_ vine planted out of a one-gallon container in 1892. The SIERRA MADRE WISTERIA covers nearly an acre over two private residential properties, whose owners invite the public to visit one day a year, usually in March. (Telephone the Sierra Madre Chamber of Commerce in February or early March at 818-355-5111.)

Donald Hodel's _Exceptional Trees of Los Angeles_ (1988) explores large, rare, and unusual trees throughout the Los Angeles region. Brief but informative commentary and locations of each tree accompany 167 species selected for inclusion because of size, rarity, endemism, beauty, cultural or historical value, age, or location.

A "City of Santa Fe Springs Historic Site," HERITAGE PARK portrays the layers of history as revealed by a single property: an adobe built in 1815 as part of a cattle ranch; a health resort based on iron-sulfur water discovered in 1874; a citrus ranch with 3,000 orange and lemon trees; and the discovery of oil in 1921, which touched off a boom that converted the area into the industrial suburb it remains today. Except for the film business, nearly all the key elements of southern California's economic development left traces on this single spot.

The park contains old trees and a replica of a small Victorian conservatory from the nineteenth-century estate gardens Harvey Hawkins built on his ranch. Once considered a horticultural showplace, today a small formal garden's hedging and Italian cypress enclose a _Ficus rubigonosa_, twin citrus trees, and bedding plants. Fountains, urns, and wooden fans and kites likewise connote the Victorian era. Elsewhere an aviary built in the 1920s overlooks remnants of a tropical garden. More significant historically than horticulturally, Heritage Park's careful restorations, quality maintenance, guides and interpretive materials, and interest in visitors nonetheless show a city retaining something of its past with intelligence and integrity. (Heritage Park, 12100 Mora Dr., Santa Fe Springs; telephone 213-946-6476.)

VI
Santa Barbara

LOTUSLAND

Victoria Padilla's invaluable *Southern California Gardens: An Illustrated History* lists over three dozen Santa Barbara estates that civic-minded owners opened to the public in 1915. Only Lotusland carries on the area's estate gardening tradition. (Even so, public visiting remains very limited, though wider access is expected in the future.) Yet this garden—so individual, creative, even avant-garde—scarcely represents tradition in any other sense. Lotusland represents adventurous gardening, pushing the limits of horticultural style to create something unlike anything else in Santa Barbara, or indeed in all of California.

Perhaps the only thing clichéd about Lotusland is its name, with its connotation of Hollywood overripeness. After a career as a European opera singer, seven marriages, and an escape during World War II on the last flight out before the Nazis occupied Paris, Polish-born Ganna Walska might well have desired a Homeric place of rest. Odysseus had spoken of a coastline whose lotus-chewing inhabitants "browsed on that native bloom, forgetful of their homeland." In 1941, Walska purchased a Santa Barbara property containing a house designed by noted architect George Washington Smith. Since 1882, its thirty-seven acres had been planted by earlier owners, including Kinton Stevens, a pioneering local nurseryman, whose son Ralph grew up on the estate. Madame Walska hired Ralph Stevens to design her garden, and his work here is considered his outstanding achievement as a landscape architect. Madame Walska continued to elaborate the gardens until her death in 1984 in her one hundredth year.

What distinguishes Lotusland is not only Walska's interest in unusual, striking plants but also her willingness to grow them en masse. She wisely did not seek to grow every species that might be cultivated here; even thirty-seven acres would not have sufficed for such a project. Despite its seeming extravagance, this garden actually pursues a set of ruthless priorities: not one of each rare plant but dozens and hundreds of each species selected for unusual beauty or effect. While botanically compendious, Lotusland offers not simply a catalog, a museum, or a collection: it is a garden, subordinating botanical to aesthetic principles with passion and discipline.

Each section of the Lotusland estate reveals a different facet of Walska's aesthetic. Paths through an introductory fern garden, cool and sheltered, emerge from tropical foliage plants under an oak canopy into a series of dry, sunny plantings, the first of many abrupt transitions. In sharp contrast to subtropical lushness, a grove of mature *Dracaena draco*, their round, fat trunks supporting umbrellas of merciless spearlike foliage, casts stark shade patterns on bare ground. Just beyond the dragon trees a courtyard surrounds the entrance to the house, painted a dark coral pink with rust-colored roof tiles and iron grillwork. Here, by the bushel, are golden barrel cactus (*Echinocactus grusonii*) and columnar *Neobuxbaumia polylopha*, the latter resembling unbranched saguaros. Yet even these unusual cacti can hardly compete with several giant *Euphorbia ingens*, showpiece specimens thirty feet high and trailing long, olive-colored branches along the stone pavement like menacing tentacles of some subterranean monster.

Madame Walska's cactus promenade, Lotusland

Alcazar Garden and California Tower, Balboa Park, San Diego (Photo: Patricia Sigg)

Botanical Building, Balboa Park, San Diego (Photo: Patricia Sigg)

Botanical Building interior, Balboa Park, San Diego

North Vista palm allee, Huntington Botanical Gardens, Los Angeles (Photo: Michael D. Mackness)

Alice Keck Memorial Garden, Santa Barbara

Temple and Neptune Pool, San Simeon (Photo: Michael D. Mackness)

Mission Carmel, Carmel

Asian section, University of California Botanical Garden, Berkeley

Cape Province Garden, Strybing Arboretum, San Francisco

Golden Gate Park, San Francisco

Japanese Tea Garden, Golden Gate Park, San Francisco

Capitol Park, Sacramento

San Francisco Conservatory of Flowers, San Francisco

From the entry court, a gravel drive extends through much of the estate, with paths branching off into several distinct gardens. A profusion of cacti and euphorbia lines each side of the drive. The botanical names given to these cacti and euphorbia—_monstrosa, stellatus, erectus, magnifica_—suggest the cumulative effect created by hundreds of curving, columnar, spiny shapes: bizarre, otherworldly, erotic, splendid.

Stepping-stones leading through the cactus and around the corner of the house present another sudden transition: from hostile desert cactus through battalions of bromeliads onto a green lawn, soft as a cushion. The dramatic presence of this garden and its creator never seems to rest, however, for the smooth baize of turf extends to another surprise. A row of several dozen blue _Agave franceschiana_ (named for Dr. Francesco Franceschi, a pioneer Santa Barbara horticulturist) edges the lawn, their fleshy leaves armed with spines and terminating in a purple needle, vicious and bloodthirsty. The temperate lawn against the desert agave sets forth one of the plainest of Lotusland's contrasts: meadow juxtaposed with desert, north to south, lushness with aridity, cool and mild with hot and harsh, benign and defensive, friendly and armed.

The lawn also contains effects that might suggest an English landscape. A giant Monterey cypress and a large oak, its branches hung with pale green ropes of donkey tail (_Sedum morganianum_) potted up under protective mesh coolie hats, might be in Hampshire were it not for the 3,000-foot Santa Ynez mountains visible to the north. Deeper into the lawn, a screen of mature Senegal date palms, their leaning trunks and fronds arching like fountains over a manicured lawn, disperses any purely English effect, blending the northern world with a profusion of palms and bird of paradise.

This double vision, both trim and tropical, recurs as the foliar screen parts to reveal a small topiary garden off the main lawn. Clipped into elephants and bears, fastigiate cones, and hedging, evergreen plants surround a clock set into the ground, its six-foot-long hands keeping accurate time in a face of gravel and blue-gray ice plant. A formal garden, its brick paths parting for an octagonal Moroccan star fountain, terminates in a small rose garden and balustrade near the house.

The path into the topiary garden is only one of several leading from the lawn. Past a grove of _Beaucarnea recurvata_—the bizarre shapes of their swollen bases, spindly trunks, and leafy topknots intensified by having been planted by the dozen—lies a small amphitheater of garden statuary. Chaucerian monks, misshapen peasants, hunchbacked gnomes, and a few dwarves populate this fanciful proscenium. Beyond the amphitheater, past several more bromeliad beds (nidularium, vresia, and aechmea by the hundred), lies a collection of miniature shade palms, mostly chamaedorea, in a rock garden whose smooth, buff-colored stones recline in a manner suggesting miniature Henry Moore sculptures.

Through a eucalyptus grove lies a garden organized not by a genus or style but by gathering species and cultivars with "blue" or glaucous foliage. Throughout Lotusland, chunks of blue-green slag glass from a local bottle plant line the paths and glint in the light. In the blue garden, the glass cunningly matches carpets of pale, gray-blue ice plant (*Senecio mandraliscae*) and blue fescue (*Festuca ovina glauca*), the Mexican blue fan palm (*Brahea armata*) and blue atlas cedar, and giant, century-old Chilean wine palms (*Jubea chilensis*). Throughout the blue garden and linking it to the lawn area, is the glaucous *Agave franceschiana*. This color theme garden is among Lotusland's most unusual areas, collecting plants sharing a single botanical characteristic yet otherwise differing in habit and foliage.

At the bottom of the main gravel drive (with which the blue garden communicates), past a lush border of *Howea forsteriana* palms, the cycads seem somewhat isolated in this garden of riches but should not be overlooked. The last area that Madame Walska planned in her eighties with the help of consultants Charles Glass and Robert Foster, the cycad collection is considered Lotusland's most important garden botanically. Although these primitive plants appear to resemble palms or ferns, their golden, seed-bearing cones at once reveal their true kinship to the conifers. Its earthen paths curving around small, grassy hillocks displaying hundreds of low-growing cycads, this well-labeled, immaculately maintained collection contains *Dioon, Macrozamia, Lepidozamiastangeria, Ceratozamia,* and *Zamia* species, and is particularly rich in African *Encephalartos*.

Not far from the cycads, approached through the Japanese garden, a bamboo screen points the way into Lotusland's aloe garden, from December to February a kind of wonderland. Amid mounded banks of foliage, tubular flowers bloom on torches, spikes, and candelabras in colors ranging from ingot red hot to goldenrod through shades of flamingo pink, coral, tangerine, light orange, mustard, and canary yellow. Even the aloes' foliar textures are exceptional, with tongues, paddles, fans, and fleshy spears colored gray and light green, rust and purple. Often freckled, banded, or speckled, aloe foliage can be borne atop smooth trunks and branches on arboreal species growing as high as thirty feet. This is a marvelous collection at any time of year, but aloe fanciers should try to see it in bloom, usually at its height in January.

The aloes merge into a bizarre fountain and pond. From two stair-cased fountains, each composed of three giant _Tridacna_ clam shells, water descends into a shallow pool, surrounded by nacreous clusters of aba-lone shells mortared by the hundred into a black, pebbled border. From the pond, painted sky blue, emerge several islands of white tufa. Yet another water feature dominates the adjacent area. Beneath two large _Podocarpus elongatus_ trees and Chilean wine palms, a pond ringed with agapanthus, agave, elephant's ear, cannas, and horsetail contains an island of papyrus and a small fountain. Leaving the water garden's lush plants, the exit abruptly alters the mood as it slopes through a mass plant-ing of _Agave victoria-reginae_, a small, choice agave signaling the change from a boggy to an arid setting.

Lotusland relies on such thematic surprises. It expresses design prin-ciples that are theatrical and flamboyant but botanically literate, bizarrely surreal but with distinctive taste and connoisseurship. There is a sense here of resources employed lavishly but knowledgeably, and instead of mere expenditure, Lotusland's horticultural and stylistic concentration shows real command. Madame Walska focused on choice species in mass plantings arranged and juxtaposed for aesthetic effect. While not without its rarities, the garden succeeds because its maker subordinated the collector's desire to the artist's control.

This is gardening on the grand scale—indeed, it would be impossi-ble without a grand scale. There is little else like Lotusland in Califor-nia, whose climate contains such abundant possibilities. These possi-bilities Madame Walska appears to have divined quickly and to have realized impressively. Was something more than grand, something cos-mic, happening behind the scenes? In _Always Room at the Top,_ her memoir written shortly after she took up residence in California, Walska reveals that like so many before and since, she was quite prepared to discern Higher Meanings in the state's culture, climate, and atmosphere. For her, Lotusland was not only a place of rest but also the locus of predestined, Infinite Truth whose symbols "consecrated profane dwellings into a sacred Grail with its fantastic gardens where blooms the Divine Lotus." Interpreted mystically or otherwise, Lotusland could have been achieved in few other places than southern California. It is not to be missed if you can possibly arrange a visit.

(In 1990, Lotusland became the second California garden sponsored by the Garden Conservancy. Because permits for wider public access have yet to be obtained, at present Lotus-

land offers tours only to groups with a botanical or horticultural affiliation which may request visits by telephoning Dr.
Steven Timbrook, Director of Ganna Walska Lotusland, at
805-969-3767. Improved access is expected in the near future;
contact the Garden Conservancy in care of The Tides Foundation, 1388 Sutter St., San Francisco, CA 94109.)

SANTA BARBARA COUNTY COURTHOUSE

In designing a structure to replace a courthouse destroyed in a 1925 earthquake, San Francisco architect William Mooser, fluent in many architectural styles, created an essay in the Spanish revival style. Although a pastiche architecturally, the 1929 courthouse is nonetheless erudite and evocative, a pleasure to view and use. In its rich detailing—tiles, stonework, hand-painted signs on courtrooms and judicial chambers, fine murals, and all manner of architectural ornament—and not the least because of its superb garden, the Santa Barbara County Courthouse remains among California's most exceptional public buildings.

The U-shaped building fills a city block, with each facade's nonrepeating, asymmetrical ornament meant to be seen individually. Although the exterior seems light and sunny, interior colors darken to chocolate brown and brick red. Leather and metal grilles emit overtones of incarceration; one wing is a jail. Pointed arches, heavy columns, and wooden ceilings evoke a medieval, almost monastic tone, a Gothicism perhaps appropriate for the adjudications taking place in the building's law courts.

The interior's outstanding architectural feature must be a Richardsonian "in and out" staircase, circular and open to the outdoors. With several other open-air arcades, this touching gesture of faith in the southern California climate leaves the main halls a few degrees—sometimes many degrees—cooler than the comfort zone, the chill perhaps warning all parties against the law's delay and likewise reminding them of its consequence.

The staircase presents a superbly composed view of the gardens, the city, and the mountains. Not unlike the building's double mood, from a playful Mediterranean exterior to inner, Gothic sobriety, the gardens repeat the north-south division, placing European turf under subtropical vegetation. The building surrounds a terraced and sunken garden on

Romantic California: the Santa Barbara County Courthouse

three sides, with the fourth open to Anapamu Street. The cool, moist north contributes evergreens—clipped yew, low-growing junipers, weeping cypress (*Chamaecyparis lelandi*), and a grove of coast and Sierra redwoods amid an opulent lawn. The south contributes ficus, bananas, and bird of paradise, but an array of palms swerves the composition decisively in a tropical direction, a vertical counterstatement to the planar, horizontal lawn.

The beautifully grown palms are numerous and diverse: several *Phoenix* species; a dozen *Howea forsteriana*, growing tall and graceful up to the eaves; three *Livistona decipiens*, a superb fan palm deserving wider use; and a dozen other species, some rare, such as the Central American *Chamaedorea costaricana* and the Himalayan *Trachycarpus takil*. Although mainly a green garden, beds of hydrangea, clivia, camellias, saucer magnolia (*M. soulangeana*), agapanthus, and *Calliandra haematocephala* provide color and variety under the canopy of palms and huge, choice Australian tree ferns.

The perimeter of the courthouse gardens, especially along Anacapa and Figueroa streets, is also worth a look. It reveals many plants of interest for rarity (such as the Mississippi "needle palm," *Rhapidophyllum hystrix*), antiquity (a dark salmon bougainvillea, with a trunk as thick as a tree, almost hides Varro's "God gave us the country; the skill of man hath built the town" motto over the Anacapa Street arch), or beauty (such as the deep purple blooms of the princess flower). But the grand prospect remains the sunken gardens viewed from Anapamu Street: architectural romance as a proscenium for horticultural opulence.

Tall trunks and lush foliage from evergreens, fern, palm, banana, and tree bird of paradise rhyme with the ornament of cornice, arcade, balcony, and towers. Garden and structure merge in splendid synthesis, creating a balanced but dynamic composition. The fine view from the courthouse's 85-foot clock tower, El Mirador, encompassing the city's red-tiled roofs, white stucco walls, street palms, and vegetation, reveals the strong influence the courthouse has exerted. The building realizes a vision of the way romantic California was supposed to turn out. In Santa Barbara, as perhaps nowhere else in the state, it did.

(The Santa Barbara County Courthouse is located in downtown Santa Barbara in the block bounded by Anapamu, Santa Barbara, Figueroa, and Anacapa streets.)

SANTA BARBARA
BOTANIC
GARDEN

One of four California botanic gardens devoted to the state's native plants, the Santa Barbara Botanic Garden occupies a site above the city in Mission Canyon. Surrounded by chaparral- and oak-covered foothills beneath rocky La Cumbre Peak and overlooking Santa Barbara Channel and Santa Cruz Island, the garden preserves natural as well as historical values. Floras from coastal, mountain, and interior regions of California converge in Santa Barbara County, and this botanic garden's exposures and elevations enable it to grow more than 1,000 of the 5,000 plant species native to California.

Dr. Frederic Clements, an ecologist who originated the "plant community," conceived the idea of establishing a botanical garden in Mission Canyon. A philanthropist, Anna Blaksley Bliss, purchased thirteen acres in 1926 and endowed a trust fund for a botanical garden commemorating her father, Henry Blaksley. The Santa Barbara Museum of Natural History administered the property until 1939, when the young entity incorporated, became independent, and changed its name to the Santa Barbara Botanic Garden. It has since grown to sixty-five acres, fifty of which are open to the public. Today the garden continues its original objectives of display and research and pursues an expanded educational program.

Its rough trails, changes of terrain, and arrangement by plant communities keep this garden close to nature. It contains ten sections, organized by habitat (meadow, desert, arroyo, and offshore island) and by genus or plant community (ceanothus, manzanita, and redwood, chaparral, and oak woodland). Visitors first encounter the Meadow section, converted in recent years to native grass species mixed with flowering annuals such as hummingbird sage (*Salvia spathacea*), seaside daisy (*Erigeron glaucus*), rose lavender (*Achillea millefolium*), and the blazing orange California poppy.

Meadow, woodland, chaparral, mountains: Santa Barbara Botanic Garden

Mission Canyon's steep sides wear a canopy of coast live oak, whose shade deepens as a path descends into a canyon of coast redwoods. Although they can survive all over California except in deserts and high mountains, coast redwoods do not necessarily thrive everywhere, requiring substantial water and suffering in too much heat and sun. Fossils show that redwoods once grew in coastal Santa Barbara County, but today the area lies well south of the species' habitat, which extends only as far as Monterey County. Yet here may be California's most successful planting outside the coast redwood's natural range. Although Santa Barbara enjoys far less rainfall than the central and north coasts, a protected canyon bottom (whose stream provides water part of the year) and coastal cloud cover encourage the fast, tall growth these trees have enjoyed since they were planted in 1930. The grove and the coast redwood's allied species—redwood sorrel (*Oxalis oregana*), California rose bay (*Rhododendron macrophyllum*), sword fern (*Polystichum munitum*), tanbark oak (*Lithocarpus densiflorus*), and bigleaf maple (*Acer macrophyllum*)—create a north coast forest's mysterious shade.

Just below the redwoods, a stream slices through a cleft in the ruins of a dam and aqueduct system completed in 1807 to provide water to

Mission Santa Barbara. Crossing a footbridge over the dam and continuing south on the canyon trail leads beneath the oaks that arch over the creek. The Pritchett Trail climbs back up through woodland, while the canyon trail continues south through a woodland preserve, fine for light

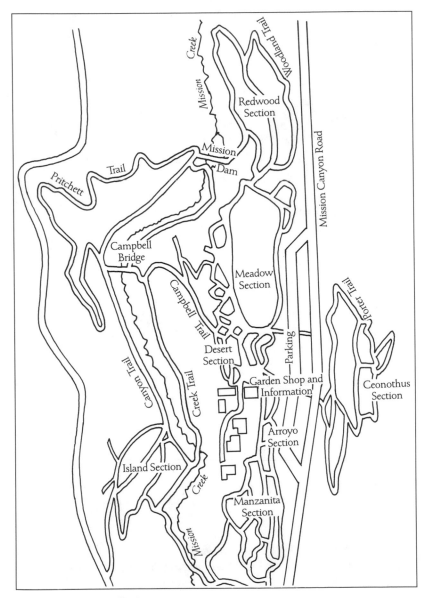

Santa Barbara Botanic Garden

hiking through interesting oaks and other trees adapting to the not always benign conditions of this area, susceptible to both drought and flood.

The Island section displays plants that either survived on isolated channel islands after extinction on the mainland or else evolved into distinct insular species. It also contains species from Baja California islands, providing instances of parallel development on islands farther north. The Arroyo section offers plants found near streams that do not flow all year. Here weeping branches give the bigcone spruce (*Pseudotsuga macrocarpa*) an especially ornamental quality. A Douglas fir (*Pseudotsuga menziesii*), the timber tree that is the bigcone's northerly relative, grows farther up the path. The arroyo section contains many fine evergreens, such as the dark green Pacific yew (*Taxus brefivolia*), weeping Port Orford cedar (*Chamaecyparis lawsoniana "Allumii"*), and chartreuse-needled *Cupressus macrocarpa lambertiana*. The berries of the toyon (*Heteromeles arbutifolia*), which ripen scarlet in the fall, appear throughout this section.

The Santa Barbara Botanic Garden also contains chaparral, desert, and riparian environments as well as areas devoted to arctostaphylos, ceanothus, and cypress species. Maps, guidebooks, and other information, including species listed according to their seasonal bloom, are available, as are educational and interpretive displays at various points. The property contains five miles of trails, offering fine views of the coastal mountains as well as the Pacific Ocean and offshore islands.

(The Santa Barbara Botanic Garden, 1212 Mission Canyon Rd., Santa Barbara. Free admission; grounds open daily from 8:00 a.m. to sunset. Other facilities, with more restricted hours, include a library and herbarium, a book and gift shop, and a nursery. The garden offers tours four days a week and by appointment, as well as field trips, classes, tours, and special programs. For information, telephone 805-682-4726.)

MISSION SANTA BARBARA
AND
A. C. POSTEL
MEMORIAL ROSE GARDEN

K nown as the "Queen of the Missions" because of its size and imposing beige stone facade, with six rose-hued engaged Ionic columns between twin bell towers, Mission Santa Barbara largely escaped the neglect that most other California missions experienced. Since its founding in 1786 as the tenth mission, the Franciscan fathers have maintained a continuous presence. Besides historical and educational displays, the mission has a courtyard garden containing a circle of California fan palms in a lawn around a fountain. Surrounding beds contain subtropical palms, banana, hibiscus, *Dracaena draco*, citrus, red trumpet vine (*Distictis buccinatoria*), and other plants that mission gardens helped make familiar in southern California.

Aloes, cacti, euphorbias, and succulents concentrate in dry beds near the sanctuary. Otherwise the courtyard garden is noteworthy for its flowers that are kept blooming all year: cannas, veronica, roses, iris, bird of paradise, hollyhocks, daylilies, asters, carnations, blue salvia, alyssum, black-eyed Susans, lobelia, yarrow, and meadow rue (*Thalictrum aquilegifolium*). In mission times, the emphasis was agricultural, and an aqueduct linked to a dam in Mission Canyon (still visible at the Santa Barbara Botanic Garden) irrigated orchards and cropland. Today there is no attempt to re-create the garden of the mission times, an effort that would render anachronistic this garden's lawn and many of its plants. Yet the courtyard retains a romantic atmosphere; as is not infrequently the case in California, strict authenticity seems both impossible and somehow beside the point.

Farther along the tour, a huge Moreton Bay fig, about a century old, presides over the tombs of many of Santa Barbara's oldest families and the remains of Mission Indians and later settlers. The fig shades a subdued cemetery garden, containing palms, junipers and evergreens, jacaranda, pittosporum, and other flowering shrubs and perennials,

Mission Santa Barbara and A. C. Postel Memorial Rose Garden

whose blooms scarcely manage to distract from the spare, almost spooky atmosphere. Many plants are gangly from too much shade, the earth is parched and bare, and the stones are gray and white: a poignant setting for a cemetery, its effect is perhaps not wholly uncontrived.

Directly across Mission Park's lawn that sweeps down to Plaza Rubio, a terrace of charming Spanish colonial revival cottages, lies the A. C. Postel Memorial Rose Garden. A city rose garden operated with the assistance of the Santa Barbara Rose Society, it contains well over 1,000 modern floribundas and hybrid teas, nearly all well labeled in formal beds among grass paths. The selection includes a few species and old roses, and modern varieties seem well selected for color and fragrance. On Plaza Rubio a small entry garden containing herbal plants, hedging, and flowering vines is under development in an apparent effort to tie this garden more closely to the mission.

(Mission Santa Barbara, 2201 Laguna St., Santa Barbara; open Monday through Saturday 9:00 a.m. to 5:00 p.m.; Sunday 1:00 p.m. to 5:00 p.m.; closed major holidays. Small admission charge. For information, telephone 805-682-4713.)

TWO
DOWNTOWN
SANTA BARBARA
PARKS

S anta Barbara's oldest park as shown on an 1853 map, ALAMEDA PARK covers two blocks with a green lawn under mature palms, eucalyptus, coast live oaks, Chinese elms, pittosporum, and Moreton Bay figs. Where diagonal paths cross at the center of the north-eastern quadrant, a small palm collection displays young, labeled specimens, some rare or unusual, such as *Chamaerops humilis argenteum*, a miniature Mediterranean fan palm whose emerging fronds have a silvery sheen. The southwestern quadrant continues in the same style, adding more evergreen trees, such as Canary Island pine, *Podocarpus gracilior*, and Montezuma cypress.

The star attraction, however, remains ALICE KECK MEMORIAL GARDEN, which fills a third quadrant. Donated to the city anonymously by philanthropist Alice Keck, the park emphasizes flowering plants. This emphasis, and its having been planted as a botanical garden and landscaped naturalistically with small streams, an informal lily pond, and other garden features, contrasts strongly with Alameda Plaza's traditional large trees in a green lawn.

Alice Keck Memorial Garden blooms all year and contains several distinct areas for plants sharing similar horticultural needs—dry and arid to wet and boggy. A plant directory and park plan is posted, and even though it dates from 1980 and thus will not identify every specimen, it remains helpful in identifying rare plants: a cream-flowered floss silk tree (*Chorisia insignis*); a winter-blooming *Dombeya calantha*; and *Leucena esculenta*, a low-growing tree with lacy foliage resembling that of a silk tree. Emphasizing colorful bloom, the park displays hibiscus, bougainvillea, an unusual, cream-flowering *Tecomaria capensis* "*Aurea*," tangerine floral carpets of *Thunbergia gregorii*, and sansanqua, reticulata, and lutchuensis camellias.

Alice Keck Memorial Garden

The 4.6-acre park was part of Alameda Plaza until it was sold in 1868. In 1913, a mansion on the property became El Mirasol hotel, from whose landscaped grounds a few trees remain. After the hotel was demolished in 1969, Alice Keck purchased the property in 1975, conveyed it to the city, and funded its design and landscaping with the stipulation that it should be an informal park, rural in feeling. Designed by Grant Castleberg, it was presented to the city on May 13, 1980.

Although there are several ficus and acacia species, Canary Island palms, and flowering trees such as the Hong Kong orchid, this is primarily a sunny, colorful garden devoted to horticultural variety. A large fern planting lines a watercourse leading into a sizable pond, and the garden features beige sandstone masonry, terracing, and crazy pavement paths as well as benches, a gazebo, and a pergola. The trees are underplanted with bulbs, perennial bedding plants, succulents, and blooming ground covers. Alice Keck Memorial Garden agreeably displays the wealth of flowering plants that can be cultivated in Santa Barbara.

(The three city blocks of Alameda Plaza and Alice Keck Memorial Garden touch at the intersection of Santa Barbara St. and Micheltorena Ave.)

SANTA BARBARA
BRIEFLY NOTED

Like several other coastal regions—Mendocino and Sonoma counties, Monterey Bay, and north San Diego County come to mind—Santa Barbara has a considerable amount of horticultural activity, with many exceptional nurseries and related businesses clustering in the area. Santa Barbara and Montecito in particular have a century-long tradition of horticultural pioneering and estate gardening, a story set forth in Victoria Padilla's masterful *Southern California Gardens: An Illustrated History* (1961). Indeed, Santa Barbara has inspired its own literature, the latest example being *Trees of Santa Barbara* (1974), by Katherine K. Muller, Richard E. Broder, and Will Beittel. The city's most famous tree is a MORETON BAY FIG TREE planted from a small pot in 1877 by nine-year-old Adeline Crabb. As the largest *Ficus macrophylla* in the United States and listed in the *Guinness Book of World Records*, its thirty-five foot circumference, bizarre buttressing surface roots, 170-foot lateral spread, and steel cable bracing make it worth at least a drive-by at Montecito and Chapala streets near Highway 101.

FRANCESCHI PARK, formerly "Montarioso," the estate of Dr. Francesco Franceschi, who while in Santa Barbara from 1894 to 1909 is reputed to have introduced more exotic plants into the state than any other source, is a fifteen-acre park perched 800 feet above the city. The plants seem to survive on their own; restoration is under way, but nearly everything remains to be done. The almost vertiginous view remains spectacular; it encompasses most of the city and Santa Cruz Island offshore. (At Ridge and Franceschi Rds.)

The FIRESCAPES DEMONSTRATION GARDEN addresses a narrow but crucial subject: fire prevention for homes in areas vulnerable to fire. Divided into four zones, the 1.7-acre garden displays labeled plants according to their degree of fire resistance. Selected for low maintenance, cost efficiency, and appearance as well as for fire resistance, the plants range from daylilies, pineapple guava, or natal plum in Zone One (nearest a dwelling) to _Ceanothus gloriosis_ "Anchor Bay," alder, or Catalina cherry in Zone Four (farthest from structures). Besides preventing erosion and resisting smog, dust, and drought, many of the plants bloom well. Safety and utility need not crowd out beauty. Zone Four permits a fine view of the Santa Ynez mountains, thick with chaparral, whose propensity to burn should motivate home owners to follow these planting and maintenance procedures. The garden is timely in every season but especially after a disastrous 1990 fire destroyed over 500 dwellings in Santa Barbara. (2411 Stanwood Dr. at Mission Ridge Rd.)

Although stretching the scope of this book somewhat, RICHARDSON'S SEASIDE BANANA GARDEN presents a unique working landscape, the only commercial banana plantation in the continental United States. Located on Highway 101 in the seaside hamlet of La Conchita about halfway between Santa Barbara and Ventura, the ten-acre banana grove perches just above sea level to take advantage of a microclimate created beneath a 300-foot palisade. Lush and quite unexpected, the tropical foliage appears almost fantastical set against the bare, sheer cliff that shelters it from wind and cold. Since 1985 the proprietors have offered fifty varieties of organically grown bananas and have opened the grounds to visitors.

VII
Central Coast

SAN SIMEON

Hollywood, as the saying goes, is a state of mind, as anyone knows who has turned a corner in Culver City or Burbank only to find a legendary studio loom into view. If the southern border of that mental and emotional zone lies somewhere in San Diego (probably near the Hotel del Coronado), surely Hollywood's northern frontier must be in San Simeon. It is not simply that Hearst and his house were a subject of what many contend was the American cinema's greatest film, or that in the twenties and thirties Marion Davies and nearly every other Hollywood figure seemed to make the trek up the coast to San Simeon's ornate halls. Besides the big budget that any spectacle requires, there is something in the place itself and in what Hearst, the architect Julia Morgan, several landscapers, and a crew of thousands did to create it—something of sham and dubious taste but also of genuine quality and passionate expertise—that embodies the Hollywood way.

The term "borrowed view" describes a landscape design that incorporates topographical, natural, or other visual features that lie outside a garden's confines. Hearst inherited the land all about San Simeon, permitting him to build with the assurance that his commanding view of ocean, range, and mountain would remain pristine. To build here was an inspiration. Few sites offer such potential, with views in all directions of an emerald landscape in winter and spring, lightening to blond and beige, marked by dark oak and chaparral, in summer and fall, and an ocean touched each evening by the golden sheen of a setting sun: a dream of California that Hearst determined to realize. So he sited his fantasy on a hill where he could borrow a view of all he possessed. The act of incorporating the surrounding domain seems to form the landscape equivalent of Hearst's collection of art objects inside San Simeon.

Neptune pool and temple, San Simeon

There was more to San Simeon's garden than simply choosing a site to appropriate its fine view. That is one kind of dominion, but so is the extraordinary modification of the hilltop that Hearst's garden represents. After the natural endowment of landscape came the engineering and art of hardscape, and although the gardens contain thousands of plants, they remain subordinate to San Simeon's distinctly architectural character. If Hearst was the producer, Julia Morgan was the director, and San Simeon resulted from a true collaboration. The first woman licensed to practice architecture in California, Morgan had a long association with Hearst and his mother, who encouraged Morgan as a student in Paris and commissioned some of her earliest buildings. Fluent in many traditional styles, Morgan first explored Hearst's idea for a Renaissance structure at San Simeon in 1919. Hearst settled, however, on what was then called the San Diego style, after the Churrigueresque buildings of the Panama-California International Exposition of 1915. (Most of those structures survived the exposition to become exterior locations for _Citizen Kane_, yet another link between Hollywood's northern and southern frontiers.)

Despite elaborate temporary villages of up to fifty people which sprang up on family holidays, Hearst had begun to tire of camping in tents at the San Simeon property. Having come into his large inheritance shortly after envisoning permanent quarters at San Simeon, he began to create the combination cathedral, art museum, spa, and horticultural Shangri-la that the unfinished but grandiose edifice would ultimately become. Something of its size and complexity is suggested by the fact that it bears several names: Hearst himself called it La Cuesta Encantada (the Enchanted Hill) or "the ranch"; maps designate it as San Simeon; and the public knows it as Hearst's Castle.

Beneath and around the main building's twin towers, five levels of terraced gardens, three smaller houses, two pools, and other outbuildings constitute an enormous property. Visitors must select one of four tours; tour number four spends the most time in the gardens, although visitors must actively encourage guides to focus on them. Even this "behind the scenes" tour proceeds inside various buildings, including the choice Casa del Mar, with its superb view down to the Pacific Ocean.

The tour begins with the Neptune Pool, over 100 feet long with round ends and a reflecting pond. A temple—a superb pastiche incorporating a colonnade, entablature, and pediment of differing classical periods—overlooks the pool, flanked by two modern curved porticos at its round ends. Geometrical chain and grid patterns in verd antique marble are set into tile beneath the pool's sky blue water, matching similar marble in surrounding paths and terraces. Cantilevered over the very edge of the hilltop, the Neptune Pool frames views through the colonnades to the untouched landscape thousands of feet below and beyond, a vertigo of height and depth, art and nature. The composition has both the unity of opposites and the sense of risk and hazard that suggested the sublime to Longinus in the first century A.D., when some of the temple columns were already old. With the high, expansive view, the deep water, terraces, balustrades, and statuary create an Olympian effect.

The scale of the plants likewise suits Hearst's ambition. The *Washingtonia filifera*—the tall palm seen throughout California, especially in the south—often seems ungainly, even ludicrous unless grouped in groves or lining a street, its absurd height suiting its companions and little else. At San Simeon, however, the palms' bare trunks reinforce a vertical architecture while remaining in scale with the towers of the main house. Crowning the hill with swaying topknots, the palms not only suit the building's immensity but embellish its suggestion of a fantastical paradise.

All trees but the oaks were brought to the site; like every other material used to build San Simeon except water, even the topsoil was hauled up the hill. The plants fit into formal gardens, with more than seven miles of myrtle and box hedging that follows the curves and angles of Italianate terraces and staircases. North of the main house's "new wing" is a walk through fuchsias, azaleas, and a few rhododendrons; curved terraces on the complementary southern exposure descend under the palms to rose beds beneath citrus trees. Two thousand roses grow throughout the property; *Lantana montevidensis* spills over terraces like lavender floral waterfalls in a pattern that has become a signature of these gardens; relics, sarcophagi, urns, fountains and ponds, terra-cotta and ceramic tile paving, statuary, and sculpted marble lamps are everywhere.

Horticultural volumes in Hearst's library indicate his interest in creating a landscape worthy of the place. Early in the project Hearst engaged his close friend, painter Orrin Peck, to design the gardens, but Peck died suddenly after less than a year of involvement. Hearst later hired Nigel Keep and a large staff to plant a forest of trees—6,000 pines to conceal a reservoir and an estimated 70,000 to 100,000 cedar, acacia, and eucalyptus to enhance the hill and its views. Charles Gibbs Adams also consulted on tree and wildflower plantings on the grounds. Today the main house is surrounded by oaks and palms, citrus, dozens of Italian cypress, arborvitae, magnolia, yews, deodar cedar, and many others now grown to maturity, a fulfillment Hearst himself did not live to see. The three lesser villas also create courtyards and glens that shelter several sun and shade gardens.

Surely Morgan herself created the architectural features of the 123 acres of terraced hilltop gardens, so well integrated with the buildings and carefully detailed with craftsmanship. Morgan was abetted by Hearst, who desired a rose garden, made specific suggestions about flowering trees and seasonal color schemes, and with willful extravagance insisted on moving trees threatened by construction or rotating them to provide the best view. Only a few years into the project no less than Bruce Porter, the noted San Francisco landscaper-artiste whose own work can be seen at Filoli, reported to Hearst that his impression of what had been accomplished at San Simeon "remains stupendous." Continuity was assured in the person of Norman Rotanzi, who started working at San Simeon in 1934 under Nigel Keep and retired as superintendent of the grounds in 1987.

Beneath the twin towers of the main house and above the Neptune Pool amid staircases and terraces filled with flowers, architectural Italian cypresses, palms, and tubbed plants set the tone of the gardens: formal in hardscape; opulent in scale; hedonistic in function; worldly and historical in culture; and lavish in beauty. To succeed, the gardens had to take into account the site's prominence and could afford to be nothing less than what they are. Were the gardens anything short of spectacular, fabulous, stupendous—the Hollywood adjectives—they would be overwhelmed by the natural beauty that surrounds this 1,600-foot summit. Whether it is a folly, an enchanted hill city, or an aesthetic reverie, San Simeon remains an unforgettable place.

(Hearst San Simeon State Historical Monument, located off Highway 1 north of Cambria, is open for guided tours. It is _highly recommended_ that tickets ($10.00 per adult) for one of four distinct tours be reserved and purchased in advance from MISTIX: telephone 800-444-7275 within California, 619-452-1950 outside California. Confirm dates of tour four, which spends the most time in the gardens but which is not offered during winter months. For San Simeon information, telephone the State of California visitor center at 805-927-2020.)

MONTEREY COURTYARD GARDENS

From 1775, when the king of Spain recognized Monterey as the capital of the remote province of Alta California, until the middle of the next century, Monterey was California's most important city. After Mexican independence in 1821, the subsequent secularization and decay of the missions, and a murky phase of plots, comic opera, and violence, an American military force claimed Monterey in 1846, and California formally became United States territory in 1848. Only days earlier, unbeknown to the outside world, John Marshall had discovered gold in the Sierra foothills. In late 1849, Monterey hosted a constitutional convention that prematurely declared California a state, a declaration Congress would not ratify for nine months. The gold rush soon pushed the old capital off the historical stage, but as so often happens, the exit of power and prosperity allowed Monterey to preserve something of its early character.

Nowhere is this historical atmosphere more prominent than in the city's old dwellings, many of them adobes, and in their courtyard gardens. (The State of California administers many of these sites, and a map and guide with hours of admission are available at Pacific House. For information, telephone the Monterey State Historic Park at 408-649-7118.) Nearest the wharf, the walled garden at the CUSTOM HOUSE is the driest and sunniest in historic Monterey. Its three gnarled peppers cast filtered shade over agave, aloe, euphorbia, opuntia cactus, the ubiquitous jade plant, and other succulents set in beds bounded by mortared abalone shells: a nice paradox in this desert garden almost at the ocean's edge and within earshot of barking seals.

Next door at PACIFIC HOUSE, built in 1847 by Thomas Larkin for the U.S. Army Quartermaster Corps and now a museum and visitor center, a paved walk lined with ferns and fuchsias leads to a large rear courtyard. Verandas overlook the courtyard's four magnolias around a central pond and fountain filled with snoozing goldfish. A huge wisteria covers a pergola to the rear, the spherical blooms of _Viburnum opulus_ _"Roseum"_ nod in late spring, and roses clamber over a stucco arcade. Although these architectural elements tend to overshadow the planting, this is a fine, sunny garden, Mediterranean in tone with bare earth and room for patterns of sun and shade to play on its white walls.

Across Oliver St. and next to JOSEPH BOSTON & CO. (an old-fashioned "general mercantile" store at Scott and Olivier streets), a tiny, well-labeled plot grows several dozen culinary, medicinal, and fragrant herbs. At Scott and Pacific streets, JACK'S TAVERN—formerly a boarding house, saloon, and California's first theater (the opening production of _Putnam, the Iron Son of '76_ played to a full house in 1850)—is surrounded on two sides by an L-shaped, walled garden. Two giant Monterey cypresses and a Sierra redwood oversee the garden. A cup-of-gold vine blooms on a south wall next to a white angel's trumpet, and strawberry trees dangle scarlet berries in dark, shiny foliage. This garden hints at Monterey's wealth of flowering plants: roses and fuchsias abound, along with terraced beds of purple salvia, princess flower, hydrangeas, white _Watsonia pyramidata_, and the furry, orange-blooming lion's tail (_Leonotis leonurus_).

Pacific Street leads south past CASA SOBERANES (c. 1840s) at number 336. Surrounded by a dense screen of sheared Monterey cypress, its well-proportioned garden slopes up from the street, from which it is perhaps best viewed. A few blocks farther, at Pacific and Madison, is FRIENDLY PLAZA, an unwalled garden with brick terraces surrounded by mortared rock beds and the lawns. Under olives, podocarpus, coast redwoods, and liquidambar are beds of miniature roses, aloe, hydrangea, rhododendron, and fuchsia. This park forms a part of the Monterey Civic Center, which is notable for Colton Hall (1849), Monterey's first "American-style"—built of stone in a neoclassical or Federal style—edifice, which Rev. Walter Colton finished in time for the California constitutional convention to meet on its second floor.

Across Pacific Street is the LARKIN HOUSE (1835), one of California's key architectural sites, to which is attached a charming courtyard garden. A Massachusetts merchant who prospered during the Mexican era and who became the only American consul to California, Thomas Larkin built his house in a style that wedded the Greek revival of New England with Spanish California adobe. Perhaps because it was the state's first two-story house, the marriage created an influential model for later dwellings in "the Monterey style." One facade of the Larkin

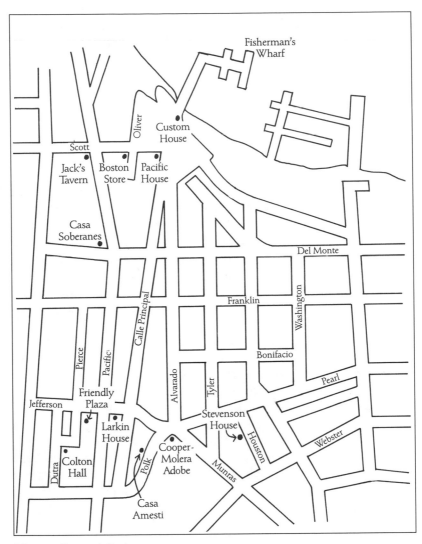

Monterey Courtyard Gardens

House, with its hipped roof over a veranda and balcony surrounding most of the two-story structure, overlooks its courtyard garden.

Inside the walled garden, a wooden trellis supports a prolific climbing "Cécile Brunner" rose and acts as a centerpiece among raised beds. The largest plants are yews, English holly, yuccas, olives, a coast redwood, a purple ornamental plum, and a citrus tree. Assorted camellias, rhododendrons, rosemary, irises, fuchsias, and roses provide color and detail in a garden that aims less for profusion than for that happy moderation suited to a courtyard's limited space. One plant merits particular mention: next to a rear gate, _Iochroma cyaneum_, a vining evergreen shrub, produces extraordinary floral clusters of tubular blue-purple flowers, creating an amazing early fall display.

A block away at 516 Polk Street, José Amesti built an adobe from 1834 to 1853. After 1918, CASA AMESTI was occupied by Frances Elkins, a successful interior decorator who restored the house, developed the gardens with her brother (architect David Adler), and bequeathed the property to the National Trust for Historic Preservation in 1954. Exterior planting sets the tone, as the naked branches of clipped box, yews, and a large juniper hold up spheres and oval trays of evergreen foliage. In the symmetrical rear courtyard garden, box, myrtle, and ivy hedging define beds between gravel paths, composing four quadrants around a small statuary centerpiece. A large tree centers three of the four quadrants, and an arcade along one side frames other statuary of hounds in repose beneath stags.

As with many other Monterey gardens, Spanish tile crowns the rear brick wall, but atypically, this garden contains few flowers, with the only color provided by the tiny scarlet yew berries, pink fruit on two apple trees, a solitary red-flowering Chinese maple, wisteria on the adobe's balcony, and a wan, retiring group of hydrangeas in a back corner. This green garden explores symmetries and foliage textures with ferns, yuccas, aloes, and ivy. The statuary especially suggests something of a _giardino segreto_, formal, green, quiet, hidden. (Casa Amesti offers tours from 2:00 p.m. to 4:00 p.m., Saturdays and Sundays only, for $1.00 adult admission. Telephone 408-372-2608.)

Across Polk Street is the COOPER-MOLERA ADOBE (1826), a complex of several buildings. A single spreading Monterey cypress is the most prominent plant on the roughly landscaped grounds, which seem to specialize in old roses trained on walls ("Gold of Ophir" [1845] and "Sombreuil" [1850]) and interspersed among other plants (e.g., "Duchess of Kent" [1838] and "Archduke Charles" [1840]). A small orchard and vineyard is tagged to indicate when the apricot or apple was introduced into California, and a fuchsia border displays scarlet and gold-tipped _Fuchsia splendens_, tubular red blossoms of Peruvian _F. corymbifolia_, and tiny lavender sprays of Mexican _F. arborescens_. (Enter on Polk or Munras; the Cooper-Molera Adobe is closed on Wednesdays.)

During a few months in 1879, Robert Louis Stevenson lived in rooms at 530 Houston Street, for which sojourn the dwelling bears the name STEVENSON HOUSE. (Stevenson recorded his impressions in an essay, "The Old Pacific Capital.") Dating from the 1840s, the house has a small dooryard garden behind a picket fence and to the rear a larger, more impressive courtyard garden, full of the blue spikes of Pride of Madeira, ten-foot white camellias and viburnum, and flowering maples under large deodar cedar, southern magnolia, grand fir (*Abies grandis*), and a dawn redwood. Even if it has little Spanish feeling, it is one of Monterey's most pleasant and varied courtyard gardens, showing how effectively a walled courtyard can establish its own environment despite traffic noise, gas stations, and the drab backs of a block of shops that hem it in. (Stevenson House can be entered at 530 Houston St. or from Munras St.; closed Wednesdays.)

LA MIRADA, on a 2.5-acre knoll overlooking Lagunita Mirada and Lake El Estero south and east of downtown Monterey, has two gardens of interest. Neither is quite typical of Monterey even though sited around yet another adobe, the Castro Adobe, owned by a succession of prominent people before Frank Work deeded it to the Monterey Peninsula Museum of Art Association in 1983. Along the driveway, the "Julia 'Pat' Peden Garden," begun in 1987, displays a sizable collection of rhododendrons, informally planted in terraced, raised sandstone beds, which with some azaleas and camellias make mid-spring the most colorful season. Many of the centerpiece rhododendrons are labeled and overlook a fine landscape of city parks and lakes through the trunks of old Monterey pines and cypresses.

Highly modified since adobe days, beautifully restored, and filled with fine art objects, the house is surrounded by small courtyards, including a superb rose garden. Replacing conventional hedging behind white bricks diagonally heeled into the ground, rows of hens and chickens (*Echeveria elegans*) sprout hot pink and golden flowers in late spring just as the roses come into bloom. The garden's star specimens are a pair of pale yellow *Banksia* roses, covered with sunny, fragrant blooms. In an alcove up a few steps from the rose garden (walled in rough-cut, beige sandstone for a rustic, English variation on the Monterey courtyard) are the quadrants of an herb garden, paved in brick under fig trees. These two picturesque courtyards, hidden behind the house, should not be missed. (La Mirada house tours, $5.00 adult admission, are given Saturday afternoons at 720 Via Mirada; the grounds may be visited without a tour; contact the Monterey Peninsula Museum of Art at 408-372-5477 for information.)

In *California's Architectural Frontier,* Harold Kirker concludes that nearly all the architecture that might seem to date from California's Spanish or Mexican period in fact represents the highly modified product of later construction and stylistic renovation by the Americans. The same conclusion appears to be true of the courtyard gardens, installed decades later to evoke an early California "look" that never truly existed. (Kirker quotes Edwin Bryant, visiting in 1846, on the peculiarity of the domestic gardens of the Mexicans, who would "allow no shade or ornamental trees to grow near their houses." Early photographs confirm that old Monterey looked almost pathetically bleak. Only after the Hotel del Monte opened in 1880 and made the Monterey Peninsula a fashionable resort did a romantic Hispanic past become a necessary fiction.) Even if historically anachronistic, however, the Monterey courtyard gardens can trace a design provenance to larger but similarly proportioned spaces in the California missions. The padres brought them by way of Mexico from Spain, which had inherited them from medieval Catholicism and from Islamic culture.

Historical authenticity aside, considered as appropriate design, the courtyards' walls screen out the world, desirable either for religious reasons or to create privacy amid a populous, busy town. (On the latter point, see S. Polyzoides et al., *Courtyard Housing in Los Angeles* [1982].) Especially in Mediterranean climates, courtyard walls, loggias, and arcades give shade from hot summer sun and trap any available winter warmth. Merging indoors and out, they would seem ideally suited as gardens for California dwellings. Their benefits seem as much psychological as practical, since many courtyards, as in some examples at Monterey, are gardened sparsely, with bare earth, dry plants, statuary, and fountains rather than intensive cultivation. While the Monterey courtyard gardens do not compare with the finest examples of the form, they contribute to the unusual atmosphere of the old capital's historic quarter. These courtyards suggest how urban spaces can adjust competing facts of density, climate, and the need for private and natural surroundings. It will also be remembered that Islamic culture considered courtyard gardens versions of paradise.

University of California, Santa Cruz, Arboretum

On a gently sloping parcel between 350 and 600 feet elevation with views of Monterey Bay and the Pacific, the UC Santa Cruz Arboretum enjoys one of the most favored situations of any California public garden. It is also an example of a site finding its best use, for this 135-acre arboretum specializes in Mediterranean plants, which are adapted to a climate having two seasons instead of four: cool, rainy winters and hot, dry summers. In Santa Cruz, the ocean mitigates the Mediterranean climate's summer heat and in most winters, protects the arboretum from hard frosts except for a few low-lying pockets. Since the arboretum began in 1964, Professor and Arboretum Director Ray Collett has guided its expansion into a collection of Australian, New Zealand, South African, and other Mediterranean climate species. The arboretum is also known for having introduced over 500 species and cultivars into commerce for the use of home gardeners.

Considerably enlarged from its modest beginning, a gift of ninety eucalyptus, the arboretum now contains over 8,000 species, grouped primarily by geographic origin—in Australian, Chilean, and New Zealand collections—or by genus, such as Eucalyptus, Erica, and Protea. The first garden at the arboretum sets a Mediterranean tone. Herbal plants (rosemary, lavender, sage, thyme, *Origanum*) offer flowers as well as pungent fragrances, and many species have the gray, olive, or sage foliage that typically protects Mediterranean plants from intense summer sun. *Perovskia atriplicifolia, Lavandula multifida, Teucrium fruticans,* and several *Salvia* species show muted green Mediterranean foliage with lavender, blue, or purple flowers, giving this small plot a kind of aesthetic unity.

An adjacent succulent garden reveals pronounced adaptations to severer climates. In 1985, Victor Reiter, Jr., a San Francisco collector, donated sixty *Echeveria* species and hybrids, notable for their unusual, fleshy structure, the colors of their stems and blooms, and their fortitude in the face of harsh circumstances. The thumb-sized stems of the aptly named _Graptopetalum amethystinum_ have flesh in the champagne range of colors, lavender when young and ripening to a creamy beige, not unlike _Dudleya virens_, whose purple flesh shades to light burgundy. Compared to these nuances, _Aloe schelpiae_'s colors assert a sharp contrast: purple leaves have coral edges and spines supporting hot orange torch flowers. Other succulents sharing a similar ecological niche include the _Lithops_, _Pleiospilos_, and related plants resembling pebbles or smooth river stones and bearing brightly hued daisy flowers for those lucky enough to catch them blooming.

At the crest of a hill, the succulent garden gives a vantage point from which to view much of the arboretum. Paths radiate from this vantage point like spokes of a wheel, leading into the arboretum's closely focused collections. This botanical garden may be best known for its collection of more than one hundred South African Protea species developed since 1973. _Proteaceae_ include several genera, among them the _Macadamia_ and the Australian _Grevillea_, but most of the arboretum's plants come from _Leucodendron_, _Leucospermum_, and _Protea_.

Over 300 protea species concentrate at the southern tip of Africa in "fynbos," the ecological equivalent of chaparral, often growing in exposed locations not unlike their habitat at Santa Cruz, where little protects them from the sun, rain, and wind. Many proteas begin blooming in September and persist through the fall, with a characteristic ring (the "involucre") of colored, feathery bracts shaped and fringed like quills around an inner capitulum, a crowded, spherical head of tiny flowers. The blooms vary widely, however, a characteristic that may suggest why Linnaeus named the family in 1735 for the Greek god, Proteus. A subject of the sea god Poseidon, Proteus tended foul-breathed seal herds at the bottom of the sea and could deceptively change his appearance whenever he wished.

The proteas' beauty arises from colored foliage and bracts encircling the flower sphere. _Protea punctata_ "light pink" has pink bracts around even pinker flowers and sage leaves likewise edged with pink held on purple stems covered with gray fuzz. Burgundy red bracts around flowers of _Protea_ "Jack Clark" bear a dusty white fluff on each tip above bright green foliage. One sign of the proteas' intense colors and various beauty is that many species contribute to the commercial flower industry not only in California but in Africa, Australia, and New Zealand.

Like the proteas, hundreds of *Erica* species—the Cape heaths—help make southern Africa one of the world's unique floral regions. The genus contains fourteen species of the familiar European heaths and eleven more in East Africa, but an astonishing 605 species are native to southern Africa below the Limpopo River, growing in concentrations so dense that the relatively small Cape of Good Hope has 103 *Erica* species. Cape heaths at Santa Cruz cluster in a specialized area, each plant blooming violet, rose, or lavender in summer and fall with hundreds of tiny bell-shaped or tubular flowers.

Somewhat remote from the arboretum's other plantings, the Edward D. Landels New Zealand Garden contains what is believed to be the largest collection of New Zealand plants on any continent. In this young garden, tree species will eventually create a podocarp forest comprised of Kauri (*Agathis australis*), the Totara (*Podocarpus totara*), Miro (*P. ferrigineus*), Kahikatea (*P. dacrydioides*), and Rimu (*Dacrydium cupressinum*), or as New Zealanders know these last four species, the black, white, red, and silver pines.

Nearer the arboretum's center once more, Slosson Gardens offers what is considered one of the world's most complete Australian plant collections. This garden also reveals rare and beautiful species, with foliage ranging from silver to olive, bright green to rose, sage to burgundy. It displays an even greater range of textures, with wispy, lacy needles; awl-shaped leaves hugging stems like scaly armature; pendulous sage-colored eucalyptus spears hung from maroon stems above beige trunks from which tan bark flakes; leathery, manzanitalike leaves and soft, fern-textured leaves. The patterns are complex and simple, smooth and furry, sharp or lenient, safe or dangerous, drooping or upright, rigid or relaxed. Here grows the exceptional *Acacia baileyana purpurea*, its lacy foliage maturing to a grayish blue, with lavender new growth casting a rosy sheen over this small tree.

Departing from the encyclopedism elsewhere, the Australian section seems the most well grown and aesthetically satisfying area at the arboretum. Instead of pinpointing heaths, conifers, or succulents, it contains an assortment of genera. Moreover, its mature plants block out the horizon, creating a visual enclosure that encourages appreciative focus. To be sure, assembling heaths or Proteaceae taxonomically has great scientific value, and in nature they grow in bleak country. But the scientific principle of selection—producing essentially a monoculture or "generoculture"—remains distinct from garden values, whose artifice ordinarily aims to simulate an idealized botanical variety seldom found in nature.

Much of the arboretum has been planned for intellectual efficiency; on a university campus, the claims of scholarship legitimately prevail over those of beauty. But in gardens, at least, the two are not the same and do not invariably coincide. The Australian section shows horticultural beauty and botanical science cooperating splendidly.

(UC Santa Cruz Arboretum, entered from Empire Grade; open daily 9:00 a.m. to 5:00 p.m.; docents lead tours and sell plants on Wednesdays, Saturdays, and Sundays from 2:00 p.m. to 4:00 p.m. For more information, write Arboretum Associates, University of California at Santa Cruz, Santa Cruz, CA 95064, or telephone 408-427-2998. Nearby the Henry Cowell Redwoods State Park provides an accessible stand of old growth redwoods, and the antique railroad is an added attraction.)

TWO
CARMEL
GARDENS

The LESTER ROWNTREE ARBORETUM, overlooking Mission Trails Park, commemorates Ellen Gertrude Lester Rowntree. Begun by community groups in 1980 on a small, gently sloping site, the arboretum is devoted, as was Rowntree, to conserving California native plants. Born in England in 1879, as Rowntree grew up in California she became aware of the unique value of native species and of their vulnerability in a society dedicated to infinite growth and constant change. During her one hundred years of life, she attained prominence in the California Native Plant Society, created a noted garden in Carmel Highlands, and wrote two books considered classics, *Flowering Shrubs of California* (1936) and *Hardy Californians* (1939).

Just inside the upper entrance to the arboretum (at 25800 Hatton Rd., where a map and brochure are available), *Arctostaphylos* "Lester Rowntree" reflects one of many honors she received. Rich in manzanita, ceanothus, and toyon species, the arboretum also devotes areas to *Fritillaria, Triteleia, Dichelostemma,* and other bulbs that bloom in spring or early summer and pass into dormancy during the dry season. A generation of newly planted trees, only a few over six feet tall, contains the coast redwood, native to this area, and its ecological colleagues, the California bay laurel and Douglas fir.

The arboretum's lowest elevation approaches the Flanders Mansion (not open to the public), where a hedge leads from the Tudor-style house to a bench beyond a small lath structure. Here the canopy of Monterey pine and eucalyptus parts to reveal a grand southerly view past the Carmel Mission towers and Carmel Bay to the rocky coast beneath forested headlands at Point Lobos. A trail leads past the Flanders Mansion through the thirty-seven-acre Mission Trail Park to Carmel Mission.

As its exterior landscaping suggests, MISSION SAN CARLOS BOR-
ROMEO DE CARMELO is one of the most well maintained and beautiful of the California missions. Although not large, its gardens contribute strongly to the mission's atmosphere, as illustrated in its fine walled
courtyard before the sanctuary. Surrounding a dry fountain, sunny raised
beds contain a tangle of geraniums, dahlias, old roses, California poppies, and the princess flower whose purple, velvet-petaled flowers grow
so superbly on the Monterey Peninsula. The centerpiece, an enormous
angel's trumpet almost the size of a small tree, supports a hundred golden
blossoms, hung like ornaments from every branch.

The courtyard's high, vine-covered walls screen out the world's distractions, focusing attention on the spiritual architecture of the mission's
dome and towers. Through an arch, the mission graveyard contains the
olive and pepper trees associated with the mission fathers, and showers
of pink, purple, and intensely red bougainvillea clamber over arcades
south of the sanctuary. A tour should not omit the beautifully reconstructed sanctuary with its catenary arch, an unusual elliptically vaulted
ceiling. Here rests the remains of Father Junipero Serra, who founded
this mission in 1770 and who was the leading figure in the history of
Spanish California. (Mission San Carlos Borromeo de Carmelo, 3080
Rio Rd., Carmel; open weekdays 9:30 a.m. to 4:30 p.m., Sundays 10:30
a.m. to 4:30 p.m.; $1.00 adult admission, telephone 408-264-1271.)

CENTRAL
COAST
BRIEFLY
NOTED

B uilt in 1853 by Pierre Hypolite Dalidet, a French vintner, the DALIDET ADOBE housed him and his descendants until it was given to San Luis Obispo County in 1953. Under coast redwoods, magnolias, and fruit trees, a country flower garden (behind a whitewashed picket fence and garden arch) grows iris, acanthus, geranium, oleander, wisteria, California poppy, agapanthus, and legions of rose and lavender valerian—almost a weed during the spring, but a colorful one. Down the block, note a remarkable Frank Lloyd Wright medical building at Pacific and Santa Rosa. (The Dalidet Adobe, at the end of Pacific St. northeast of Santa Rosa St., San Luis Obispo, is open Sundays from 1:00 p.m. to 4:00 p.m. from Memorial Day to Labor Day and by appointment. Telephone 805-543-6762.)

The MISSION SAN LUIS OBISPO DE TOLOSA sanctuary forms one side of a small courtyard of lawns, brick paths, and flowers under a large oak's filtered shade. The garden's distinctive feature, a long grape arbor, divides beds of familiar mission garden plants (bird of paradise, citrus and figs, yucca, cacti, agave, and succulents) as well as annuals, acanthus, amaryllis, and tree ferns. In a tight situation (two of its sides are a parking lot and a driveway), the courtyard garden improves its unfocused surroundings. (Enter the Mission San Luis Obispo de Tolosa courtyard garden from Dana St. between Broad and Chorro, San Luis Obispo.)

Herbaceous perennials and other plantings extend over 300 yards along a lawn in front of the CALIFORNIA POLYTECHNIC INSTITUTE, SAN LUIS OBISPO, Business Administration Building. The curving border reflects expert knowledge and superb maintenance— most species and cultivars are labeled, the plants look perfect, and not a weed dared to challenge a spring border of pink *Armeria maritima*, golden *Geum quellyon*, cream and lavender digitalis, pink columbine, purple *Salvia pratensis* and rose-red *S. greggii*, and royal purple *Campanula glomerata superba*.

In time two Sierra redwoods will come to dominate their neighbors—
Grevillea robusta; a bed of Proteaceae; a _Magnolia soulangiana_; a gazebo and
a trellis; and an immaculate cactus and succulent bed, with flawless,
almost sculptural specimens in neat gravel. Offering local residents both
design ideas and examples of plants suited to the climate, the border illustrates how a focused goal and capable hands can produce an exceptional
garden within limited space. (Follow California St. parallel to train tracks
to the Cal Poly San Luis Obispo campus; garden structures and lawn
become visible just after the rows of Canary Island palms lining California St. end; weekday campus parking is difficult, but parking is free after
6:00 p.m. and on weekends.)

A mail order nursery devoted to "old, rare, unusual and selected modern roses," ROSES OF YESTERDAY AND TODAY welcomes visitors
to its test and demonstration garden on the property from which it ships
bare root roses to fanciers in all climates. Located in Brown's Valley, a
redwood- and fern-lined canyon east of Watsonville, this small but
choice garden will reward the persistent rosarian. In this climate, the profusion of color comes in May and June, but many varieties bloom through
the summer or in the fall, in whose cooler weather some types produce
fewer but higher-quality blossoms. In mid-September, the slightly sloping garden beneath the redwoods contained a spectrum of bloom from
the palest pink of "Souvenir de la Malmaison" (1843) to the deep red,
fragrant "Lissy Horstman" (1943). Climbing roses, such as "Dortmund"
(1955) with masses of single red flowers, white at the base of each petal,
enclose the garden, which is fenced against the deer.

Many varieties have shapes, habits, scents, and especially colors that
modern hybrids have all but lost. The subdued yellow of "Autumn
Delight" (1933), pale pink with lavender notes of "Marchioness of Lon-
donderry" (1893), and the clear pink of "Baroness Rothschild" (1868)
illustrate the hues to be seen in traditional roses, upon which the corals,
oranges, and silvers of modern hybrids can scarcely be said to have
improved.

With labeled shrub, pillar, and climbing types, species, old-fashioned,
and historical varieties, and roses with outstanding color and fragrance,
this garden is not only useful but beautiful during its blooming period.
Although the interesting nursery catalog (available at a small charge)
contains a map and directions, a detailed area map is highly recommended before setting out for the property, which is somewhat remote.
(Roses of Yesterday and Today, 802 Brown's Valley Rd., Watsonville, CA
95076; admission is free. The demonstration garden is open seven days
a week from 9:00 a.m. to 3:00 p.m.; nursery office is closed weekends.
Telephone 408-724-3537.)

VIII
San Francisco

olden Gate Park began in the 1860s, when some leading San Franciscans acted to create a park suited to a great city. The fact that San Francisco was not yet a great city was only one of many obstacles to be overcome in realizing the park. Squatters actively urged their dubious titles to the "outside lands" against the claims of the city, which then extended no farther than Divisadero Street. Raked and stirred by stiff, chill ocean winds that funnel through a streamline, shifting sand dunes buried two-thirds of the 1,013 acres designated for park use. Frederick Law Olmsted, who designed New York City's Central Park, advised civic leaders in the mid-1860s that it would be impossible to make a park on this lifeless, forbidding acreage, particularly citing the absence of existing trees and doubting any could be grown in the future. In 1871, newly appointed park engineer William Hammond Hall nonetheless began to reclaim a blockwide strip at the park's eastern edge now known as the panhandle. In retrospect, the effort to launch what would become a great urban park takes on a visionary quality, an act of imagination and almost of faith.

Within five years, Hall filled the park's eastern third with thousands of eucalyptus, Monterey cypress, and Monterey pine. Planted not only for beauty but to stabilize soil and block the wind, the trees established the pattern of alternating woodland and grass meadow that still characterizes park landscaping. Without microclimates created by the forest, the park would seem far less amenable to its human visitors and its botanical residents. In the park's western end, Hall also began to level and reclaim sand dunes stretching all the way out to the ocean, making good progress until a political dispute caused him to resign in 1876. Golden Gate Park entered a decade of decline until Hall, otherwise engaged as California state engineer, was summoned to revive it in 1886. After a fashion he did so, by choosing the most important figure in park history,

John McLaren, to be its new superintendent.

Hall created a master plan of roads and paths, stabilized the soil, and initiated tree plantings. McLaren, whose tenure lasted until his death in 1943 at the age of ninety-six, nonetheless confronted a forbidding task in 1887. During the next decades, he pushed the green edge of horticulture westward to the ocean by improving the soil with street sweepings (horse-drawn conveyances being the era's dominant mode of transport), by importing loam from areas with better soil, and by planting hundreds of thousands of trees. (McLaren's *Gardening in California: Landscape and Flower* [1909] records his reclamation techniques and horticultural opinions about hundreds of plant species.) Throughout his administration, the park periodically aroused political controversy over what would be permitted or excluded. Raymond H. Clary's *The Making of Golden Gate Park* (1980) covers the park's history, making the point that as always, the park remains vulnerable to fashions, schemes, and lack of interest in every generation.

Yet the park survives remarkably well. Notwithstanding assorted museums, sports facilities, recreational areas, and major traffic arteries, Golden Gate Park's ambience and its horticultural areas remain largely intact. Three features—the Japanese Tea Garden, Strybing Arboretum, and the San Francisco Conservatory of Flowers—are separately treated. A sketch of Golden Gate Park's other horticultural areas follows.

Although most of the park's gardens cluster in its eastern third, QUEEN WILHELMINA'S GARDEN forms an outpost within sight of the Pacific Ocean near the extreme northwestern corner, north of where 47th Avenue meets Kennedy Drive. The garden takes its cue from a windmill built in 1902 to conceal a pump supplying well water to irrigate the park. The windmill towers above a saucer-shaped depression, sheltered from ocean winds by Monterey cypress. Formal beds of tulips bloom in a lawn amid Iceland poppies, primula, and magenta, purple, and blue *Senecio hybridus*. The display reaches its height during April.

Far away in the park's northeastern corner is the first of several specialized gardens, FUCHSIA DELL. A grove of majestic old Monterey cypresses forms a broken canopy to shelter several hundred fuchsias from winds scouring the park. Many young fuchsias have been trained on trunks so as to display their pendulous blossoms at eye level. A few callas, white viburnum, bergenia, calceolaria, clivia, hydrangea, tree ferns, and Japanese maples accompany the fuchsias, which are pruned in the spring to flower later in the year, when the garden becomes one of the park's most elegant precincts.

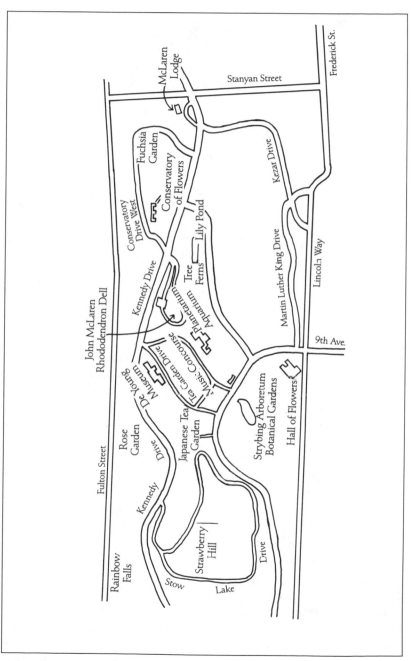

Golden Gate Park

Primeval picturesque, Golden Gate Park

East of the San Francisco Conservatory of Flowers, a small DAHLIA GARDEN fills a teardrop bed amid a traffic circle overlooked by a terraced "Arizona garden" of desert plants. Although not large, the display offers beautifully grown plants and intensely colored flowers of cactus, pompon, single, anemone, and many other dahlia types. The velvety, thickly textured petals seem to thrive under the gray sky of a San Francisco August: the dahlia is the city flower.

A sunken garden with formal beds of seasonal bulbs and annuals acts as a kind of front yard for the San Francisco Conservatory of Flowers, with succulents and flowers on sloping twin panels spelling out brief messages. Across Kennedy Drive, behind some barrel-shaped yews, a superb grove of Tasmanian tree ferns (*Dicksonia antarctica*), among the park's oldest such plantings, has several dozen specimens up to twelve feet high. With their shaggy, brown trunks clothed in the chartreuse leggings of baby's tears, the TREE FERN FOREST creates a prehistoric effect. Forest evergreens, such as incense cedar and the Sierra redwood, tower over the ferns, intermixed with bananas and the Mesozoic-looking *Gunnera*, the latter recognizable by its low-growing habit, three-foot-wide leaves, and cones covered with hundreds of crimson seeds.

Such species add a reminder that although it has a cool climate, San Francisco also ordinarily has a frost-free one. Other plants in the tree fern dell include the columnar, tropical _Sparmannia africana_, callas, acanthus, New Zealand flax, clivia, and a thick oxalis carpet covering the ground as it would a redwood forest floor. Protected from wind yet under a break in the canopy, the tree ferns' unfolding new growth has a precision and refinement seemingly at odds with their suggestion of primitiveness. One can almost imagine the dinosaurs munching on the fronds. San Francisco's weather seems to embellish the grove's stagy, Jurassic ambience, moodily primeval in a fog. Morning or afternoon sunshine slanting through the filligree can be magical, especially after a rain with silvery water dripping from every tree tip.

Farther south over a small rise, another tree fern glade falls away to a soupy, swampy pond. Intensifying the primeval landscape, picturesque Monterey pines precariously overhang the lake, their gnarly roots exposed along a bare palisade. Along the path's outer curve, a stand of even larger Tasmanian tree ferns, from whose dense foliage emerge gangly trunks of Australian tree ferns (_Cyathea cooperi_), blankets a shaded slope. The assemblage makes one of the park's most imaginative landscapes.

Backtracking only slightly, a path forks uphill into the JOHN F. McLAREN RHODODENDRON DELL, the larger of the park's two major rhododendron plantings (the other being within Strybing Arboretum). An irregularly defined area south of Kennedy Drive and east of the oval containing the Music Concourse, the McLaren Rhododendron Dell may be entered from almost any direction, although a marked entrance (McLaren's statue surrounded by _Rhododendron_ "Pink Pearl") is on Kennedy Drive. The eighteen-acre dell contains more than 3,500 plants of 300 species, many of them enormous specimens of old-fashioned hybrids imported from England and transplanted here following the 1915 Panama-Pacific International Exposition.

Divided by paths meandering among thousands of unlabeled plants, the dell's vastness makes specific directions impossible. It is not difficult, nonetheless, to locate examples of the Loderi series among the oldest shrubs. Sir Edmund Loder's hybrids descend from his cross of _Rhododendron griffithianum_ with _R. fortunei_, the latter a fragrant Chinese species brought back to England in 1856 by the remarkable plant hunter, Robert Fortune. The resulting Loderi series preserved its powerful fragrance that has been called "ambrosial." Large shrubs produce enormous trumpet blooms opening from dark rose-lavender buds into white with a touch of the palest pink. If the flowers do not attract your eye, surely the extraordinary scent of Loderi "King George" will find you: allow yourself to be led by the nose. The powerful fragrance can be intoxicating—sniffing it makes you want to inhale it again and again—with the sweet smell of an ice cream parlor lightened by a spicy, pungent overtone.

The subtly pink "King George" is only one of an enormous variety of colors found throughout the Rhododendron Dell. In recent years, the Monterey pine and cypress forming the canopy have begun to die, many having lived well past a century. Their passing leaves the area in something of a transitional phase. New cover trees—ginkgo, Japanese maples, and the three redwood species—are being planted, but will not reach shade height for years, even decades. Some rhododendrons thrive in new-found sunlight; others are stressed; and where the overstory remains, other rhododendrons continue, for the time being, in customary circumstances. An area of Exbury hybrids (famous hybrids developed between the World Wars by Lionel de Rothschild at his estate by that name, located on the south coast of England, where he kept 250 acres of rhododendrons), displays small shrubs flowering yellow, pale orange, gold, or cream.

It may seem unusual to find a California climate that so well suits a genus associated with the moist, northern maritime conditions of southern England and coastal Scotland and Wales. But north of Monterey, the cool northern Pacific creates a sliver of rhododendron territory—roughly coextensive with the redwood belt—that gradually widens as it extends north up the coast into British Columbia. (There are a few native California rhododendrons but nothing like the hundreds that originate in central and southern Asia.) As the rhododendron dell demonstrates, San Francisco's cool, marine climate favors this magnificent genus. Timing is important for seeing the area at its peak, which comes between late March and early May during most years but can begin earlier or persist a month later depending on rainfall and weather. In season, the spectacle becomes one of the park's finest horticultural features.

Not far away, the park includes a small planting of palms east of the De Young Museum and north of the Music Concourse. The park also contains a ROSE GARDEN entered from Kennedy Drive or the Presidio Bypass. Behind a double row of rectangular beds for shrub roses, a lattice screen supports climbers, with a semicircular central section surrounded by standard roses. The shrubs are largely modern hybrid teas, floribundas, and grandifloras, with a few miniatures, tree types, and old roses (e.g., "Blush Noisette," an early Noisette hybrid pink with a spicy sweet fragrance, and "Austrian Copper," a single rose whose hot coral orange hue is not as unpleasant as it sounds). Although scarcely a Bagatelle, the rose garden makes an agreeable addition to the park as its roses come into bloom in May.

Throughout the park, one can see century-old trees in maturity—some in senescence. In the central third, the effects associated with McLaren are quite visible, as forest meets meadow and a waterfall, stream, or lake creates picturesque landscapes. The western end is the most rustic and least gardened, best for hiking, rambling, and musing on the difficulties Hall and McLaren encountered in converting a wasteland into a superb urban park.

(Most city street maps designate park features, but two maps are available at the San Francisco Conservatory of Flowers, the Strybing Arboretum book shop, and park museums. The glossy, more expensive map is inferior; the cheaper, blue-ink-on-paper has greater detail and is more attentive to horticultural features.)

THE
SAN FRANCISCO
CONSERVATORY OF
FLOWERS

Perhaps it is their paradoxical construction, a fragile glass membrane fastened to a sturdy cast iron skeleton. It could have to do with the essential whimsy of creating a tiny tropical biosphere in a place that knows hard winters, a kind climate enclosed by a cruel one. Maybe the extreme artifice of the glass bubble needed to shelter exotic nature explains it. Whatever it is, something about greenhouses inspires people to behave oddly. As he learned the infirm General Sternwood's opinions of his sinister family in *The Big Sleep*, Chandler's Philip Marlowe found the atmosphere oppressive, the vegetation meaty, morbid, and menacing. He couldn't wait to get out. Joan Didion, by contrast, felt drawn inside commercial greenhouses near her Sacramento childhood home. On one occasion something livid in the greenhouse atmosphere perhaps inflamed the belief, widespread among adults, that they can say virtually anything, however implausible, to an unaccompanied child. In "Quiet Days in Malibu," she remembered being shooed away by a nurseryman who accused her of "using up the air."

Greenhouses, the least natural garden space, make it possible to grow plants far away from, yet within, their own climates. In theory, some equatorial connoisseur, for reasons known only to himself, could enclose an arctic or temperate glasshouse, cooled to cultivate beeches and elms, alpine flowers, or tundra. But in practice it has been the northern world that has found fascination in keeping tender plants through hard winters. This interest extends back to high-windowed royal orangeries that nursed tubbed citrus through stone-gray French Januaries and to the Hampton Court lean-to vinery that annually persuades a "Black Hamburg" grape to fruit despite the wan English summer. (Planted in 1768 and still producing crops of over 800 pounds of fruit, that famous vine is now protected by its fifth greenhouse, an aluminum model built in 1970.)

With the Victorians, however, the fashion ceased to require any pretense of utility; fruiting, flowering, and otherwise, all plants were grown; the more exotic, the better. A taste for tropica supplied a steamy outlet for suppressed Victorian desire as well as a symbol of imperial benevolence and scientific progress. As the Belgian Royal Glasshouse complex at Laeken Palace demonstrates, wintergardens scarcely ceased to be emblems of royal (and later plutocratic) privilege. But during the nineteenth century, the great structures became popular institutions, representing the latest industrial materials (glass and cast iron) and technological methods (prefabrication and modular coordination) suited not only for greenhouses but also for elegant shopping arcades and soaring railroad station shelters.

A survivor from the Victorian vogue, the San Francisco Conservatory is Golden Gate Park's oldest building, uncrated from prefabricated parts shipped around Cape Horn in 1876 and arriving just before the death of James Lick, who had acquired them for his San Jose estate. Leading San Franciscans purchased the greenhouse on behalf of the city and hired the firm of Lord & Burnham of Irvington, New York, to erect the wood and glass structure in Golden Gate Park. Designed by an unknown architect, the building was completed in 1879; it was manufactured in England, then the center of glasshouse construction in the decades after Joseph Paxton pioneered the modern glasshouses at the Duke of Devonshire's estate at Chatsworth (1841) and London's Crystal Palace (1851).

Neither building has survived, but Burton and Turner's Palm House at the Royal Botanic Gardens at Kew may still be seen. The San Francisco Conservatory of Flowers is often said to derive from the Kew Palm House, its curving volumes and tubular wings perhaps admitting a general resemblance. Nevertheless, the buildings differ greatly in size (the Palm House being much larger in height and square footage); in style (the conservatory's gables, cupola, and spiked crusts of Victorian ornament having no counterparts at the Palm House); and in general plan. From its central dome, the San Francisco glasshouse extends two wings, each of which turns a corner into another, smaller wing, perpendicular to the main axis, with a central entry wing creating an E-shaped building. The plan thus differs markedly from the Palm House's simpler footprint, a rectangular central gallery with two wings, curved into semicircles at their termini. (The San Francisco Conservatory would seem more closely to resemble the greenhouses at Lyndhurst on the Hudson River, also E-shaped and in the "curvilinear" style.)

A mild climate glasshouse: the San Francisco Conservatory of Flowers

But what truly distinguishes it from Kew and from most glasshouses is that palm trees grow *outside* the San Francisco Conservatory as well as under its whitewashed glass skin. In Golden Gate Park, robust Canary Island palms thrive outdoors in a frost-free climate, their thick, columnar trunks contrasting with the conservatory's curving, horizontal volumes. Yet as Mark Twain supposedly concluded, San Francisco cannot claim to possess a tropical or even a warm climate. ("The coldest winter I ever spent," went Twain's apocryphal remark, "was a summer in San Francisco." If he ever said so, he evidently reconsidered the matter; Twain later built a conservatory at his house in Hartford, Connecticut.) Elsewhere it is possible to grow palm trees next to a greenhouse. But in few climates must it seem necessary to have a greenhouse next to which palm trees can grow.

Under the central dome emerge some themes that characterize the conservatory's collection. Focused on tropical plants (vines, palms, shrubs, aroids), the display emphasizes foliar color, exotic flowers, and large specimens. The six-foot stems supporting three-foot leaves make the elephant ear (*Xanthosoma sagittifolium*) impressive not only for its size but also for its pale green blush, cleanliness, and efficient design. (On hot days, when the misting system releases a spray of water, the wide leaves collect and channel water down grooves in the stems to the base of the plant.) Note also the ropy aerial roots of an "imperial philodendron" (_Philodendron speciosum_) which have clung to a cast-iron pillar supporting the dome since being planted in 1883.

The plants under the dome also introduce the conservatory's emphasis on foliage color, a compensation for the tiny flowers of many tropical understory plants. A common color scheme reveals dark and pale green, white, or pink variegations on the upper leaf and maroon or red-purple undersides, the latter characteristic of _Calathea oppenheimiana_ and found throughout the genus _Calathea_. At fifty-five feet, the dome also shelters large palms: a sizable _Livistona chinensis_; a Philippine _Veitchia merrillii_; and the gray-fronded _Cryosophila warscewiczii_, its trunk armed with needles. Two glass corner cases display orchids, rotated in bloom from the conservatory's large collection, said to contain North America's best collection of _Dracula_ and _Masdevallia_ orchids.

Under a low, arched ceiling, the east wing displays permanent plantings of tropical vines and foliage plants. As a golden cone ripens on a _Cycas madagascariensis_, nearby cream stripes follow midribs of _Caladium bicolor_, from which dark pink veins extend into arrowhead-shaped leaves. The enthusiastic Rangoon creeper (_Quisqualis indica_) drapes nearly the length of the wing on an overhead support, above a festival of foliage: bold, creamy veins of African mask _Alocasia amazonica_; purple foliage and tiny pure pink blooms of _Setcreasea pallida_; and fuzzy flowers of the chenille plant (_Acalypha hispida_), dark rose cattails drooping by the dozens.

Through a partition, the east wing enters a water garden containing that most traditional greenhouse plant, the _Victoria amazonica_ water lily, familiar from old picture postcards showing it bearing the weight of an uneasy Victorian child. (The plant aroused great interest when it first bloomed in 1849 in Europe, where many botanical gardens continue to award it a greenhouse all to itself.) At San Francisco, its pool is ringed by mild-mannered ferns, sharply contrasting with dozens of lascivious salmon, pink, and red anthurium and with the angry scarlet bracts of the lobster-claw (_Heliconia caribaea_).

The sunny, dry west wing contains the zebra banana (_Musa acuminata_), several gingers, and bromeliads (note buds like creamy white beads on the flowering spike of the Honduran _Aechmea luddemanniana_). A small gazebo marks a transition to its westernmost gallery. Paved with interlocking bricks interrupted only by a few Australian tree ferns, an area devoted to holiday and seasonal floral displays presents showy mass plantings frequently of overwhelming color and fragrance. A spring display, for example, may surround Easter lilies with blue, magenta, dark purple and white cineraria, under hanging pots of epiphyllum cactus bearing waxy, intensely colored salmon pink, pale golden, and fuchsia flowers: only three species, but the hundreds of blooms intensify vivid colors to make an impressive, dramatic floral event. With a cool ocean breeze blowing in through open flaps in the ceiling, the effect can be unforgettable.

Compared to the treasures within Kew's historic architecture, the aesthetically conceived and impeccably maintained tropical plantings at the Jardin des Plantes in Paris, or the endless botanical variety at the Jardin Botanique National de Belgique at Meise, the San Francisco Conservatory of Flowers does not equal the scale or the renown of the great European indoor gardens. Yet the conservatory remains a polished gem, carefully maintained to the quality of its traditional European counterparts. Its existence indicates the city's essentially European self-conception, its interest in making itself fit to be spoken of as a place where civilized people live.

This interest—expressed throughout Golden Gate Park and in many other tangible and intangible ways, from fine hotels to health care to well-functioning public transportation—signals a conception of the city as a social realm, a forum of public amenities. In southern California cities, the good life remains essentially a private matter and hence can seldom promise anything more than mere hedonism. As acquisition of the conservatory attests, early in their history San Franciscans imagined how the city might develop. This memorable public garden offers only one example of the steps San Francisco took to realize itself.

(The San Francisco Conservatory of Flowers, located on Kennedy Dr. in northeastern Golden Gate Park, is open from May to October, 9:00 a.m. to 6:00 p.m., and from November to April, 9:00 a.m. to 5:00 p.m. $1.50 adult admission. On greenhouses, see Stefan Koppelkamm, *Glasshouses and Wintergardens of the Nineteenth Century* [1981].)

STRYBING ARBORETUM
AND
BOTANICAL GARDENS

G olden Gate Park was a mature park by the 1930s, when construction of Strybing Arboretum actually began. William Hammond Hall, the first superintendent, desired to establish an arboretum, but the overwhelming task of reclaiming a thousand-acre territory forced him to defer that project. Early in John McLaren's superintendency, a site was selected. Plantings of conifers began in the mid-1890s, and maps began to label the site as the park's arboretum. Lack of funds prevented further development, however, until Helene Strybing's bequest to the city following her death in 1926. Little is known about Strybing or her reasons for making this bequest, but she specifically instructed that her legacy be used to develop a botanical garden of plants native to or characteristic of California.

As funds became available in the 1930s, Eric Walther (who after starting as a young park gardener in 1918, would later become arboretum director) and McLaren drafted a master plan. Construction began in 1937 according to the plan, which defined and organized plantings by geography and ecology rather than botanical relations. The first tree formally planted was a *Drimys winteri*, a South American magnolia relative that reflected Walther's enthusiasm for magnolias, which remain a continuing emphasis. (As do several arboretum guides, *Magnolias and their Relatives in Strybing Arboretum* reflects the erudition of Dr. Elizabeth McClintock, resident botanist and an authority on plants throughout Golden Gate Park.)

The arboretum officially opened in May 1940. A second installment of Strybing's bequest became available in 1939, making possible an expanded phase of development, with plants contributed by nurseries, private individuals, and established botanical gardens from the United States and throughout the world. By 1957, when Walther retired, 5,000 specimens had been planted on forty acres. In 1954, the Strybing Arboretum Society formed to support arboretum programs, and in the early 1960s, additional acreage was developed pursuant to a master plan drafted by Robert Tetlow. Today the Strybing Arboretum fills seventy acres with over 6,000 labeled species.

At the main entrance, a small concourse divides the Helen Crocker Russell Library and a County Fair Building from a bookstore, a demonstration garden (displaying ideas and plants for home patios, trellises, paving, fencing, and seating), and a "mixed border," which interprets the English perennial border in California plants. A gate leads from the concourse into an undulating main lawn of several acres. The street entrances, concourse, lawn, a fountain, and finally the Zellerbach Garden at the arboretum's northwestern edge form one of its few axes. Like the oval main lawn, the arboretum's plan consists of a series of circular and oval beds connected by curving, serpentine paths.

The easiest tour progresses in a circular fashion, with stops at specialized gardens and collections. For the most part, these are geographic, although some focus on genera (rhododendrons, redwoods), themes (a garden of fragrance, a biblical garden), or plant categories (succulents or dwarf conifers). Only a few trees shade the main lawn (horsechestnut, deodar cedar, *Tilia cordata* "Rancho," and a southern magnolia "Samuel Sommer," the first of many magnolias). Proceeding north and west leads to a small "garden of fragrance" in raised rock beds, planted with common myrtle, pennyroyal (*Mentha pulegium*) and spearmint (*M. spicata*), sage and lavender, and spicy freesia and the sweetly aromatic cheddar pink (*Dianthus gratianopolitanus*).

Golden Gate Park's other large rhododendron collection (with over 300 species and cultivars) lies nearby. Although the *Guide List to Plants in Strybing* (available at the bookstore on the entry concourse) shows rhododendrons scattered throughout the arboretum, they concentrate here. This diverse genus offers flowers in a range of colors; some are fragrant and others scentless; some specimens grow into small trees, while others remain two to three feet high; some bloom in huge trumpet flowers, a dozen per stalk, while others keep to a miniature scale. Unlike the park's other rhododendrons, the arboretum labels its specimens. Of note during April are the scarlet "Noyo Chief"; the pale yellow blooms, not without a touch of green, of "Saffron Prince"; and an even paler yellow, the Himalayan *Rhododendron dalhousiae*, whose strongly defined trumpet flowers have a citrus scent.

The rhododendrons merge into a "primitive garden," with black tree ferns (*Cyathea medullaris*), the massive, menacing leaves of *Gunnera tinc-*

toria, iris, *Ginkgo biloba,* and cycads around a bog. (Compare this small area to the grandiose garden on the same theme near Tree Fern Dell in the park.) A fountain marks the "Cape Province Garden," specializing in unusually adapted plants from one of the world's most botanically rich areas. (At the southwestern tip of Africa, Cape Province has 8,500 plant species in 35,000 square miles; California, four times as large, has only 5,000 native species.) The garden focuses on flowering bulbs, heaths, proteas, succulents, and daisies. Blooming during spring are the unusual daisies of *Watsonia meriana,* whose ray petals, white on top and purple underneath, have spoon-shaped ends that make a kind of pinwheel, *sputniki* effect; the lavender and gold-centered daisies of *Nylandtia spinosa,* flowers appearing at the tips of stems covered by shiny leaves edged by little needle hairs; and magenta flowers by the hundreds on a woody shrub, *Orphium frutescens.*

Beyond the Cape Province area, an Australian section includes euca-lyptus, callistemon, the "lilly-pilly tree" (*Acmena smithii,* bearing seeds shaped like half-inch apples), and a meadow of rose and pink straw-flowers (*Helipterum*). A South American section displays the dark blue claw flowers of *Salvia guaranitica,* salvias, fuchsias, bromeliads, a large Mayten tree (*Maytenus boaria*), and a rare Brazilian pine (*Araucaria angustifo-lia*). Behind the formal, semicircular Zellerbach Garden and its wisteria-covered trellis, a perimeter path enters an Asian area. It contains rarities such as the Himalayan *Michelia champaca* and a large, vigorous *M. doh-sopa,* the white bracts of the dove tree (*Davidia involucrata vilmoriniana*), and Japanese timber bamboo *ma-dake* (*Phylostachys bambusioides*). The Asian area descends from a bluff into a sheltered hollow containing a striking *Picea smithiana,* a weeping spruce whose new spring growth streaks its darker mature foliage with pale green highlights. At the bottom of the hollow, landscaped by Henry Matsutani and echoing a small part of Kyoto's Katsura Imperial Gardens, a wooden "moon viewing" platform overlooks a lake under a large *Magnolia delaviyi,* camellias, and Japanese maples (*Acer palmatum "Senkaki"*).

Another large lawn near the moon-viewing platform extends to a backdrop of Sierra redwoods and other evergreens. (A weeping *Sequoiaden-dron gianteum "Pendulum,"* not unlike a bedraggled setter just in from the rain, overlooks the lawn. No more than a curiosity, its trunk contorts indecisively and lower branches ambiguously creep on the ground, making it at once a tree and a ground cover.) Several firs (*Abies* species), cryptomeria, and other needled evergreens border the lawn. The arbore-tum's coast redwood trail begins near this area, plunging through deep shade and companion plantings of giant chain fern, oxalis, *Rhododendron macrophyllum*, dogwood (*Cornus sessilis*), and salal.

Behind the redwood trail is an utter contrast, a dry garden in a rocky amphitheater with aloes, agaves, yucca, succulents, and cactus. The arboretum's California section selects plants suited to a rock garden, meadow, arroyo, pond, chaparral, and mixed woodland. A promising new area, the New World Cloudforest, includes a young, very rare *Magnolia dealbata*, whose wide, tender leaves give it an interesting tropical appearance. A grove of dwarf conifers presents an array of foliage colors: chartreuse *Chamaecyparis obtusa "Crippsii"*; bright yellow *C. lawsoniana "Hillieri"*; rusty-tinged *Thuja occidentalis "Sulphurea"*; and specimens with blue foliage, such as *Picea pungens "Montgomery."* The pungently scented conifers surround a lake filled with water lilies and edged with dark purple irises.

Strybing Arboretum is an imposing public garden, not only because of its large size. Its staff honors a tradition of seeking out rare plants—perhaps a necessity in this unusual, cool Mediterranean climate—not often seen elsewhere in California. In a sense, the arboretum offers one of many specialized facilities in Golden Gate Park, a museum of plants resembling the equally specialized Steinhart Aquarium or De Young Art Museum. Golden Gate Park represents, however, the successful horticultural transformation of sand and scrub into a civilized landscape of woodland, meadow, lake, and flowering dell. The arboretum embodies the refinement and the culmination of that process.

(The Strybing Arboretum and Botanical Garden is located in Golden Gate Park just inside the Ninth St. entrance. Free admission; open weekdays 8:00 a.m. to 4:30 p.m. and weekends 10:00 a.m. to 5:00 p.m. Facilities include a bookstore and the Helen Crocker Russell Library, a collection of over 10,000 botanical and horticultural books; telephone 415-661-1514; open daily 10:00 a.m. to 4:00 p.m., though the Russell Library is closed on holidays. Tours are given daily. Telephone the Strybing Arboretum Society at 415-661-1316.)

THE JAPANESE
TEA GARDEN
IN
GOLDEN GATE PARK

I t would seem that Californians have never been able to keep quiet about their fine weather, and San Franciscans can claim an equable climate if not a warm one. Many plants seem to thrive in it, and so do many people. In 1894, to capture the attention of the snow-bound eastern and midwestern states and to mitigate local effects of a national business depression, San Francisco put on the California Mid-winter Exposition. On sixty acres of what is now the Music Concourse, a midway was constructed of fanciful and international exhibits. The Japanese Tea Garden began as the fair's most popular attraction, a Japanese village developed by George T. Marsh, an importer of Japanese art goods and student of Japanese language and culture. After the exhibition, Marsh sold the village to the park commissioners, who placed Makota Hagiwara in charge of the Japanese Tea Garden.

Although remnants survive from the 1894 village—the *romon* or main gate, the teahouse and pond, and the drum bridge—Hagiwara enlarged and changed the garden, importing plants from Japan. He also built a home for his family and lived on the site, and after his death in 1925, his daughter and son-in-law took over management. Family members operated the garden until World War II relocation forced them out, regrettably not the first instance of discrimination against them, although unquestionably the worst. (The garden was even renamed the "Oriental Garden" in 1942; the original name was restored ten years later.) There has been considerable activity since 1960, when Nagao Sakurai redesigned the pond area in front of the teahouse. (Elizabeth McClintock's *The Japanese Tea Garden, Golden Gate Park* [1977] discusses the garden's history, architectural features, and plants.)

The main emphasis has shifted to the garden's western portion, where a torii, a five-story pagoda painted white, gold, and bright orange, and a similarly painted temple gate (structures from the Panama-Pacific

The Japanese Garden in Golden Gate Park

International Exposition of 1915) crown a steep slope above a pond. A waterfall drains down the slope, planted to display the Fraser collection of dwarf conifers that originated with the Hagiwara family. After passing through several owners, the collection was returned to this spot in 1965. It is only one of several plant and garden ornament collections now housed in the garden, which must plan carefully to avoid this source of crowding as well as to cope with the great numbers of visitors to this very popular garden.

Plants around the pond include pink flowering plums, rose-tinged heavenly bamboo, dark purple *Prunus cerasifera* "*Atropurpurea*" on either side of the torii, and the copper and red of *Acer palmatum*, nearly as vivid as the orange pagoda itself. Paths around the main pond reveal many Japanese garden accoutrements: stone lanterns, a broken stepping-stone bridge, a waterfall, and rock formations. Behind the pagoda, cryptomeria shades a small Zen garden, from which a "Maple Lane" leads up to a plateau, the site of an eighteenth-century Japanese statue of Buddha. (In 1977, E. J. Schuster, who earlier redesigned the pagoda grounds in 1969, landscaped Maple Lane, adding a *So*, or "sprinkled hailstone" pavement.)

Where the garden's Japanese maple canopy parts, tall Monterey cypresses in Golden Gate Park tower above, intensifying the small scale and precise pruning inside the Japanese Tea Garden. Following the paths presents a sequence of bright light and filtered shade, unless a foggy or rainy day alters the textures of the plants, the pavement, or the pagoda. In 1966, a new wing added to the neighboring De Young Museum and housing the Avery Brundage Collection of Asian art included large picture windows overlooking the Japanese Tea Garden. This "borrowed view" and the art collection give a new relevance and purpose to what is regarded as the oldest Japanese-style garden in the United States.

(The Japanese Tea Garden is located on Hagiwara Tea Garden Dr. at Martin Luther King Dr. Open Monday through Saturday 10:30 a.m. to 5:30 p.m., Sundays and holidays 10:30 a.m. to 5:45 p.m. $2.00 adult admission; open free on New Year's Day, Easter, Memorial Day, July 4th, Thanksgiving, Christmas, and the first Wednesday of each month. Visitors may purchase tea and gifts at the teahouse and shop inside the garden.)

SAN FRANCISCO
BRIEFLY NOTED

Surely among the most unusually sited gardens in any California city is a surprising creation that clings to Telegraph Hill above the wharf. Grace Marchant, a former Hollywood stuntwoman, developed the garden over many decades. After her death in 1982, part of the plot was found to have encroached on private land, and more than 4,000 donors raised the money to purchase and preserve the garden through an arrangement with the Trust for Public Lands. Sloping east and north, GRACE MARCHANT GARDENS is the largest of a series of tiny plots lining the vertiginous Filbert Steps between Sansome and Montgomery and commands exceptional views of San Francisco Bay, Treasure Island, and the Bay Bridge. Where the Napier Lane footpath crosses the Filbert Steps, a small gate marks the gardens, recognizable as the area's largest plot and covered by a chartreuse carpet of baby's tears. (If unlocked, the gate can be opened for a closer look, but everything can be seen from the Filbert Steps.)

Befitting the garden's compact scale—about a half-acre—trees are small (Japanese maple, pittosporum, and even an avocado) and shrubs large. One rose engulfs a large camellia with apricot blossoms; a princess flower reaches fifteen feet; and golden flowers hang from an angel's trumpet that is almost a small tree. Nearby are several bananas, their foliage tinged with copper along a red midrib, and scattered throughout the property are bearded iris, aloes, ferns, canna, bergenia, acanthus, elephant ears, and fuchsias. Small stepping-stones lead up the hill past a tiny stream trickling down a channel between foot-high cliffs clad in baby's tears, giving this garden a storybook quality that even its proximity to the docks and downtown office blocks does not quite dispel. Surrounded by houses somehow finding purchase on the steep cliff, this garden's charm is such that San Francisco should have dozens more like it. Perhaps it already does. Those with strong legs and hearts may wish

A view of bridge and bay from Grace Marchant Garden, San Francisco

to explore the paths and staircases throughout Telegraph Hill, such as those along Greenwich one block north. (Grace Marchant Gardens, south of the Filbert Steps between Montgomery and Sansome; parking is easiest along the Embarcadero. Be prepared for steep, numerous steps.)

Graced by many fine neighborhood parks, San Francisco also conceals a number of fine private gardens within its densely populated city limits. Joan Hockaday's fine book, *The Gardens of San Francisco* (1988), explores the city's horticultural history, tours some of its private gardens, and besides a thorough treatment of Golden Gate Park, also turns up a few of San Francisco's less well known public gardens.

One of these is the GOLDEN GATE BRIDGE SOUTH TOWER GARDEN, at the city's northern tip, affording splendid views of the Golden Gate, Marin Headlands, Angel Island, Alcatraz, and San Francisco Bay as far as the Bay Bridge. Designed by Irving Morrow as consulting architect and Joseph Strauss as chief engineer, the Golden Gate Bridge was completed in 1937. Its engineering achievement and its fine use of the art deco style make the span doubly impressive viewed up close from this unaccustomed vantage point. But the bridge is not the only source of excitement. As Harold Gilliam's *Weather of the San Francisco Bay Region* explains, continental and oceanic air masses surge through this "weather funnel." Cold Pacific air and fog can pump through the Golden Gate into San Francisco Bay at high speed. Particularly during the summer, the onshore flow can extend through the Carquinez Straits as far as the Sacramento Delta, a powerful force that here, at the funnel's narrowest point, can create thick fogs of dramatic intensity.

Its exposure to fogs and strong winds makes gardening difficult on this site, so the garden's quality is doubly remarkable. The cool conditions cause some of its perennials to bloom at unexpected times. Ginger and Pride of Madeira flower in September, as do pink, burgundy, and yellow abutilon. Mexican bush sage (*Salvia leucantha*) performs impressively, with impeccable leaf spears on stems supporting purple floral spikes. Bright pink *Amaryllis belladonna*, yellow and red cannas, a bed of semidouble dahlias, hydrangeas, agapanthus, and annuals enliven the late summer floral display. A pedestrian path up to the visitor center has a planting of geraniums surrounding a small knot garden of succulents, ornamental kale, purple alyssum, and ground covers in shades of purple, green, and gray. The area, less than five acres, also contains a small rose garden, informational displays on the military history of Fort Point, and plaques with engineering data and other facts about the bridge.

IX
San Francisco
Bay Area:
The Peninsula

FILOLI

iloli was one of a number of estates built on the peninsula during the first decades of this century. Similar projects included Senator Phelan's Villa Montalvo in Saratoga, W. H. Crocker's New Place, and other Hillsborough estates, many funded by fortunes traceable to the gold rush. (The fashion for art-filled mansions in formal gardens later culminated well to the south, at San Simeon.) The ambition that spurred the pioneer fathers led their sons and daughters to be ambitious, for themselves and for their state, in a different way. Their estates reflected a desire to advance California society toward what they felt would be its next stage, acquiring aesthetic culture. That generation, many of whom were educated abroad, equated culture with European art and society. Their country seats—their desire for country seats in the first place—reflected that equation.

In *On the Edge of the World: Four Architects in San Francisco at the Turn of the Century* (1983), Richard Longstreth points out that this period viewed the formal garden as the way to unify a great house with its site. Certainly Filoli's gardens take their cue from the neo-Georgian mansion they enclose, extending its symmetrical plan right into the garden's axes. The house was carefully sited to fit into ancient coast live oaks existing on the property and to obtain views of lakes, watershed, and wooded mountains to the north and west.

The attention to site has a personal meaning as well as a cultural context. William Bourn had inherited a fortune from his pioneer father and enlarged his patrimony by developing the Empire Mine into the nation's largest gold mine. He was also instrumental in developing the water and power utilities necessary for the growth of San Francisco. Besides serving as president of San Francisco Gas and Electric Co. and Spring Valley Water Co., Bourn helped realize the Panama-Pacific International Exposition of 1915. Fight for a just cause; love your fellowman; live a good life: Bourn named "Filoli" for his personal credo.

Educated at Cambridge University, Bourn was also a patron of the arts. His friendship with Willis Polk facilitated Polk's success as one of the era's most prominent San Francisco architects. Noted both for his restless eclecticism and his command of historical styles, Polk designed everything from commercial office buildings to cottages. Built from 1915 to 1917 (with gardens installed during the next few years), Filoli was Polk's third residential commission for the Bourns, having two decades earlier designed the Empire Cottage at their Grass Valley gold mine and their city house at 2250 Webster Street.

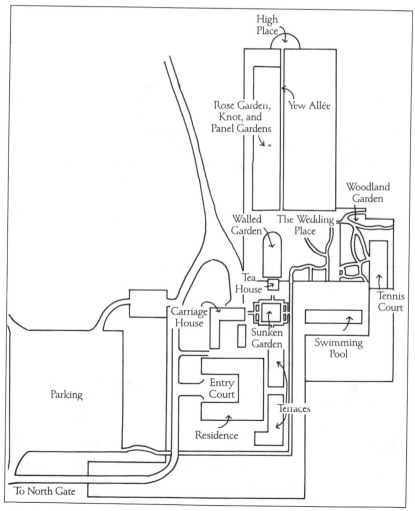

Filoli

Bruce Porter, who collaborated frequently with Polk, had also done previous work for the Bourns. A painter, sculptor, writer, and stained glass artist, he executed murals and stained glass for the Pacific Heights house and may also have contributed to the Empire Cottage gardens. At Filoli, Porter's garden plan extends the mansion's lines and terraces south and west into interlocking rectangles formed by sunken and walled gardens, water features, and garden buildings. The rectangles communicate by means of cross-axes, staircases, and portals through high walls. Changes of level reveal unexpected views along the axes, especially north to the Crystal Springs reservoir. (Bourn engaged Porter after rejecting another designer's plan because it failed to emphasize this prospect, which reminded him of Muckross House, a family property in County Kerry, Ireland.)

Isabella Worn also contributed to the Filoli gardens, creating color schemes and supervising the plantings during her collaboration with Porter. As well-known Bay Area "social decorators," she and her sister provided flowers for weddings, parties, and other occasions. The sisters performed this function for the Bourns through the 1930s, when Filoli was sold to Mr. and Mrs. William P. Roth. Well known in horticultural circles as a collector of camellias, rhododendrons, roses, and rare plants, Mrs. Roth continued to develop the gardens in consultation with Isabella Worn, who thus provided continuity between the only two families to own and live in Filoli. It was Mrs. Roth who gave the house, gardens, thirty-nine acres of land, and an endowment for maintenance to the National Trust for Historic Preservation in 1975. Later family gifts created a property of 654 acres. Adjacent land to the north, the watershed and lake of the Crystal Springs reservoir, will remain undeveloped.

Approached from the east, two wings of the U-shaped house enclose a gravel courtyard edged by Japanese maples and magnolia that are underplanted with azaleas, camellias, and rhododendrons. Focusing on an entry portico, the austere courtyard finds a measure of relief in potted annuals on the steps and purple wisteria and white *Clematis armandii* clambering above the door. Here appear several plants—hollies, Japanese maples, and cylindrically pruned Irish yews (*Taxus baccata "Stricta"*)—that reappear throughout the grounds. Near the house, allées of blue atlas cedar and London planes likewise prefigure the formal plantings that distinguish Filoli's gardens.

The sixteen acres of formal gardens begin to the south with a sunken garden. This square area terminates a cross-axis formed by double rows of Irish yews on either side of a swimming pool, behind which is a

A formal garden in the wilderness: Filoli

small pool house in front of olive trees sheared into cylinders. The pool and yews lead the eye to a honey locust tree (_Gleditsia triacanthos_ "Sunburst"), its golden yellow spring foliage contrasting with the muted olives and with the dark green forested mountains farther west.

The sunken garden sets a reflecting pond amid lawns and beds of annuals (in spring, columbine, Siberian wallflower, and pansies). Through a gate, another axis leads to a walled garden centered on a teahouse, a miniature brick orangerie with marble floors and high windows. The subdivisions of the walled garden include a gentle slope of curving terraces called "the wedding place," a camellia grove under oaks, and a small formal garden around a sundial inscribed "Time Began in a Garden." (Other contemporary developments in Eden—labor, mortality, the knowledge of good and evil—raise a question whether this ambiguous sentiment makes quite the happiest choice for a garden motto.)

A gate through the wall near the wedding place leads into a "natural garden," with white-flowering dogwood and more camellias, rhododendrons, and azaleas shaded by Japanese maples and massive oaks. This informal area's paths wind through dense vegetation before reaching a tennis court, whose rectangle extends to the pool house, forming the other end of the axis from the sunken garden. The pool house view also reveals a row of pleached plane trees lining a high brick wall and the weeping limbs of twin Camperdown elms, whose tortuous, twiggy branches form a tent of shade all the way down to the ground.

Under the pleached planes, past climbing *Hydrangea anomala petiolaris*, and through the wall again (its south exposure supporting climbing roses such as "Altissimo" [1967], a fine, vivid red floribunda), the path leads into another narrow yew allée before emerging into a rose garden whose formal beds are hedged in precisely trimmed box. (The 600 roses begin blooming in mid-May.) Here an "open knot" garden (i.e., without flowers filling spaces between the knots) weaves strands of miniature gray hedges of lavender cotton and contrasting vegetation of germander, dwarf myrtle, and red dwarf Japanese barberry.

Containing an herb garden and an enormous panel garden of annuals, the long, rectangular garden eventually leads to the end of the estate's longest yew allée, "the high place," a lawn within a half-circle of Vicenza stone columns that commands a view north to Crystal Springs Reservoir. This prospect made "the high place" Mr. Bourn's favorite spot on the estate. The return to the house passes a long perennial border, displaying creamy-white *Viburnum opulus*, lamb's ear, catmint, bridal wreath (*Spiraea x vanhouttei*), and yellow *Kniphofia uvaria*.

Porter's plan of brick walls, hedging, and allées forms a series of garden rooms unified visually by the more than 220 barrel-shaped Irish yews. The gardens display an exquisitely high level of horticulture, with tens of thousands of bulbs and annuals kept in bloom from early spring until well into the fall. Pollarding, pleaching, hedging, and similar pruning techniques—rarely seen in California, a bastion of blandly "naturalistic" garden thinking, to which topiary and other severe pruning methods are anathema unless smuggled in under the aegis of bonsai—reach a similarly accomplished level. Nor do the Filoli gardens overlook unusual botany, with rare plants from the Bourn-Roth era as well as recent contributions by local horticultural societies.

Filoli combines plants used formally or spatially—the flat-topped Irish yews, the hedging, knot gardens, and allées—with romantic, colorful, or eccentric horticulture: vines flowering on brick walls, the golden honey locust at an axial focal point, or the paradoxical Camperdown elm. Terraces and balustrades, a sunken garden, walls and staircases, and water features structure the garden and organize its profusion of fine plants. About the time he planned Filoli, Bruce Porter linked formal

California gardens, by way of the mission fathers' transplanted memories, to precedents in southern Europe. With a touch worthy of Oscar Wilde, he dismissed as "dowdiness" the naturalistic garden, based as it is on the idea "that art has to simulate Nature in her least artful moods." Instead he offered the pleasure of finding the plan of a house, with its sense of shelter and human occupation, extended into the garden.

Especially in a great garden, Porter advised that although Nature finally has her way, "she plays the more beautifully when man has set his early thought and art upon the boundaries within which she shall play—under his control and by his guidance." Writing in 1915, the year it was begun, Porter may have had Filoli in mind. It is as much the brick and stone hardscape as it is fine plants that distinguish these gardens from the surrounding terrain, beautiful but rugged. If that wilderness is nature, the ordering rectangles and axes seem to say, this garden is nature selected for the choicest cultivar, controlled by precision pruning, and combined for color rhymes and foliar textures. Placed in marvelous countryside around a fine house, planned so that architectural plants frame the views and hardscape structures space, and cultivated with expertise, Filoli perfects the formal estate garden in California.

(Filoli, Cañada Road, Woodside. Tours, which include both the house and the garden, must be arranged in advance and cost $8.00 per adult. For tour reservations, telephone 415-364-2880. Tours are conducted from mid-February to mid-November; visitors must be 12 years of age or older. The Friends of Filoli also offer guided nature hikes for a small per-person fee; telephone 415-364-2880. Quotations from Bruce Porter come from his "Introduction" to Porter Garnett, _Stately Homes of California_ [1915].)

SUNSET
MAGAZINE
HEADQUARTERS

S unset *Magazine* began in the 1890s as a Southern Pacific Railroad magazine to attract tourists and increase passenger travel to the west. The early format changed long ago, but a regional emphasis has remained constant and the magazine speaks with a voice that makes it almost a cultural influence in the western states. Besides travel, food, and home improvement titles, Sunset also publishes a full line of gardening books. The *Sunset Western Garden Book* performs the same function for gardeners that the magazine does for readers: addressing peculiarly western needs, tastes, landscape, climate, and experiences that traditional print media, headquartered on the eastern seaboard, still find it convenient to overlook.

Even if some features retain a this-could-never-happen quality— smiling, bearded males assembling clever canapés, apparently unaided, in spotless kitchens—*Sunset Magazine* nonetheless arouses considerable loyalty by fostering a sense that it is produced by people whose lives resemble those of their readers. Values of active participation, of community and personal initiative, and cheerful, Emersonian self-help pervade the magazine's travel, home projects, food, and gardening features. The 1951 move of the firm's headquarters from San Francisco to Menlo Park, in other words, had its desired effect. Amid a postwar migration from the cities, Sunset followed its audience, reasoning that its staff could reach readers better by creating the magazine in a suburban environment.

Although the building and gardens of *Sunset* headquarters are essentially suburbia writ large, the seven-acre property's extravagant scale causes a difference in degree to become one of kind. Furthermore, in most suburban establishments, Cliff May did not design the house, nor did Thomas Church create the garden. Each designer in his way symbolizes postwar suburban living. May is credited with originating the ranch house style, which for three decades dominated suburban housing in the western United States. (His influence was especially strong in California, even if translating his design ideas into typical tract dwellings often travestied May's own elegant, livable houses.) Church, whose ideas are outlined in his book, _Gardens Are for People,_ was closer to the contemporary international design idiom in the fifties but had nearly as wide an influence.

Church recognized that most gardens were limited by the small size of suburban properties. As did May's ranch house, Church's designs also incorporated the desire of westerners, many of whom lived in agreeable climates, to let the outdoors inside and to use their gardens as extensions of their homes. Hence the wide eaves, shallow pitch, and shake roof of the one-story Sunset headquarters, its outdoor porches, patios, and fireplaces, roof cutouts and picture windows, and sprawling, low-rise scale will seem utterly familiar. So will many of the plants, arranged in beds around a generous lawn. It is a typical backyard, really, except for its grand proportions. That Sunset had the wit and confidence to go to the masters further distinguishes it. May and Church both turned in designs that were functional but spatially opulent, low-key but aesthetic and intelligent.

Two wings of the "house"—editorial offices, test kitchens, and entertaining areas, gracious living presumably adapted to gracious working—open onto an enormous lawn panel. Over an acre in size, the lawn is surrounded by a path that curves past beds of trees, flowering shrubs, and seasonal annuals that form a botanical tour of the Pacific Coast, with each region represented by native species or by plants widely grown from the Pacific Northwest to the California desert. The theme, it must be admitted, is only loosely observed, emerging most clearly only at the beginning and the end of the tour.

The path through the first area, the Pacific Northwest, forms a kind of peninsula moving away from and then returning to the main lawn. A sizable coast live oak shades beds of rhododendrons in front of a screen of Douglas fir. A smaller sandstone path winds through woody shrubs and small trees: Himalayan evergreen dogwood (_Cornus capitata_), purple Japanese maple, mahonia, huckleberry, and holly. The sunny corner abruptly changes to deep shade under a California buckeye shading ferns, azaleas, irises, and more rhododendrons.

At the oak, a small rose bed inaugurates a border of flowering annuals and bulbs as the detour rejoins the main path. Another coast live oak, a mayten tree, and a fine weeping Lawson cypress shade camellias and fuchsias. Bare branches of the New Zealand tea tree lean over the path, and a southern magnolia shades sword ferns and holly. Another detour branches away from the main path around a putting green, lined by calceolaria, primula, bergenia, and agapanthus in front of *Hydrangea macrophylla* and the lily magnolia (*M. quinquepeta*), shaded from the afternoon sun by a screen of coast redwoods planted in 1951 and well over 100 feet tall.

The final section begins with lavender-blue flowering ceanothus. A forty-foot-tall *Yucca australis* towers above a small dry climate garden of succulents, agaves, cacti, aloes, and euphorbias (including the curiosity, *Euphorbia caput-medusae*, its snakelike sprouts suggesting the head of Medusa to the botanist who named it). The collection also contains California native plants suitable for garden use, such as the Matilija poppy, and exotic bromeliads, such as *Puya alpestris*.

This aesthetically pleasing garden reflects the Sunset philosophy: experimental exotic introductions balanced by native species; conservation of existing trees with installation of new ones; bedding plants for flowers through most of the year; and gardens designed for outdoor living (the putting green, fireplaces, and patios). The lavish scale, inherited from another era, might seem out of step with current thinking at Sunset and elsewhere which advocates saving water by reducing lawn size. Yet a public garden remains one of the most appropriate places for a large lawn. Here the lawn performs a symbolic as well as an aesthetic function, connoting Sunset's suburban demographics right down to the golf course "Astoria Bent" grass that creates a beautifully manicured turf, the Platonic backyard lawn that everyone wants and nobody has.

Although he could design a formal or axial plan as well as anyone, Church is known for his creative use of angled lines, asymmetry, and especially for the sweeping curves of biomorphism. Whether in the sculpture of Noguchi or Calder, Harley Earl's finny tribe of General Motors products, or the Formica boomerang pattern, this line turned up everywhere in the 1950s, edging a golf course green or defining the coping of kidney-shaped swimming pools. Everywhere the line is moving, curving, and pulsing like protoplasm, flight, or primitive urges flung out into the world which return to be held in your hand.

This idiom, so familiar as to be scarcely noticeable, remains a product of conscious design; it may look simple, but the sweeping line and proportions are not easy to get right. At the Sunset garden, the tension arises from a square lawn and its pair of peninsular limbs surrounded by a curving path and occasionally varied by island beds. After nearly four decades, the plan's simplicity remains subdued but dynamic, intelligent but with a pleasingly light touch. And besides being a garden for people, there is plenty of room for plants.

(Sunset headquarters, Willow and Middlefield Rds., Menlo Park, open only during workdays; closed weekends. Free admission; gardens open 9:00 a.m. to 4:30 p.m. for self-guided visits; a map is available. Tours of the headquarters, providing a glimpse of publishing operations, are offered daily. Telephone 415-321-3600.)

HAKONE
JAPANESE
GARDENS

L ocated in the hills above the village of Saratoga, Hakone Japanese Gardens began as Oliver and Isabel Stine's fifteen-acre estate. After visiting Japan, Mrs. Stine began a Japanese garden, designed by Naoharu Aihara and completed in 1918, with traditionally crafted structures for family weekends and entertaining. (Because the property is near Congress Springs, Mrs. Stine named it for mineral springs in Japan's Fuju Hakone National Park.) As the site slopes down a steep hill, Aihara designed a "hill and water garden" (*tsukiyama-ansui*) in the "strolling pond style" (*chisen-kaiyo-shiki*).

In 1966, after several subsequent owners, the City of Saratoga purchased the garden to save it from subdivision. Two years later, Kyoto-trained Tanso Ishihara assumed supervision during an extended renovation of the six-acre parcel, completed shortly after his death in 1980.

As Ishihara wrote (with Gloria Wickham in "Hakone Gardens, Saratoga," in *California Horticulture Journal*, October 1974), it is possible to regard Hakone Japanese Gardens using traditional Japanese garden concepts. Hakone, for instance, has a "master waterfall" and "cascade-screening trees," juniper and dwarf Japanese maple through whose foliage one views the partly obscured cascade. An island in a pond supports a traditional dwarf black pine and a Momoyama stone lantern, their miniature scale shifting attention away from the island's tiny size. Symbolizing the Buddhist god of mercy, a "master stone" marks a viewing place above the three-cascade *kasane-ochi* waterfall, ordinarily furnished with a lower stone suitable to accommodate the garden owner's meditations on horticultural beauty.

Although Hakone Japanese Gardens contains several distinct areas, it gives little sense of being compartmentalized. The centerpiece garden places a pond in a relatively level area beneath a slope up to the "upper house," the garden's oldest structure, built on the "Moon-Viewing Hill" in 1917 with traditional mortise and tenon joinery and wooden pegs.

As is customary in Japanese gardens, few plants seem prominent for their flowers alone. Instead, evergreens, deciduous plants with unusual branch structure or bark, or plants with foliar color, texture, or shape establish nuanced rhythms and visual variety. Such plants include dwarf Japanese maples' lacy rust-red leaves, the dark greens of hinoki cypress, pines, and madrone, variegated juniper and pittosporum, and the chartreuse and near-yellow of bamboo, creeping fig, and deciduous maples.

Ornamental koi, symbolizing love, fertility, and longevity—the koi life span can exceed that of humans—provide another source of color, from pure orange varieties to those blotched with cream, silver, gold, black, and pale blue. The fish add a note of ease, drifting silently through the still pond. Since a clearly stated principle summons up its opposite, the placid pool lies beneath a series of small waterfalls, the largest of which comprises three falls cascading down the steep hillside behind the garden's largest pine, a Monterey pine spreading over a Kasuga lantern.

The pine's enormity points to another principle of opposition at Hakone, between the plant allowed to grow freely and the pruning,

Craftsmanship and tradition: Hakone Japanese Gardens

shaping, and influencing of growth to achieve conventional effects. In Japanese horticulture, the most extreme example of such methods is bonsai miniaturization. Other examples at Hakone are the island plants trimmed in the snow-collecting horizontal shapes and plants at the foundation of buildings sheared into green spheres.

At Hakone, several permanent structures guide visitors to particular views: covered with white and lavender Japanese wisteria vines, a waterfall-viewing pavilion exaggerates the cascade of water, the hill's foreshortened steepness, and the height of the upper house. Ascending to the upper house reverses the effect, when the pond and its miniature trees seem tiny in relation to the height of the upper house, the descent of the waterfall, and the size of the Monterey pine spreading above it.

Since 1987, the Japan Bamboo Society of Saratoga has created a two-acre *Kizuna-en* bamboo garden near the Japanese garden. Designed by Kiyoshi Yasui, the garden propounds some obvious municipal symbolism (e.g., five large stones for Saratoga city council members, a wall of twenty-six field stones representing Muko-shi council members) connoting the sister-city relationship between Saratoga and Muko-shi, a Kyoto suburb. Organized in several terraces crossed by stepping-stones and appointed with stone lanterns, the garden displays a developing collection of bamboos exceptional for size or rarity. Plans call for a bamboo research facility on the site.

Above the pond and waterfall under large redwoods is a collection of hundreds of camellias donated by the estate of Richard R. Roggia in 1974. Steep trails present an unusual vantage point on the Japanese garden below. Hakone Japanese Gardens provides historical, symbolic, and horticultural examples of Japanese garden traditions, treating them with knowledge and respect.

(Hakone Japanese Gardens, 21000 Big Basin Way, Saratoga; open Monday through Friday 10:00 a.m. to 5:00 p.m. and Saturday and Sunday 11:00 a.m. to 5:00 p.m.; closed legal holidays. Free admission. Tours on Saturday and Sundays from 2:00 p.m. to 4:00 p.m., April through September, or arranged by telephoning 408-867-3438.)

VILLA
MONTALVO
ARBORETUM

A reform mayor of San Francisco who later served as a U.S senator, James Duval Phelan built a country home in Saratoga in 1912. After graduating from college in classics and philosophy, he studied European cities on a two-year grand tour and devoted much of his public career trying to make San Francisco an urban center fit to be considered in the same class as London, Paris, and Berlin. His estate suggests both the Anglo-Irish culture of his family and the Mediterraneanism of his youthful imagination. (He named it for Garcí Ordóñez de Montalvo, in whose *Las Sergas de Esplandían* [1519] the name "California" first appears.) A friend of Golden Gate Park while mayor from 1897 to 1902, Phelan hired John McLaren to design his gardens. Like the house, the gardens suggest Italy and the Mediterranean, with a touch of the English countryside.

The estate overlooks the Santa Clara Valley, backing up to the forested hills to the west. The eastern view is almost obscured by huge trees that after nearly eight decades tower above a lawn that slopes away from marble stairs below a balustraded terrace. The house, a cream-colored Italianate villa flanked by twin porticoes clothed in white wisteria, surrounds a colonnaded rear courtyard. Doric columns flank an oval lawn (a pool in Phelan's day), with a fourth side composed by a small pavilion, brick paths, hedges, tubbed citrus and palms, and bedding plants. (Unfortunately, the 1989 earthquake damaged parts of the courtyard and house, toppling statuary and severing trellises.)

To the north and west, before disappearing into the forest, a lawn slopes up to a white lath gazebo under red horsechestnuts (*Aesculus carnea* "*Briotii*"), blooming dark salmon-pink in spring, a superb flowering tree seen all over the San Francisco Bay area. Reminiscent of an English landscape, the largest garden area places an undulating lawn between a corridor of skyline trees—a characteristic McLaren composition—on a gen-

A neoclassical courtyard, Villa Montalvo

tle slope that terminates in a formal garden. The opulent lawn drifts through a mixed forest of palms, southern magnolia, birch, oak, variegated English holly, deodar and blue atlas cedars, bunya bunya, eucalyptus, and tulip trees. The formal garden at the foot of the lawn also suffered from the recent earthquake, but its plants survived well enough, with rare ornamental and exotic fruit trees set among Italian cypresses, box hedging, and citrus focusing attention on the Ionic columns of a "Love Temple."

From the formal garden, the plan's three distinct units emerge along an axis from formal house through informal landscape to formal garden. The house (by William and Alexander Curlett with E. C. Gottschalk), McLaren's naturalistic lawn and trees, and the formal garden give a sense of spatial flow within this enclosed, axial composition, any one of its three units providing fine views of the other two. As they did in Phelan's time, trails penetrate the dense wood covering the hillside behind the house and about the garden; the arboretum contains a 1.5-mile nature trail through chaparral, mixed evergreen forest, and coast redwood plant communities. A small amphitheater behind the house provides a venue for musical and dramatic performances; the arboretum is part of an arts center.

(The Villa Montalvo Arboretum and Center for the Arts, 15400 Montalvo Rd., Saratoga, off of Saratoga Los Gatos Rd. [Highway 9] between Saratoga and Fruitvale aves. Open Monday through Friday 8:00 a.m. to 5:00 p.m.; Saturdays, Sundays, and holidays 9:00 a.m. to 5:00 p.m. Free admission. For information, telephone the park staff at 408-867-0190.)

SAN
JOSE
GARDENS

Its gardens remind us that the Santa Clara Valley was once not only one of the world's richest orchard areas but also that its miles of apricots and prunes in the spring were said to have made it among the most beautiful. MISSION SANTA CLARA DE ASIS, located on the University of Santa Clara campus, is the mission's fifth site. The present sanctuary dates only from 1928, yet its heritage reaches back to a mission founded in 1777 which once had the largest Indian population of any in California. Instead of the dry mission garden style, the entrance to Mission Santa Clara is landscaped in what is almost a midwestern mode: lawns, shrubs, and walkways lined by tree roses, pansies, and impatiens.

South of the sanctuary, a large garden opens onto the university campus, where an early adobe wall gives a suggestion of a courtyard. Especially when it blooms in April, an ancient wisteria and its gnarled, foot-thick trunks make a long trellis the most prominent garden feature. Midway along the trellis uprights, a Lady Banks rose planted in the late 1800s mixes pale yellow blooms with thousands of lavender wisteria flowers for an exceptional display. Out in the garden, under mature, statuesque palms, more *Banksia* roses climb on the Adobe Lodge (with the adobe wall, the oldest university campus structures in the western United States). Supporting a tiled half roof that extends the rooflines of the Adobe Lodge, the wall forms a unified composition lined with a row of ancient olives, a series of tubbed aspidistra, and surrounding palms. (Mission Santa Clara de Asis, at the University of Santa Clara, is entered from The Alameda.)

The five-acre SAN JOSE MUNICIPAL ROSE GARDEN, dating from 1931, sets formal beds in a large park around a large circular pond and fountain. A wooden trellis supports climbing roses, although nearly all plants are modern hybrid teas, grandifloras, and floribundas, with a few miniatures and polyanthas. The varieties—the deep red "Olympiad" and subtle shell pink of "French Lace," for example—seem carefully chosen. Most bear labels, and the flowers coming into first bloom in late April suggest that San Jose is an exceptional place for roses. (San Jose Municipal Rose Garden, Naglee Ave. between Dana Ave. and Garden Dr., open from sunrise until one hour after sunset.)

San Jose's major tourist attraction, the WINCHESTER MYSTERY HOUSE, seems not only a piece of history but also the architectural symptom of psychological disquiet. Her husband and infant daughter having met untimely deaths, Sarah Winchester allowed a psychic to convince her that only continuous building would protect her from the same fate. Since Sarah was blessed (or cursed) with an ample inheritance from the Winchester Rifle Company, she kept carpenters busy around the clock after 1884.

Whatever its job-creating merits, however, the gambit inevitably failed when Winchester died in 1922. The following year tours began of the 160-room house, full of architectural curiosities—stairs to nowhere, spider web windows, and many features incorporating the number 13—and surrounded by gardens and the structures necessary to run what was then a large working farm. (A self-guided tour leads to

A California folly: Winchester Mystery House

points of interest, each with taped commentary by actors in folksy personae. Since disembodied voices constantly emanate from speakers concealed in shrubbery, the effect in the garden is nearly as bizarre as anything inside the house.)

Several garden courtyards and structures are included in the tour, such as a greenhouse whose roof has thirteen glass cupolas, a design detail credited to Mrs. Winchester. The set piece, a front garden on Winchester Boulevard, offers a typical California rural estate garden of the period. One convention, the palm drive, is still seen through much of the state; the Winchester House differs only because the number of its *Washingtonia filifera* palms—thirteen—had a private significance for their owner. Front garden paths curve between box hedging, fountains, and statuary and under large, exotic trees.

Like every Victorian entry garden, it is designed to impress. Yet it also has a personal touch of ambivalence, since the reclusive Mrs. Winchester required a huge hedge to screen the garden from the prying eyes of passersby. The entry garden also displays the eccentricities that gained Winchester House its notoriety—a "door to nowhere," for instance, an external door on the second floor with no balcony, landing, or staircase. Giving new meaning to the pastiche concept, the house's Eastlake-Queen Anne architecture, a wonderland of finials, turrets, a five-tone paint scheme, and leaded glass front door windows inset with roses, appears to best advantage from the front garden. (Winchester Mystery House, Winchester Blvd. between Interstate 280 and Stevens Creek Blvd. The self-guided garden tour is free; admission is charged for guided mansion tours, the Historic Firearms Museum, and the Winchester Antique Products Museum. Open daily except Christmas. For hours, subject to slight seasonal changes, telephone 408-247-2101.)

A botanical garden, cultural center, and bird and wildlife sanctuary, OVERFELT GARDENS was deeded by Mildred Overfelt to the City of San Jose in 1959 in memory of her parents, William and Mary Overfelt, members of a pioneer San Jose family that operated a grain and dairy farm on the site since the 1850s. Opened in 1966, the park has just over thirty acres, whose planted areas include a grove of palm species that do not mind summer heat and winter lows well below freezing, small rose and iris gardens, a coast redwood grove, and lawns.

The most unusual features are permanent structures in a Chinese cultural garden. Elaborate stone, marble, and tiled pavilions commemorate Confucius, Sun Yat-sen, and Chiang Kai-shek. Except for a "Plum Pavilion" overlooking a pond and grove of ornamental plums and red jade apple (*Malus purpurea*), however, as yet there is little Chinese landscaping, perhaps a development left to the future. Most of the park, indeed, remains in its natural state. (Enter Overfelt Gardens on Educational Park Way, off McKee Rd.; open 10:00 a.m. to sunset; telephone park ranger for information or tours at 408-251-3323 or 926-5555.)

Superior horticulturally is the KELLY PARK JAPANESE FRIEND-SHIP GARDEN, a smaller version of Koraku-en, a noted seventeenth-century Edo-style garden in Okayama, San Jose's sister city. What first seems to be a single pond in a level garden proves to be the first of three lakes. As the upper lake narrows, it spills over a tiny falls into a stream meandering under stone footbridges before reaching a prospect of the second and third ponds on lower levels. Dedicated in 1965, the 6.5-acre, sloping garden contains many large trees, particularly the coast redwoods and deodar cedars screening its boundary along Coyote Creek.

From the second, smallest pond, water hurtles down a steep rapids, noisily objecting to boulders that impede its flow. Past a teahouse, water lilies, and tubbed iris and across a wooden zigzag footbridge, the path continues under a willow's umbrella shape. It winds around the third lake past azaleas and rhododendrons by a smaller, steeper watercourse (drainage from the first pond can be alternated to follow a long, meandering route or this short, steep falls) under blue atlas cedars. The circular path passes beneath a small bluff before regaining the higher ground at the first pool. Besides meticulously pruned shrubs, the garden is noteworthy for its wide lawns and lavish use of space, carefully composed views on the sloping site, picturesque water features, and fine trees: a grove of *Trachycarpus fortunei* palms near the entrance, some Sierra redwoods, and many flowering ornamentals. (Kelly Park Japanese Friendship Garden, entered from a gate on Senter Rd. between E. Alma and Phelan aves.; open 10:00 a.m. to sunset; free admission; telephone 408-295-8383.)

THE
PENINSULA
BRIEFLY
NOTED

ear San Francisco Creek in Menlo Park, the shops, restaurants, and galleries of the ALLIED ARTS GUILD are connected by a series of small courtyards. Although an entry garden's roses, bedding plants, and trellis gesture toward an English cottage style, the guild's true gem is its "court of abundance," with citrus trees in box-hedged beds symmetrically plotted around a brick and ceramic tile fountain. Yellow pansies, white daisies, and chartreuse leaves and orange fruit of citrus stand up to strong sun intensified by the beige walls and red tile roofs of buildings (designed by Pedro de Lemos and Gardner Daily in a "primitive California Spanish" style in the late 1920s) enclosing the courtyard. In the Spanish manner, tubbed plants in unmatched pots line brick paths. The gardens and shops of this craft-oriented complex are perhaps a local resource only but are no less valuable for that. (Allied Arts Guild, 75 Arbor Rd. at Cambridge St., Menlo Park; open Monday through Saturday 10:00 a.m. to 5:00 p.m.)

Not far away in Palo Alto, the ELIZABETH F. GAMBLE GARDEN CENTER offers a more purely horticultural community resource. On a small estate surrounding a 1902 home and carriage house, the garden center has a resident horticulturist and large volunteer staff, library, educational programs, tours, and master gardener's programs. The estate has been renovated to preserve existing large trees and create new bulb and flower courtyards. Defined by low lattice fences painted forest green, with brick paths throughout, the installations provide a trim, unified look and are simply planted, for example, with the fuzzy gray lamb's ear, lavender salvia, roses, and *Tanacetum haradjani* around a small circular lawn. The 2.3 acres contain several gardens with flowering shrubs and vines and the plots of a master gardener demonstration garden. The site's diverse activities seem to make it almost a model local gardening center. (Elizabeth F. Gamble Garden Center, 1431 Waverley St., Palo

Alto; gardens open daily with free admission; office hours are weekdays, 9:00 a.m. to 12:00 noon; telephone 415-329-1356.)

The trees of San Mateo's Central Park are designated the SAN MATEO ARBORETUM, although the park has many uses. The large trees, many labeled, include oaks (*Quercus agrifolia* and *Q. lobata*), Canary Island and Senegal date palms, evergreens (large coast redwoods, a Spanish fir [*Abies pinsapo*], and a Lawson's cypress), eucalyptus, and deciduous black walnut and ginkgo. Large bunya bunya, Atlantic cedar, and Moreton Bay fig trees shade a sand-filled children's play area. (Central Park, El Camino Real at 5th Ave., San Mateo; open 6:00 a.m. to 10:00 p.m.)

Central Park also contains a JAPANESE GARDEN, designed by Nagao Sakurai and dedicated in 1966. A gate opens into a mostly level garden designed in the stroll style. Black pines pruned in the planes of the snow-holding pattern hew to aesthetic convention despite its lack of function in a snowless climate. As is not uncommon with Japanese gardens in California, dubious siting works against intended effect; the fenced garden cannot altogether overcome out-of-scale high-rise buildings near the park.

Azaleas, pink and white camellias, blue and lavender cineraria, a flowering cherry, and the salmon-pink of a fine red horsechestnut provide some color among a foliar surface primarily composed of greens and dark purples. A teahouse and pavilion (the latter containing a map and plant list) overlook the garden's pond, into which two small waterfalls drain. The garden contains several stone lanterns—*takara, yukimi, oribe,* and *funatsuki-ishi* types—and a river stone beach slopes down to the koi-filled pond. (San Mateo Japanese Garden in Central Park, open weekdays 8:00 a.m. to 4:00 p.m., weekends 11:00 a.m. to 5:00 p.m. Admission free. Telephone 415-377-4700.)

X
San Francisco
Bay Area
East

UNIVERSITY OF
CALIFORNIA
BOTANICAL
GARDEN

Although now located in Strawberry Canyon high above the Berkeley campus, the University of California Botanical Garden initially occupied a site near the present Moffitt Undergraduate Library. In 1891, Edward Lee Greene, a botany professor, began a botanical garden to provide living plants for university teaching and research. The early collection specialized in *Nicotiana* (whose best-known species is *N. tabacum*, the tobacco plant), on which genus a later director, T. Harper Goodspeed, published the definitive work.

In the 1920s, the university's growth forced the botanical garden to relocate. Goodspeed convinced the university that a site in Strawberry Canyon east of campus would be ideal. The university owned 400 acres in the canyon, and the property had remained relatively undisturbed biologically. Moreover, because of its topography, the canyon drew cool, humid, marine air across the bay from the Golden Gate, moderating summer and winter extremes to permit cultivation of a wide range of plants. The botanical garden began to move to its present site in 1926. Professor J. W. Gregg of the university's Department of Landscape Design prepared a plan reflecting Goodspeed's decision to plant not according to botanical taxonomy—the customary arrangement for botanical gardens—but by geographic origin.

Shortly after settling into its new site, the botanical garden acquired over a thousand rhododendrons, many of which survive as large specimens in the Asian section. The acquisition was later strengthened by a plant-gathering expedition to China by Joseph F. Rock, a pioneer in introducing Asian rhododendrons to the West. It inaugurated a tradition of botanical experts and horticultural patrons whose efforts and contributions helped develop the botanical garden. Later expeditions included several South American explorations of Andean flora, recorded in Goodspeed's *Plant Hunters in the Andes* (1961).

A glimpse of the Asian section, University of California Botanical Garden

The botanical garden continues to be involved in traditional pursuits: collecting, documenting, and preserving new and rare plants; educating students and the public; scientific research; exchanging seeds and materials with other botanic gardens; and the cultivation, introduction, and display of living plants, today comprising more than 10,000 species on thirty-three acres. The site's canyon topography and elevation between 625 and 890 feet provide a variety of exposures, and the site receives an average annual rainfall of twenty-six inches, with cool, wet winters and dry summers.

One benefit in visiting a university botanical garden, especially one as large and well established as Berkeley's, is that nearly all plants are accurately labeled. The drawback of such compendious erudition, however, is that it is impossible to see everything, much less to describe it, so this rendering of the garden's wealth will necessarily have to pick and choose. Following the course of Strawberry Creek (which divides the garden roughly into upper and lower sections) will lead through most of the garden.

At the top of the creek in the Asian area, during April a rare *Paulownia glabrata* tree sends out trumpet flowers resembling the lavender of the jacaranda, fewer in number but larger in size. Fed by a small waterfall, a Japanese pond drains into a gorge lined by the old rhododendrons for which this garden is famed: *Rhododendron falconeri*, from Shutan; *R. arboreum* from India and Ceylon; and *R. delavayi* from Yunnan, China, to name only a few. The rhododendrons bloom in unexpectedly vivid colors under mature coast redwoods, Monterey pines, and smaller evergreens of exceptional beauty, such as the weeping, blue-green *Taiwania cryptomerioides*. Several Chinese dawn redwoods shade a *Paeonia suffruticosa* from China's Hubei province, a tree peony whose showy, blush-pink blooms nearly match those of the rhododendrons for size and beauty.

At the bottom of the canyon past two large Sierra redwoods, the garden changes abruptly to a cycad and palm area. It is a reminder that this site, from which cold air drains, remains free of hard frosts even if cool and wet for much of the winter. Besides familiar cold winter palms— *Phoenix*, *Trachycarpus* (though *T. martianus* and *T. wagnerianus* are rarely seen), *Rhapis*, and *Washingtonia* species—the indoor Tropical House displays a few more tropical palms in a warm glasshouse. Consistent with a specialty of this botanical garden—plants of economic value—the Tropical House also displays edible tropical plants, such as the Burmese dwarf banana (*Musa rubra*); cinnamon (*Cinnamomum zeylanicum*), whose bark provides the spice; and Arabian coffee (*Coffea arabica*), a surprisingly

_____

ornamental plant whose shiny green leaves when new are tinged a rusty hue.

The North American section next to the palm house displays flowering plants—purple-flowered *Tradescantia hirsutiflora* from South Carolina and a white-flowered beach plum (*Prunus maritima*) from Rhode Island— under a New Jersey bear oak (*Quercus ilicifolia*) and a Massachusetts paper birch (*Betula papyrifera*). Up the hill, an herb garden offers a selection of

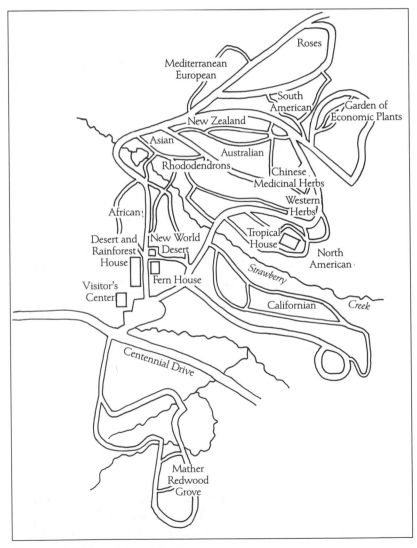

University of California Botanical Garden

Western and Chinese medicinal herbs. Above the herb garden, an Australian section contains many plants that have become part of the California landscape: eucalyptus, melaleuca, and callistemon. New Zealand contributes less familiar, distinctive plants, such as _Casuarina torulosa_, a 25-foot, open tree with needles like a pine but colored with a red-purple tinge; an exceptional weeping evergreen, _Dacrydium cupressinum_; and the small, true-blue flowers of "Chatham Island forget-me-not" (_Myosotidium hortensia_) held above tropical, curly leaves.

Farther up the slope, a South American section offers assorted _Puyas_: _P. hamata_, _P. dyckioides_, and _P. coriaceae_. All but one of 160 Puya species originates in high Andean elevations, and the genus is noteworthy for its flowers, which bloom in some of the most vivid color combinations of any plants in the world. Here also grows _Calceolaria salicifolia_, resembling the horticultural variety but with much smaller bright yellow flowers. At the top of the property a "garden of old roses," with superb views down the canyon to the bay and the Golden Gate Bridge, attempts to illustrate the history and genealogy of roses. Near the roses, also at high elevation, a "Mediterranean-European" garden presents not only the usual cistus, lavenders, and rosemary but also the chartreuse-flowered _Euphorbia dendroides_ from Italy and magenta _Gladiolus byzantinus_ from Tunisia. It also offers trans-Alpine and central European natives (e.g., Austrian _Geum montanum_, Swiss _Helleborus foetida_, and Hungarian _Rosa canina_) and the blue-purple, bell-shaped flowers prolifically furnished by the Norwegian _Campanula persicifolia_, all particularly fine in the spring.

North of Strawberry Creek, nearest the garden entrance, a southwestern exposure supports three dry gardens, representing southern Africa, the New World Desert, and California. Several towering cactus species emerge from the New World Desert's thickly planted beds. These columnar cacti include the night-blooming _Cereus peruvianus_ and _C. jamacaru_ from South America; _Trichocereus pascana_, whose seven-foot column resembles a saguaro, its chartreuse flesh bristling with gray spines; and the Bolivian _T. terschekii_, twenty feet tall and clothed in a pattern of menacing hairpin spines. The area features _Trichocereus_ and many other South American cacti collected during the Andean expeditions from 1935 to 1958.

Above the New World Desert, the southern Africa section overflows with aloes, succulents, ice plant ground covers, euphorbias, grasses, and especially with flowering bulbs: pale gold _Gladiolus carneus_, salmon _Ammocharis tinneana_, and clear pink _Watsonia vanderspuyae_. It also displays dark pink flower towers of *Echium wildpretii* and lavender *E. strictum*, both quite different from their blue-flowered relative, the pride of Madeira.

The University of California Botanical Garden also has a large California section, containing more than one quarter of the state's native plant species, organized by region and habitat. The five-acre Stephen Mather Redwood Grove, planted in 1936, commemorates a University of California graduate who became the first director of the National Park Service. It features a coast redwood grove and associated flora, with a "Miocene Sequoia Forest area" for descendants of plants that grew with redwoods in ancient times. (A caveat: although this area's valid educational and research purposes are to be respected, no one who has not visited a native stand of old growth redwoods should allow themselves to forgo that fine experience on the strength of a walk through the young trees of this small, developed grove, noisy with traffic.)

The University of California Botanical Garden is an erudite, compendious collection. As the specimens named here only suggest, it is full of rare plants known only to experts or connoisseurs. The garden takes advantage of an exceptional site, with views down a canyon thickly wooded by oak, redwood, and Monterey pine, across the San Francisco Bay, and through the Golden Gate to the Pacific Ocean. It successfully balances its educational and scientific purposes with aesthetic display, amply proving that there need be no insurmountable conflict between utility and beauty. The garden likewise largely succeeds in integrating individual plants into a coherent scheme. There is no substitute for quality, and this is one of the finest gardens of its kind in California.

(University of California Botanical Garden, Centennial Dr. in Strawberry Canyon, Berkeley, above the UC Berkeley Stadium and below the Lawrence Hall of Science. Free admission; open 9:00 a.m. to 4:45 p.m.; closed Christmas Day. Tours are offered Saturdays and Sundays at 1:30 p.m.; there is also a book and plant store. Telephone: 415-642-3343.)

BLAKE GARDEN

The Blake House and Garden occupy eleven acres in the Berkeley Hills overlooking the Golden Gate and San Francisco Bay. Designed by Walter Bliss, the house was one of two built in the early 1920s by Anson and Edwin Blake on family property. Anson Blake's wife, Anita Day Symmes Blake, and her sister, Mabel Symmes, developed the garden over several decades into the distinct areas that still characterize the landscaping. In 1962, after Anita Blake's death, the UC Berkeley Department of Landscape Architecture assumed control of the property, which had been deeded to the university five years earlier. Eventually the house was prepared for the university president's use, and it remains private.

The public may, however, visit the large, varied gardens surrounding the house. A small but choice formal garden stretches along a reflecting pool and lawn perpendicular to the house, shaded by an allée of southern magnolias, their trunks and branches patched with pale green moss. The axis terminates in a vine-covered rock grotto, behind which a curving staircase ascends to a terrace between twin columnar yews. A pond drains from the grotto along a blue tile spillway into a reflecting pool filled with water lilies. Modest scale restrains these epic-sounding formal features from any sort of oppressive grandeur. The formal garden's level symmetry contrasts with precipitous grades and naturalistic planting elsewhere on the property.

Even the formal garden, despite its boundary hedges of red-tipped *Syzygium paniculatum*, cannot be described as overly disciplined. Behind the hedges, small paths circulate around miniature statuary, some of it Oriental in theme, and beds display camellias, azaleas, ginger, ferns, rhododendrons, agapanthus, and other flowering plants under small *Azara microphylla* and *Deutzia taiwanensis* trees. Past twin lilies (*Doryanthes palmeri*) west of the formal garden, callas, Tasmanian tree ferns, and clivia grow against the Spanish-style facade of the house.

Reflecting pool and magnolia allée, Blake Garden

North of the formal garden, looming like a dark, enchanted forest, a coast redwood grove follows the bed of a slow creek that forms several ponds and bogs. A path, springy with rust-colored redwood litter, descends through underplanted sword ferns, sorrel, and shade plants like camellia, calla, and clivia. Despite the exotics, the creek recalls the original vegetation of the Berkeley Hills, which at one time supported native stands of coast redwood. Below the house, the creek emerges from arboreal gloom into a clearing containing the rare *Brugmansia sanguinea*, a Peruvian shrub bearing scarlet, bell-shaped flowers in the spring.

Directly beneath the house's western exposure, the sunniest part of the garden catches views of the San Francisco skyline and the Golden Gate on which it would be difficult to improve. The steep slope descends to a kidney-shaped lawn surrounded by beds of plants accustomed to hot, relatively dry conditions: several irises, Spanish lavender, California poppies, salvia, and just past a low-growing oak, a fine group of pride of Madeira, not far from its close relative, tower of jewels (*Echium wildpretti*), which bears a single spike of dark rose flowers.

To the south of the house another lawn is bounded by a lilac vine (*Hardenbergia comptoniana*) trained on arching supports into a tunnel of purple and lavender flowers that leads to another formal area. Under eucalyptus, melaleuca, loquat, avocado, and *Magnolia delavayi* are *Iochroma cyaneum* and beds of magenta and purple cineraria daisies. The Blake Garden, quiet and secluded and well off the tourist route, becomes especially fine on a foggy or slightly wet day in spring, when water drips, leaves glisten, and sun breaks through the clouds to illuminate the colors of the flowers.

(Enter the Blake House and Garden at 70 Rincon Rd., Kensington. Free admission and parking. Open Monday through Friday 8:00 a.m. to 4:30 p.m.; closed weekends and holidays. It is unwise to approach without an excellent map, as straight streets are unknown in this hillside area. For tours and information, telephone 415-524-2449.)

TILDEN
REGIONAL PARK
BOTANIC GARDEN

Through good fortune or good planning, the San Francisco Bay area finds itself ringed with regional parks, watersheds, and other protected lands. Not only do these areas provide recreation or clean water but they also help to preserve the landscape and views that remain vital to a regional identity. Open space also supports specialized uses whose importance extends beyond a single locality. The Botanic Garden in Tilden Regional Park is one such facility, devoted to native plant species from ten floral regions of California.

The garden traces its origin to a research program on California native plants conducted by the U.S. Forest Service in Berkeley. Its nursery reminded Howard McMinn, a Mills College professor of botany, that northern California had no botanic garden for California native plants. In 1938, McMinn brought the East Bay Regional Park District and the Forest Service together, the former providing land and the latter providing its native plant collection. Construction began in Wildcat Canyon in the Berkeley Hills in 1940 under the direction of James Roof. After the interruption of World War II, the garden's clearance and development slowed considerably, even though population growth in the 1950s continued to endanger native species. From 1952 to 1962, Roof undertook expeditions to collect native plants all over California, from San Diego County to the Siskiyou Mountains.

The current plan divides the garden into sections representing ten floral and geographic provinces. (Each section identifies plants with a different color label, sometimes also giving details about the county of origin or elevation.) At an elevation of 940 feet, the garden lies near the northern boundary for growing many southern California species and likewise near the southern limit for northern California species. The site also lies at the edge of the fog belt, moderating extremes of humidity and temperature and increasing the number of species cultivated here.

Wildcat Creek roughly bisects the seven-acre site, with the Sea Bluff section and the forested floral provinces of the Redwood, Sierran, and Pacific Rain Forest sections west of the creek, and to the east the Franciscan, Santa Lucia, Valley, Channel Island, Southern California, and Shasta Cascade sections. Since the garden has several thousand plants, the following descriptions will sketch only a few plant species from some of the sections. Nearest the entrance and visitor's center, plants from six inland northern counties, the Shasta Cascade section, include the Engelmann spruce (*Picea engelmannii*), the weeping or Brewer spruce (*P. brewerana*), the blackfruit dogwood (*Cornus sessilis*), the pale gold Siskiyou iris (*Iris bracteata*), and purple Del Norte iris (*I. innominata*).

The Tilden Botanic Garden is known for its Sierran meadow of plants native to elevations above 6,000 feet in the Sierra Nevada. Spring-blooming species include the lavender triplet lily (*Triteleia laxa*) from Tuolumne County and the yellow mariposa tulip (*Calochortus luteus*), whose bell flower has a slightly chartreuse cast. The Sierran section would not be complete without a grove of big trees (*Sequoiadendron giganteum*), which are close enough to their coast redwood cousins for comparison of the trees that inspire the forestry superlatives, tallest, oldest, biggest.

Native rhododendrons, the California rose bay (*Rhododendron macrophyllum*) and the Western azalea (*R. occidentale*), typify the Pacific Rainforest section of north coast plants. Descending a steep trail and crossing Wildcat Creek leads to the quite different Santa Lucia section, comprising coastal counties from Santa Barbara to Santa Cruz. Although the coast redwood's native range extends well into this region, it is also known for the bristlecone fir (*Abies bracteata pinaceae*), the dark blue-flowered Nipomo ceanothus (*C. impressus*), and "rock lettuce" (*Dudleya caespitosa*), a seacliff plant sending out wide, maplelike leaves and a flower spike.

In the Channel Islands section, the offshore islands of southern California contribute Santa Cruz ironwood and the showy island bush poppy (*Dendromecon harfordii*) that sends out brilliant single yellow flowers. The Southern California section supports the Cuyamaca cypress (*Cupressus stephensonii*) from its restricted range on the southwest slope of Cuyamaca Peak in San Diego County and the gray-green, needle-tipped spears of *Yucca whipplei* from Ventura County. The most vivid flowers of this section appear on the giant coreopsis (*Coreopsis gigantea*), which bears dozens of brilliant yellow daisy flowers above lacy foliage.

Terraces and California native plants, Tilden Regional Park Botanic Garden

The botanic garden specializes in ceanothus and manzanita (*Arctostaphylos*), with nearly complete collections of these two genera. It is difficult to give more than a suggestion of the wealth of plants in the Tilden garden; several sections and subsections have not been mentioned here. The garden is uncrowded, well organized, and full of unusual plants. If some are dormant or out of bloom during a given season, others will offer persuasive evidence of the beauty and interest of California native plants. The fine trees at the Tilden Botanic Garden are worthwhile all year, and in few other places can so much of California's botanical patrimony be viewed so easily.

(Tilden Regional Park Botanic Garden, Wildcat Canyon Rd. near South Park Dr., is open 10:00 a.m. to 5:00 p.m. Free admission; daily tours are provided during summer months; group tours by appointment. For information, telephone 415-841-8732.)

OAKLAND
GARDENS

Oakland's city center has a pair of rooftop gardens. Although significant as engineering, the KAISER CENTER ROOF GARDEN seems hardly more than a novelty, a blandly landscaped mezzanine to neighboring office towers. A posted landscape plan marks ten flower beds, a lake, and fountain and lists small trees and flowering shrubs planted with beds of annuals at the edges of seating areas and paths that curve around wide lawns. (An elevator to the roof garden above the parking structure is behind the Kaiser Center at Harrison and 20th sts.)

A more adventurous roof garden at the OAKLAND MUSEUM (the 1969 building is by Kevin Roche, John Dinkeloo & Associates, with landscaping by Dan Kiley and Geraldine Knight Scott) places three levels of concrete planters, terraces, and staircases above the street. Designed to echo the hanging gardens of antiquity as well as to relieve museum fatigue, the raised beds support screens, hedges, and mass plantings of pittosporum, leptospermum, and hawthorn, beds of bergenia, California poppies, and geranium, and allées of evergreen pears. Terraces enclose contemporary sculpture (e.g., John Mason's *Yellow Cross Form* [1966]). Stairs from museum roof terraces slope down to a sunken sculpture garden in a lawn shaded by mature trees. Capably executed and well used by the public, the sunken garden excites children to a frenzy. The top of the roof terrace, surrounding a planting of olives, reveals fine views of the Oakland Hills, downtown, and Lake Merritt. (The museum, entered from Tenth and Oak, is open Wednesdays through Saturdays 10:00 a.m. to 5:00 p.m. and Sundays 12:00 p.m. to 7:00 p.m.; closed Mondays and Tuesdays. Telephone 415-273-3401.)

On a peninsula extending into Lake Merritt, the LAKESIDE HORTICULTURAL CENTER contains several small gardens, some sponsored by community horticultural societies, such as the hundreds of

A downtown palmetum, Lakeside Horticultural Center, Oakland

dahlias near the entrance which are cultivated by the American Dahlia Society. Besides its fine, large trees, the center includes a collection of rhododendrons, fuchsias, and azaleas; a small Japanese garden; a citrus grove; a lath house sheltering cymbidium orchids, epiphyllum, and tree ferns; a dry garden of cactus, yucca, aloe, and agave; beds devoted to bearded irises, chrysanthemums, and spring bulbs; and a "Resource Garden," demonstrating "the use of composted sewage sludge with water-saving plants and conservation irrigation."

Since 1982, a palmetum maintained by the Northern California Chapter of the International Palm Society has given the Lakeside Center a collection of distinction, the most inclusive outdoor palm collection north of Santa Barbara. Besides familiar palms, the palmetum proves that many rare species can prosper in the Bay area: *Trachycarpus takil* and *T. wagnerianus; Parajubea cocoides, Ceroxylon hexandrum,* and *C. quindiuense* from the Andes of South America; *Ravenea glauca* from Malagasy; *Livistona drudei* from Australia; *Arenga engleri* from Taiwan; and many others. Planted with coral trees, banana (*Musa basjoo* from the Ryukyu Islands), black tree fern (*Cyathea medullaris*), and other tropical and subtropical species, the labeled, well-maintained, compact palmetum presents an impressive array of cool-climate palms. (Lakeside Horticultural Center, 666 Bellevue, Oakland. Free admission; open Monday through Friday 10:00 a.m. to 3:00 p.m.; Saturday and Sunday, May 1 to October 31, 10:00 a.m. to 5:00 p.m.; Saturday and Sunday, November 1 to April 30, 10:00 a.m. to 4:00 p.m.)

Beneath an incense cedar allée, a staircase descends past an amphitheater of curving rose beds beneath massive Italian stone pines at the MORCOMB AMPHITHEATER OF ROSES. A water staircase meets a reflecting pool at a second axis that begins in a circular plateau of roses enclosed by junipers that add their pungence to the flowers' sweet fragrance. The second axis slopes past the reflecting pool and coast redwoods to twin pavilions marking the lower entrance at Jean Street. There a plaque indicates that the seven-acre rose garden, designed by landscape architect Arthur Cobbledick, dates from 1937. The several thousand shrub roses, many labeled, begin to bloom late—in early May—because the site is shaded by tall oaks and evergreens. Majestic Italian stone pines above the amphitheater come close to stealing the show from the roses. (Open daily from dawn to dusk east of downtown Oakland, the Morcomb Amphitheater of Roses can be entered at Vernon and Monte Vista or between the two pavilions from 700 Jean St.)

Dunsmuir House, Oakland

Viewed from below, the grand siting and phantasmagoric, see-through gilded spires of the OAKLAND MORMON TEMPLE can be unforgettable, almost a hazard to safe freeway driving. Designed by Harold Burton, completed in 1964, and sheathed with gleaming Sierra white granite, the windowless, towering edifice has a Himalayan, over-the-rainbow quality that is both noble and unforgiving. Sloping away from the temple, a fountain cascades slowly down a stone streambed crossed by Oriental-style metal bridges between beds of annuals, privet and holly hedges, and a *Washingtonia robusta* palm allée. Six Canary Island palms cross the facade, with two more where the *Washingtonias* end at the entry gate. The palms' exoticism, architectural quality, and formal placement reiterate some of the temple building's own design tensions. Although a parking lot occupies much of the eighteen-acre site and garden terraces surrounding the temple itself were torn up for renovation at the time of this writing, the temple gardens may merit a closer look when reopened. (Oakland Temple, Church of Jesus Christ of Latter Day Saints, 4770 Lincoln Ave., Oakland; visitors center open 9:00 a.m. to 9:00 p.m. daily; telephone 415-531-1475.)

At Oakland's southern border, DUNSMUIR HOUSE AND GARDENS preserves an estate built by Alexander Dunsmuir, heir to a British Columbia mining and lumber fortune. After a twenty-year liaison, Dunsmuir married Josephine Wallace and built a white colonial revival mansion for her as a wedding gift in 1899. Less than six weeks later, while on their honeymoon, Alexander died; Josephine herself would live less than eighteen months longer. San Francisco businessman and civic leader I. W. Hellman, Jr., purchased the property in 1906 as a summer home for his large family, in whose hands the estate remained until the City of Oakland acquired it in the 1950s.

Once far larger, today the estate comprises about forty acres at the bottom of a curving valley formed by the Hayward fault, which creates the "sag pond" overlooked by a gazebo and lined by ornamental trees and bog plants. Up a slope on a southwest exposure is a dry garden crowded with beautifully kept cacti, agave, aloes, and succulents. The valley widens beyond a line of statuesque Monterey pines and incense cedars, and the house presides over a vista reflecting the influence of John McLaren, who assisted the Hellmans in landscaping the site. The lavish lawn, large trees, and forested border resemble McLaren's work at the Villa Montalvo in Saratoga and throughout Golden Gate Park.

Designed by Eugene Freeman, the two-and-one-half-story mansion surveys the sweeping lawn and imposing trees from a veranda under a portico of three massive Corinthian columns. The vast lawn curves south under hillsides forested with eucalyptus, bunya bunya, deodar and atlas cedars, California bay laurel, and pittosporum, ending where a jacaranda shades a bed of purple, lavender, and gold bearded iris. The lawn, curving drives and borders, huge trees, and water running through the protected valley alongside the imposing mansion preserve an informal but opulent country estate. (Dunsmuir House, 2960 Peralta Oaks Court, Oakland. Grounds open Monday through Friday 9:00 a.m. to 3:30 p.m.; house tours Sundays and Wednesdays. For information on Christmas programs, concerts, and tours, telephone 415-562-0328.)

J ohn Muir spent most of each year making a living as a fruit rancher in a domestic, even idyllic estate in the Alhambra Valley, despite his consistently argued preference for wild over tamed nature. (Positive and progressive in its time, that position may have hampered later environmental thinking. Outside forces now affect wilderness so closely that it must be artificially managed to remain "wild." Calling wilderness sacred may help preserve it, but it is possible that it leaves the secularized, everyday environment—the one people live in, and the one that kills us when we poison it—vulnerable to mistreatment. And other landscapes, natural even if they are not wild, also merit protection: the crucial resource of "working landscapes" that are productive, beautiful, and symbolic of a valuable way of life.)

Muir's father-in-law, Dr. John Strenzel, was an influential figure in California horticulture. Muir managed Strenzel's and his own ranches and raised peaches, cherries, pears, and grapes on 2,600 acres, leaving only a few months a year for his cherished High Sierra rambles. The nine-acre JOHN MUIR NATIONAL HISTORIC SITE preserves Muir's house (which Strenzel built in 1882 and Muir occupied with his family from 1890 to 1914) and the 1849 Vicente Martinez Adobe. A "Victorian garden" of trees dating from Muir's time surrounds the home; a pair of *Washingtonia filifera* palms flank the front door in typical period style, framing views of the orchards, ornamental trees, and the valley. A veranda and sunroom overlook a small lawn and flower beds, and a self-guided tour leads through vineyards (zinfandel, muscat, and tokay grapes) and orchards (prune, walnut, apricot, pear, peach, fig, almond, and cherry) to the Martinez Adobe. The gardens are a secondary emphasis, but exhibits inside the house present Muir's life and influence well, and the orchards are unusual, a remnant of Muir's own working landscape. (John Muir Historic Site, Alhambra Ave. at State Highway 4, Martinez;

John Muir National Historic Site, Martinez

open 10:00 a.m. to 4:30 p.m. except Thanksgiving, Christmas, and New Year's Day; adult admission $1.00. Telephone 415-228-8860.)

The University of California, Berkeley, campus has some fine trees, including a grove of *Eucalyptus globulus* (some nearly 200 feet high) well over a century old. Like the other University of California campuses, Berkeley has seen great changes in the 1980s, but *Trees of the Berkeley Campus* (1976, available from the U.C. Cooperative Extension) remains informative, particularly as there appears to be no labeling program for campus planting.

North of campus, the City of Berkeley maintains a small but choice rose garden. Yet another hillside garden sited to take maximum advantage of a view of San Francisco, the Golden Gate, and the distant Marin mountains, the BERKELEY MUNICIPAL ROSE GARDEN can present a spectacle in late afternoon or sunset. Carved into a natural amphitheater by the Works Project Administration from 1933 to 1937 and built of local stone, the crescent terraces step down beneath coast redwoods and incense cedars. Creeping fig covers western exposures of raised beds, making a green surface when viewed from the bottom of the garden where Codornices Creek drains into a small reflecting pond. Halfway down the garden a graceful, semicircular wooden trellis (which has been credited—on undocumented evidence—to the legendary local architect Bernard Maybeck, who did live and work in this district) follows the curve of the beds, supporting the clear yellow "Golden Showers" and the richly dark red "Étoile de Hollande," among many others.

The garden's shrub roses are estimated to number between three and four thousand plants. In 1985, the terraces were replanted to the original 1937 color scheme. About the first of May such well-chosen, labeled roses as the pale pink "Pristine," fragrant "Sutter's Gold," dark red "San Antonio," and clear white, old-fashioned "Blanc Double de Coubert" come into their first bloom. (Berkeley Municipal Rose Garden, open dawn to dusk, is on Euclid Ave. across from Cordonices Park.)

It is no criticism to say that the most exceptional thing about the HAYWARD JAPANESE GARDEN is its unusual site on a peninsular mesa high above San Lorenzo Creek. The 3.5-acre Botany Grounds, after housing a high school agricultural studies program for nearly sixty years, was acquired for park use in 1962. Designed and constructed in 1980 by Kimio Kimura, the Japanese garden is an inspired use of this remarkable site. Dense riparian boscage screens surrounding buildings yet casts no shade on the Japanese garden, creating a feeling of simultaneous enclosure and exposure. The chasm of the San Lorenzo Creek bed many feet below on nearly every side emphasizes the sense of remoteness.

Two large oaks near the entrance and a spreading Italian stone pine inside form orienting landmarks as paved paths meander before finally reaching a group of small wooden structures. Crafted in traditional styles, these pavilions present views over the creek's lushly wooded, precipitous banks and a small lake with a waterfall, zigzag bridge, and river stone beach. Many plants, heavily pruned in the Japanese manner, reflect not only a high level of maintenance but also contrast sharply with the untrammeled vegetation that curtains the far edges of the garden.

Juxtaposing horticulture with wilderness so starkly may serve to correct one of the many cultural misreadings to which the Japanese garden style falls prey in the United States. California seems especially prone to sentimentalism on this score, imagining that the Japanese garden reproduces or somehow approximates nature. In fact, no more artificial techniques could be imagined than those used in the Japanese garden. The result seems "natural" only by reference to the formal gardens of France, Italy, or the Iberian peninsula but ceases to be so when compared— a comparison the Hayward Japanese garden, with refreshing candor, virtually forces one to make—to nature itself. (Hayward Japanese Garden, Botany Grounds Park, Hayward. Open daily 10:00 a.m. to 4:00 p.m. Telephone 415-881-6715. Visitors may park on City Center Dr. and follow signs to the Japanese garden on foot, or approach from Crescent Ave.)

XI
North Coast

MENDOCINO COAST BOTANICAL GARDENS

Even at the height of summer, a thick onshore cloud cover often shrouds the north coast. The marine layer that keeps the redwoods green also hides the sun, and Fort Bragg often reports the coolest summer temperatures in California. A white sky dominates the Mendocino Coast Botanical Gardens during the summer, admitting light but not much sun during what is elsewhere the hottest part of the year. In 1961, Ernest and Betty Schoefer purchased property here that satisfied several requirements: it had both ocean and highway frontage, year-round water from Digger Creek, flat terrain with forest cover to shelter plants from the stiff ocean wind, and a humid climate with cool summers and fairly mild winters. The site, in other words, offered ideal conditions for cool-weather, coastal horticulture.

Retired nursery owners, the Schoefers spent sixteen years developing, planting, and operating the site as a private botanical garden until 1977. After five years of intervening ownership, in 1982, the California Coastal Conservancy purchased twelve acres and a five-acre coastal access easement and transferred the parcel to the Mendocino Recreation and Park District. Today a nonprofit corporation operates the garden, and in 1990, the Coastal Conservancy purchased thirty-five more acres, to be integrated into the expanding botanical garden. As did the Schoefers, plant fanciers continue to come to the Fort Bragg area to enjoy a climate ideal for fuchsias, begonias, and rhododendrons. With strong support from the community and from these experts, who have donated major plant collections, the Mendocino Coast Botanical Gardens has grown into one of the state's most significant and beautiful public gardens.

The garden has three distinct areas. Nearest the entrance, the most finished area devotes specialized sections to perennials, camellias, ivy, roses, heather, succulents, and Mediterranean plants. It also displays rhododendrons, a genus planted throughout the property which provides a transition into the second area, a naturalistic fern canyon under a Bishop pine forest along Digger Creek. In the third area, a coastal bluff whose tree cover changes to the shore pine capable of surviving in harsh conditions, a rugged landscape overlooks the Pacific Ocean crashing on a rocky, dramatic coastline.

Hence the botanical garden ranges from the exotic to the native, from a horticulturally finished perennial area to one where the flora is largely untended, and from art to nature. The perennial garden sets an archipelago of island beds (like those associated with the designs of Alan Bloom) in a grass lawn. Some of these island beds emphasize foliage plants, with purple-leaved plums (*Prunus cerasifera* "Krauter Vesuvius") whose color matches the oval leaves of the low-growing smoke tree (*Cotinus coggygria* "Royal Purple"). A larger bed displays dwarf, prostrate, and contorted conifers, half a dozen cultivars of dwarf Japanese maple (*Acer palmatum dissectum*), and a weeping cedar of Lebanon (*Cedrus libani* "Glauca Pendula") that creeps along the ground, almost a vine.

Even under a dull sky, the perennial garden flowers colorfully through the summer and into the fall, with the ruby darkness of chocolate cosmos (*Cosmos atrosanguineus*), the deep, true blue of gentian sage (*Salvia patens*), and an outstanding *Convolvulus tricolor* "Rainbow Flash," whose single flower has a yellow center, a cream ring, and a dark blue and purple outer margin. Appearing throughout the perennial garden, dahlias are concentrated in their own bed near an adjacent Mediterranean garden. Dozens of Scottish heathers (*Calluna vulgaris*) bloom well into the fall on purple, rose, and lavender varieties such as "Beale's Red," "Spring Torch," and "Mayfair." Luxuriant reds, pinks, yellows, and whites of tuberous begonias, left to overwinter in the ground, appear just before the first rhododendrons.

This garden never leaves visitors very far from rhododendrons, as background plants as well as concentrated in distinct beds. Besides familiar hybrids such as "Loder's White," "Cynthia," and "Countess of Haddington," are the California natives (*Rhododendron occidentale* and *R. macrophyllum*) that grow wild on the north coast; tender *Vireya* species; and the most recent additions, endangered Asian big-leaved rhododendrons (e.g., *R.* "sino grande," *R. giganteum*, and *R. Macabeanum* "Nymans"). The genus *Rhododendron* provides one of the most exciting tales in the history of plant exploration, one with some chapters yet to be written. It is likewise notable for its breeding propensities: the genus contains more than

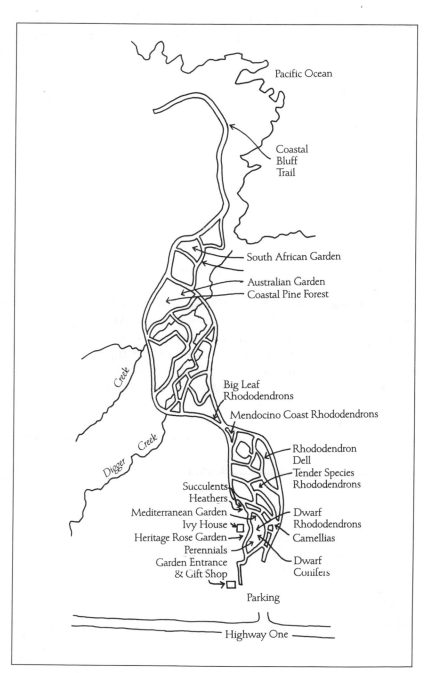

Pacific Ocean

Coastal
Bluff
Trail

South African Garden

Australian Garden
Coastal Pine Forest

Creek

Big Leaf
Rhododendrons

Mendocino Coast Rhododendrons

Digger Creek

Rhododendron
Dell

Tender Species
Rhododendrons

Succulents
Heathers

Mediterranean Garden
Ivy House
Heritage Rose Garden
Perennials
Garden Entrance
& Gift Shop

Dwarf
Rhododendrons
Camellias

Dwarf
Conifers

Parking

Highway One

Mendocino Coast Botanical Gardens

800 species, and the international register records 10,000 named varieties. Although varieties flower over several months in Fort Bragg, blooming usually peaks in April.

Just beyond the perennial garden is the Ivy House, an open-air structure sheltering over 400 ivies donated by the American Ivy Association, a standard reference collection said to be the world's largest. (Although there are only six ivy species, there are hundreds of named varieties, infinitely adaptable as vines, topiary, potted bonsai specimens, and even as small trees.) Near the Ivy House, a small "heritage rose garden" contains curiosities such as "Laneii," stems bristling with forests of thorns, and the prostrate *Rosa wichuraiana*, an evergreen species introduced from Japan in 1891. A superior Mediterranean garden displays a splendid crimson spot rock rose (*Cistus landanifer*) that blooms profusely during autumn, its single flowers bearing yellow stamens and a dark red spot near the base of each white petal. Spikes of a nearby blue salvia (*S. farinacea*) reveal a good deal of purple, and coral pink flowers with purple sepals hang from *S. coccinea*.

A small succulent garden contains many curiosities, such as *Aloe plicatilis*, whose straplike leaves fan laterally from two sides of a central growth point, a habit quite different from the aloe's usual star pattern. *Cotyledon orbiculata* "Ausana" produces curly, spatulate gray-green leaves and multiple bloom stalks hung with bright coral trumpet blossoms. The latter is only one of many vivid color combinations—hot pinks, pale lavenders, bright yellows, and tangerines—abounding in the succulent garden's flowers and fleshy stems.

The Mendocino Coast Botanical Gardens places fuchsias throughout the property but concentrates such varieties as the double red "Mephisto," the red and purple "Royal Purple," and the classic "Swingtime" in their own bed. The trail into a rhododendron dell mixes fuchsias with rhododendrons before reaching a fern canyon sheltered by Bishop pines (*Pinus muricata*). The Bishop pines not only protect the plants below from steady ocean winds but as summer fog condenses on their pine needles, it waters canyon vegetation drop by drop through rainless summers. Several paths meander along Digger Creek and through the canyon, whose ferns—mostly *Woodwardia*—keep company with blue-belled Australian creeper (*Sollya heterophylla*), false lily of the valley (*Maianthemum dilatatum*), and extensive new plantings of big-leafed rhododendrons.

As the trail proceeds past a new South African garden and through a stand of young, laterally branching Monterey cypress and shore pine (*Pinus contorta*), it finally attains a bluff with splendid views up and down the shingly beach and stony coastline. In season, migrating gray whales heave and puff offshore. The wind snaps; the waves crash, exposing the rock cliffs, layered black, brown, and green; the surf tosses up kelp and ocean smells; the bluff is cold and exposed, lonely but beautiful. Here you have left the garden and entered rudest nature, emphasizing the Mendocino Coast Botanical Garden's remarkable accomplishment: harmonizing plants and setting with unusual success in a not always friendly climate.

(Mendocino Coast Botanical Gardens, 18220 N. Highway 1, Fort Bragg. In summer, open 9:00 a.m. to 5:00 p.m.; from November to April, open 10:00 a.m. to 4:00 p.m.; closed Thanksgiving, Christmas, and New Year's Day. $5.00 adult admission. There is a small book and gift shop and a plant sale area. For information, telephone 707-964-4352.)

KORBEL
CHAMPAGNE
CELLARS
GARDEN

I t seems fitting that one of California's most unusual public gardens should be placed in one of its most beautiful regions. The Korbel Champagne Cellars occupy property in western Sonoma County along the Russian River, just where climate and terrain change from vineyard to forest. The western approach by River Road presents an especially fine view of the Korbel estate and its wooded surroundings: neat rows of bright green grapevines stretch out on a river plain flat as a table, framed by a shaggy, mountainous backdrop of rugged timberland. The West accustoms one to seeing an evergreen, mountainous landscape only at high altitudes. Yet here forests clothe the land near sea level as the Russian River slows down, twisting and turning, before it empties into the Pacific only a few miles away.

The marine influence also sets this garden apart. Winters here are cool and wet and summers sunny with hot days but cool nights, a fine climate for growing premium chardonnay, pinot noir, and chenin blanc grapes. It is equally fine for flower gardening, and it is extraordinary flowers that make the first impression at Korbel. Lining the winery's brick facade, a long floral border shines in hues bright enough to be seen from the highway. Its strong colors, however, only suggest the more nuanced effects of a garden restored and redesigned by Valerie Heck, a member of the family that owns Korbel, and by Phillip Robinson, who still supervises its care.

History is important here, an almost palpable presence. The main winery building dates from the nineteenth century, and the Korbel firm was established in 1862. Also built in the 1860s, a white frame "summer house" crests a small hill, shaded by second-growth redwoods and overlooking the river plain. There the Korbel family planted trees and roses, built terraces and fences, and otherwise ornamented the property. Still growing in the garden, for instance, is a linden tree that, according to family lore, the wife of one of the three founding Korbel brothers brought as a sapling from a spa in Czechoslovakia and planted here as a "lightning tree."

After 1906, however, the family no longer lived in the house, and the garden fell into disuse. Seventy years later, Valerie Heck and Phillip Robinson began their restoration. They knew that formerly the garden had been sunnier; the redwoods, cut in the mid-nineteenth century, had not yet regrown to their present substantial size. They also knew that somewhere underneath a cloak of vinca there had been a rose garden, whose restoration would draw on Robinson's background growing roses. As they cleared, they began to see the old garden's outlines: terraces, lawns, hedges, paths, and steps. Using resources at hand, gardeners renewed the neglected soil with pomace, the seeds, stems, pulp, and other organic matter left over from the winery's annual crush.

It would be inaccurate to call this very finished garden an English cottage garden. The paths are not straight; there are no walled or hedged enclosures and no dooryard; it is not flat; there are no rectangular beds and few fruit trees, vegetables, or herbs. Robinson instead conceives of it as a gigantic "Grandma garden," composed mainly of perennial flowering plants and the old roses in which he specializes. Close scrutiny, moreover, will detect the presence of exotics, rarities, and experimental plants. Perhaps most important, Robinson's expertise with floral color harmony and with contrasting the textures of foliage shows this garden decisively moving beyond the cottage garden's quaint constraints.

Partly because of the climate, whose cooling marine influence persists even at the height of summer, the Korbel garden contains plants seen only rarely in California—hostas, for instance. But this garden also blooms with choice flowering plants because an expert horticultural hand and aesthetic eye govern what fills it. The "chocolate cosmos" (_Cosmos atrosanguineus_), for instance, dark reddish-brown in color but clearly a cosmos in petal and shape, serves up a surprisingly true chocolate fragrance; summer poinsettia, _Euphorbia heterophylla_, a distant but recognizable cousin of the Christmas variety, offers a tiny bract of delicate coral hue.

Besides its rarities or keepsake varieties, the Korbel garden creates an impression of profusion and fertility. Robinson quotes Sackville-West on how to treat a flower bed: "Cram, cram, cram, every chink and cranny." It is not that the sight of bare earth offends the eye but rather that horticultural extravagance delights it. Nor is it that the Korbel garden, like any other, lacks obstacles that must be overcome: it is not large,

Roses, vineyards, and redwoods, Korbel Champagne Cellars

and the redwoods throw too much shade; it is sloping, with little level ground; and it is rainy and cool in winter, dry and hot in summer. It is rather that within these constraints, the planting creates an effect of command, facility, and artistry.

The garden overflows with all manner of plants: variegated Chinese maple (*Abutilon pictum "Thompsonii"*) rhyming with a variegated elderberry near the entry gate; white *Nicotiana*, purple basil, and wax begonias surrounding camellias in a "boat bed," tapering at both port and starboard ends; clematis, blue thistle (*Eryngium amethystinum*), snow-on-the-mountain, and a variegated *Euphorbia marginata*, a fragrant bed of white morning glory, lemon verbena, and strawberry geranium (*Saxifraga stolonifera*); and old-fashioned flowers like the white trumpets of foxglove, the miniature Viola "Magic," and the delightful "poor man's orchid" (*Schizanthus pinnatus*), speckled white and purple. There are even a few subtropicals: tree dahlias, a Polynesian elephant ear, and a potted "sensitive plant" (*Mimosa pudica*) shyly folding up when touched.

The paths, curving up and down as the elevation changes; vegetation spilling over borders; the scarcity of straight lines or hard edges; the color harmonies and foliar contrasts: these tendencies produce an effect distinctly informal yet highly finished. As Sackville-West advised, this garden plants "only the best things in it, and only the best forms of the best things, by which I mean that everything should be choice and chosen."

The rose garden makes the main exception to the principle of informality, presenting fine roses in the traditional manner, dressing up the beds with box hedges and decently clothing their naked canes. The roses include nineteenth-century varieties from Korbel family days—an old lemon-white Noisette, "Lamarque" (1830), for instance, and "Souvenir de la Malmaison" (1843), a pale "blush" pink Bourbon rose with a flat, saucerish flower—as well as twentieth-century hybrid teas. Examples of the latter include "Forty-Niner" (1949), an unusual bicolor with petals cherry red on top and yellow beneath, and the aptly named, deep red velvet "Night," also known as "Lady Sackville" (1930). The garden sports that curiosity, *Rosa chinensis viridifloria*, a variant of the ever-blooming Chinese species whose petals mutated into serrated, leafy sepals without a true flower, causing this "green rose" to be sometimes known, ominously, as *Rosa monstrosa*.

Here is a garden on the one hand rooted in its locality, with native coast redwood hedging the parking area and saplings shading a picnic deck near the wine-tasting rooms. The garden also lies hard by the business end of the winery; bundles of aerial tubes cross overhead, conveying juice to and fro on its journey to becoming sparkling wine. On the other hand, the garden adventurously exploits an array of exotic plants that thrive in this marine climate. Despite the horticultural abundance, one gains an impression of mastery and focus instead of diffusion and distraction. It is a fine example of what can be accomplished when a horticulturist's hand unites with an artist's eye. The existence of the garden also speaks well of the Korbel Champagne Cellars' commitment to quality and to placing its product in a civilized context.

(Korbel Champagne Cellars, 13250 River Rd., Guerneville. Garden open from mid-April through October, Tuesdays through Sundays, with free, guided garden tours offered on the hour from 10:00 a.m. to 4:00 p.m. Confirm hours and dates by telephoning 707-887-2294. Korbel also offers an excellent tour of its winery and cellars. Those interested should not overlook one of the finest small redwood groves on the north coast, Armstrong Redwood Grove, nearby at the end of Armstrong Rd. north of downtown Guerneville.)

LUTHER BURBANK MEMORIAL GARDEN

Familiar to Californians who see its dark, shady canopy commercially cultivated in the Central Valley and who pay steep prices for its hairy fruit, a kiwi vine clambers over a garden shelter containing a photographic summary of Luther Burbank's life. The pictures record Burbank's achievements and suggest the celebrity that caused scientists to question whether he was quite the "genius" or "wizard" that an ignorant, enthusiastic press portrayed him to be. Identifying him with the idea of progress, the popular mind placed Burbank in the company of eminent industrialists and inventors. As the photographs show, after attending the 1915 Pacific Exposition in San Francisco, Henry Ford, Thomas Edison, Harvey Firestone, and other dignitaries journeyed north to Santa Rosa to meet Burbank, whose botanical discoveries were felt in some way to resemble their technological achievements.

Despite commercial puffery, a casual approach to record-keeping, and a strain of mysticism and spiritualism that tended to discredit him in the eyes of the scientific world, as a plant selector and collector, hybridizer, and nurseryman, Burbank did produce geniune achievements: between 800 and 1,000 hybrids and introductions. Some of these new plants can be viewed at Luther Burbank Memorial Gardens, where he lived and worked. The "plumcot," for instance, a plum-apricot hybrid, produced fruit that did not ship well and thus never succeeded commercially. Yet by producing edible fruit from diverse parents, the plumcot added to Burbank's reputation as a plant wizard.

The "paradox walnut," a more successful hybrid between the native California black walnut and the English walnut, could grow to sixty feet in sixteen years, far speedier than other walnuts. Unlike other fast-growing trees, the "paradox" produced a hard wood of superior grain prized by the cabinetmaker. The Shasta Daisy, the result of a seventeen-year breeding program, remains one of Burbank's most widely grown introduc-

Burbank's house and greenhouse, Luther Burbank Memorial Garden

tions. The garden also contains such Burbank innovations as the "Tower of Gold" red hot poker (*Kniphofia uvaria*), a white agapanthus, and one of Burbank's celebrated failures, the "spineless" cactus. (Although not truly spineless and unsatisfactory as forage for desert livestock, the spineless cactus nevertheless survives throughout the American Southwest.)

The Burbank garden also contains a frame house that Burbank occupied during middle life and in which his second wife lived for fifty-one years after Burbank died in 1926. It has been well restored, as has a greenhouse that Burbank designed and used for propagation and in early stages of hybridization and selection. He carried on the rest of his breeding programs at Gold Ridge Farm near Sebastopol, which may also may be restored and opened to the public in the near future. There Burbank pursued trial-and-error horticulture on an industrial scale, growing thousands of seedlings to increase the chance of finding a useful variation. In a single year, one observer counted fifteen bonfires—one composed of 65,000 hybrid berry seedlings—necessary to destroy the rogues that Burbank rejected in searching for a new plant with desirable qualities.

Burbank lived and did most of his work in Santa Rosa, however, where the garden area nearest his home, tack house, and greenhouse is under renovation to emphasize his plant introductions, with estimated completion for 1992-93. The rest of today's site does not follow historical principles, and many plantings—the liquidambar, ginkgo, Chinese elm, camellias and other shade plants, and everyday annuals—seem to have few links to Burbank.

The white picket fence around the property sets a symbolic, premodern tone that, significantly, does not extend through the garden. Burbank was a horticultural innovator and popularizer, and for all his spiritual and mystical leanings, he debunked nature by commercializing it, adapting industrial production techniques to fabricate new plants. He then marketed them with sophisticated business acumen, selling geographic rights to a new hybrid or commercial variety in what was essentially a limited franchise agreement. The memorial garden's historical and botanical presentation suggests both Burbank's horticultural achievement and the popular esteem in which he was held. The visits by Ford, Edison, Jack London, Paderewski, David Starr Jordan, and other luminaries reflected yet a third aspect of Burbank's modernism: his courting of and commercial manipulation of his own celebrity. Perhaps the kiwi, lately the symbol of a dreaded, fashionable cuisine, suits him after all. Burbank, in other words, had a very modern career. It is his fame and repute, as much as his horticultural legacy, that are on view in Santa Rosa.

(Luther Burbank Memorial Garden, Santa Rosa and Sonoma aves., Santa Rosa. Garden is open free of charge all year; Burbank house tours are given April through October, Wednesday through Sunday 10:00 a.m. to 3:30 p.m. for $1.00 admission. For information, telephone 707-576-5115. For biographical information, see Peter Dreyer, *A Gardener Touched With Genius: The Life of Luther Burbank* [1985].)

NORTH COAST
BRIEFLY NOTED

WESTERN HILLS NURSERY deserves inclusion here not simply because it sells rare, choice plants but for the garden in several surrounding acres. Located in coastal Sonoma County in high country between Pacific Coast Highway and the village of Occidental, the nursery grows unusual evergreens (dwarfs, those with weeping or fastigiate habit or having golden, blue, or other colorful foliage), ground covers and ornamental grasses, subtropicals, and rare deciduous trees. The garden emphasizes foliar color (New Zealand flaxes in purple, yellow, or pale pink), flowering plants (Chinese maples or coral trees), and distinctive botany. This remote nursery, open limited hours, is worth the journey for those interested in the surprising range of plants possible to cultivate on the north coast. (16250 Coleman Valley Rd., Occidental; Wednesday through Sunday 10:00 a.m. to 5:00 p.m.)

Visitors to the Mendocino Coast Botanical Gardens may wish to stop briefly at the GEORGIA PACIFIC TREE NURSERY in Fort Bragg, where a short nature trail travels through a small arboretum of timber species: coast redwoods, Monterey cypress, Port Orford cedar, Sitka spruce, Monterey pine, Douglas fir, and giant sequoia. Although not unlike many demonstration forests found throughout the region, this nursery affords a glimpse of the vast corporate greenhouses, sheltering acres of seedlings. A green carpet under glass, the spectacle suggests the awesome effort required to reforest, and perhaps also the sobering scale of the cutting. A lumber mill is visible through the trees. (Highway One in Fort Bragg.)

The centerpiece of the MARIN GARDEN AND ART CENTER must be its octagon house, a library of books on art and gardens. One of few remaining examples of a mid-nineteenth-century housing fad, these two-story dwellings were the geodesic domes of their day. (The Colonial Dames of America have beautifully restored and opened another octagon house at Gough and Union sts. in San Francisco.) The property contains offices, libraries, a playground and "bottle house" (a children's storybook cottage), indoor and outdoor theatrical venues, a restaurant, a gift shop, an art gallery, an antique shop, and a long list of memorial trees and groves. As this catalog suggests, the assortment of buildings somewhat diffuses the garden's effect. Nonetheless some of the center's over seventy tree species remain exceptional, such as a massive giant sequoia and a fine southern magnolia, nearly as wide as it is tall. The grounds offer many flowering plants, from a wisteria covering a passage-way to rhododendrons, camellias, azaleas, and flowering pears, plums, and cherries. Despite many meritorious specimens, the whole adds up to rather less than the sum of its parts. (Sir Francis Drake Blvd., Ross; tele-phone 415-454-5597.)

Approaching through mature eucalyptus leading to an ornate Span-ish colonial church, visitors should check in at the ST. VINCENT'S SCHOOL office after passing through the first of two large garden court-yards. Flanked on three sides by arcades and decorated with lions, urns, and other garden ornament and religious statuary, the evergreen, dry gardens are Mediterranean in proportion, planting, and feeling. The western courtyard is dominated by the sanctuary's towers and by mature palms in six slightly raised beds informally planted with pine, cedar, and southern magnolia, with sky blue plumbago and purple bou-gainvillea around a statue of Christ blessing a child. (St. Vincent's, begun to care for gold rush orphans in the 1850s, is today a "multi-service cen-ter for children with special problems," primarily those with serious emotional disturbance.)

The eastern courtyard, overlooking San Pablo Bay, surrounds a cen-tral fountain and octagonal lily pond. Planted with evergreens—yew, arborvitae, laurel, and upright junipers clipped into cubes—the garden makes a Spanish impression, with its stucco, paved paths, and stone benches, bare earth, and few blooming plants. Dating from 1927, both gardens appear to receive benign neglect, giving them an air of romantic desuetude. However much they might benefit from an infusion of water and care, strong basic designs and resilient planting permit the courtyard gardens to survive nicely. Although subdued, they are far from negligi-ble. The vivid surrounding architecture, the institution's noble work, and the tough plants surviving without tender treatment sustain a picturesque and poignant atmosphere. (St. Vincent's Dr., off Highway 101 north of San Rafael; telephone 415-479-8831.)

XII
Central Valley

BOURN
COTTAGE

The gold rush came so early in its history, and stamped its identity so indelibly, that California still calls itself "the Golden State." Along Highway 49 through the Mother Lode, much evidence of that era remains—general stores, saloons, cemeteries, and "the diggin's" themselves. Ramshackle and swaybacked now, the miners' structures were mostly temporary; that any survive at all is remarkable. The days when a prospector could stake a claim and dig a fortune were little more than a flash in the historical pan. Mining soon industrialized, legalized, and capitalized, ceasing to be the wild, instinctive adventure it had started out to be.

The Empire Mine illustrates what happened when the roaring gold rush slowed down to a well-run business. Mr. and Mrs. William Bourn, Jr., needed an establishment for their infrequent but regular visits to their mine, which Mr. Bourn had inherited from his father at age twenty-one in 1877. In the 1890s, they hired architect Willis Polk to design a cottage and landscape plan for the surrounding thirteen acres. (Polk had just finished their formidable San Francisco mansion and in 1916 would execute his third commission for the Bourns, Filoli, an elegant country estate in Woodside; see San Francisco Bay Area: The Peninsula.) Known for his stylistic facility, Polk built a two-story English hunting lodge of brick and cracked granite, the latter material a by-product of the Empire Mine just down the hill. The formal regularity of brick and the rugged, sharp-edged rock suggest only the first of many tensions to be observed in the Empire Cottage and its gardens. Although rustic and rural, the estate is designed to be civilized. These are your digs when you own the second largest gold mine in the world.

The forest cover in these foothills is mostly long-needle ponderosa pine, growing a hundred feet tall and more at this elevation of 2,500 feet. The trees must part, however, for the wide lawns that surround the cottage, introducing a second contrast, the forest and the meadow. As it happens, the manicured turf also owes something to the mine. From 1850 until mining stopped in 1956, workers had extended 367 miles of tunnels underground. Having filled the shafts to a level 200 feet below ground, subterranean springs provide a reservoir of pure water to keep the lawns and gardens green during dry summer months.

Besides the ponderosas, dozens of introduced trees planted around the turn of the century have grown to great size. These include deodar, liquidambar, maples, oaks, elms, birches, a ginkgo, and—surprisingly, given the occasional heavy snows at this elevation—a southern magnolia as fine as any in California. Introduced plants contact the native trees most noticeably in the vines that clamber up the ponderosas. A gargantuan Chinese wisteria all but smothers one tall pine, while a Virginia creeper hugs another tightly, dressing up its columnar trunk like a lace-finished pantaloon. These examples point to another dynamic in the estate garden, that between the native and exotic plants.

With its red brick laid in a herringbone pattern, a terrace at the cottage signals another motif. Annuals bloom in narrow beds near the house, and below the terrace a wide lawn with two circular fountains (each with forty jets, perhaps an echo of the extravaganzas at Versailles) slopes down to a wall with stairs to a lower level. As the grade changes, the style shifts from English to Italianate, north to south, rock to brick, lawn and terrace to a hillside water garden. Water issues from an animal's head into a small basin, then down a staircase—a *catena d'acqua* or *cordonata* cascade—to a rectangular reflecting pool below the terrace, the axis of this unit slightly out of line with that of the house's terrace and entrance.

These features quote the Italian hillside garden: the terrace's square corners and volumes, a staircased fountain causeway and rectangular reflecting pool, the changed elevation, and even the geometrical units angled together askew in that touch of irregularity that an Italian villa's site plan not infrequently discloses. Several olive trees and eight columnar Italian cypresses horticulturally underscore the change in style. Drawing predominantly on the English country house, with a nod toward the French *jets d'eau* and a strong allusion to Italian landscape architecture, Polk's Empire Cottage shows how worldly the northern California elite could be at the turn of the century.

Their Sierra business trips, in other words, did not have to seem like errands into the wilderness. So the Bourns and their designers carefully inserted elements of formality into this rugged forest—terraces, rose gardens, symmetrically arranged cypresses, a small allée of red maples in the dooryard—even as they built a house with cracked granite unearthed from the mines, rooting their establishment in the riches that made it possible. The cottage, after all, lies just up the hill from the mine, the life of work barely out of sight from the life at home.

Behind the cottage, the estate rose garden has been restored to its original formal plan. From the cottage dooryard and across the carriage entrance, staircases lead under an arbor that, combined with holly hedging, forms an axis into the rose garden. Historical principles guided the restoration. Experiencing poor health, William Bourn, Jr., sold the Empire Mine in 1929, and thereafter its rose garden declined. Self-consciously devoted solely to "old roses," the restored garden contains no rose discovered or introduced after that year. Consequently, many old roses at Empire Cottage—_Rosa gallica officinalis_, for instance, introduced before Chinese tea roses began to arrive about 1789, the year of that other revolution—flower only once annually, in late spring or early summer.

The ever-blooming or—from the French, who dominated rose hybridization in the nineteenth century—"remontant" habit initially appeared in types such as hybrid perpetuals, here illustrated with "Baronness Rothschild" (1868), "Baronne Prévost" (1842), and "American Beauty" (1860). Since they can be traced back as early as 1867, several hybrid teas grow at the Empire Cottage, including the favorite "Dainty Bess," introduced in 1925 and thus just sneaking in under the wire. But the hybrid tea did not gain its contemporary preeminence until after a medley of new types, each with some advantage new to rose cultivation, had come forward to displace earlier kinds, from Noisettes, hybrid Provence, hybrid Damask, and Bourbons, to hybrid perpetuals. Describing more than 6,000 varieties, Singer's 1885 _Dictionnaire des Roses_ suggests the almost Darwinian proliferation of hybrids, races, and cultivars during the 1800s. Like an earlier champion eclipsed by a new rose, Singer's compendium was itself followed in 1906 by Simon and Cochet's _Nomenclature de tous les Noms de Roses connus_, setting forth nearly 11,000 entries.

As Thomas Christopher's _In Search of Lost Roses_ (1989) relates, despite its remoteness from the (mainly French) centers of rose cultivation, the California gold country drew the latest European roses to it nearly as reliably as it attracted tens of thousands of people coming to work the mines. A century later, many of these plants somehow survived in cemeteries, churchyards, and abandoned gardens of Placer, Nevada, El Dorado, and other Sierra foothill counties. There they waited to be rediscovered by rose-rustling devotees of the "old rose" movement; with

Texas, the Mother Lode proved to be one of the two richest sources for old roses in the United States.

So it seems fitting that the Empire Cottage rose garden specializes in old varieties. It keeps to an impressive but manageable scale; with about 1,000 plants, the garden presents only about sixty varieties, ranging from the trellis-smothering "Gold of Ophir" (also known as "Fortune's Double Yellow," introduced from China by Robert Fortune, who in 1845 found it growing in "a rich Mandarin's garden at Ningpo") to "Belle Poitevine" (1894), whose vigorous foliage supports ever-blooming lavender flowers with a strong, spicy fragrance. Like other late-blooming types, "Belle Poitevine" is a hybrid rugosa, a hardy, free-blooming Japanese species; a white form, *Rosa rugosa* "Alba" (1845) and the single dark pink "Frau Dagmar Hastrup" (1914) bloom in September, as does *R. rugosa magnifica*, a light purple, double type with a strong citrus fragrance. Rose fanciers, however, should time visits for May or June.

Besides the Empire Cottage and gardens at the Empire Mine State Historic Park, an active community organization conducts "living history" days, in which volunteers dressed in period costume assume the roles of machinists, smithies, and ironworkers from the Empire Mine's heyday. The park displays gold mining techniques, the history of the mine and of the Bourn family, Grass Valley's Cornish heritage, and a large exhibit preserves the mine and its technology. An expensive enterprise requiring technology, engineering, and geologic expertise, hardrock mining stopped here because it ceased to be profitable, not because the gold ran out; the Empire Mine is said to hold far more gold than was ever extracted during its heyday. The area is nearly as rich in history as it is in gold, a commonwealth embellished by the restored Empire Cottage.

(Empire Mine State Historic Park, 0.7 mile off Highway 49 at Empire St., Grass Valley. Open daily 9:00 a.m. to 5:00 p.m.; $3.00 adult admission. There are daily tours of Bourn Cottage and gardens. Telephone 916-273-8522.)

CAPITOL
PARK,
SACRAMENTO

uriously enough in retrospect, finding a site for a state capital created a prolonged dispute through California's early years as the thirty-first state. The capital moved several times before settling in Sacramento in 1855, and Berkeley, San Jose, and Monterey made efforts to spirit away state government as late as the 1930s. Construction of the State Capitol Building, designed by Miner F. Butler, lasted from 1860 until completion in 1874. Plans for a landscaped park to surround the emerging Greek revival edifice began in 1869 by building up the forty-acre site with rich silt dredged from the nearby Sacramento River. The earliest plantings in 1870-71, comprising 800 trees and more than 200 varieties of shrubs imported from around the world, established a tradition that persisted to create a graceful downtown park with wide lawns under trees of cosmopolitan origins and superb quality.

Botanically speaking, Capitol Park has grown in spurts. A row of deodar cedars lining the capitol building's western facade is only one example of the original trees remaining in Capitol Park. But in the decades after the original plantings, ignorance reclaimed the identities of many specimens until 1905, when Alice Eastwood, head of the California Academy of Sciences Horticulture Department, was hired to identify and label the plants with common and botanical names and their places of origin. Another wave of new plantings began in 1950. A restoration of the capitol building, completed in 1982, also revived interest in Capitol Park. Well maintained and seemingly in fine shape, today the park contains more than 450 species of trees, shrubs, and flowers.

Although its lanes and paths extend the downtown street grid, Capitol Park, except for Tenth Street, is closed to vehicular traffic; its eastern reaches are particularly quiet. Lining the perimeter, an imposing row of mature California fan palms (*Washingtonia filifera*, the state's only native palm) establishes a visual boundary between city and park, which is otherwise unfenced and may be entered at any point.

As befits a park with a strong civic purpose, commemorative features exist throughout Capitol Park, including memorials to all conflicts since the Civil War. The most recent, the Vietnam War Memorial, overlooks a rose garden near Capitol Avenue and 15th Street in the park's east end. An axial pedestrian lane—"the mall"—extends Capitol Avenue into the park. Bisecting Capitol Park, the mall orients its eastern half, guiding the eye between an allée of clipped, columnar yews to a view of the Capitol dome.

Across the mall from the roses, a small cactus garden dates from 1914, when California schoolchildren sent plants to Governor Hiram Johnson to symbolize California's deserts. North of the Father Serra Memorial, another specialized garden contains more than 300 winter-blooming camellias. Sacramento's floral symbol, the camellia inspires an annual festival in Land Park, and in the city's older neighborhoods, camellias grow to be small trees.

During the summer, Capitol Park is a green park, dominated by its lawns and great trees. The verdure only heightens the effect of two large flower beds planted with summer annuals on either side of the mall. When red salvia fills the round beds, for instance, it creates twin saucers of scarlet thirty feet wide, visible throughout the eastern part of the park. Oleander, pomegranate, crepe myrtle, and the berry-red, peapod-shaped flowers of the Brazilian *Erythrina crista-galli* can scarcely challenge the massed salvia's vibrant red color.

Trees nonetheless remain Capitol Park's distinctive feature. The *Capitol Park Tree Tour*, a free brochure available at the State Capitol Museum Tour Office, plots three park tours with over 300 trees and nearly as many species keyed by number to labeled specimens. Aside from their beauty and value in embellishing the Sacramento city center, collectively these trees form an impressive arboretum. The park's trees, in fact, suggest a further theme, an almost celebratory statement about California.

Near the capitol building's eastern steps, for instance, rows of citrus line the mall, scenting the summer air with fruit hung decoratively thirty feet above the ground. These pungent trees symbolize a key species that contributed not only to California's economic development but also to its myth as an Eden of wealth, warmth, and health. Even if infinite commercial expansion and earthly paradise have proved to be at odds with one another, at one time both dreams contributed to the state's history and to its self-image.

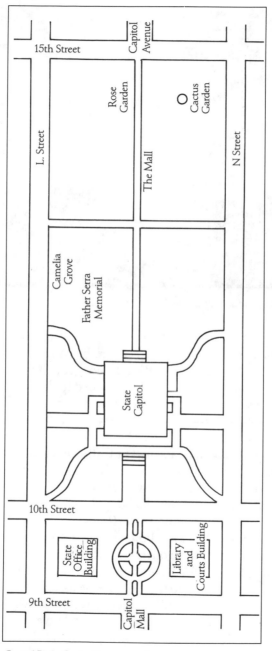

Capitol Park, Sacramento

The towering trees and dome of Capitol Park (Photo: Patricia Sigg)

California's greatest trees, the coast redwood and sequoia or Sierra redwood, also thrive in Capitol Park. Besides enriching the state materially and spiritually, these noble giants added to the state's lore and legend, tall trees inspiring tall tales that turned out to be true. The dawn redwood (*Metasequoia glyptostroboides*), known only in fossils until discovered in a remote part of China in the 1940s, also grows to statuesque proportions in Capitol Park, near its distant California kin.

If not as favored as coastal regions, Sacramento's climate and abundant water for irrigation foster a wide range of species growing far from native habitats. Consider, on one hand, Capitol Park's tropical pines, such as the exceptional Jelecote pines (*Pinus patula*) from Mexico on the Capitol's east facade, their long, bright green, drooping needles glistening in the sun like tinsel. On the other hand, look for a hardy tropical, such as the cooking banana (*Musa paradisaica*), in the park's northeastern sector, its lush leaves barely floating on the weak summer breeze.

Palms flourish no less well than evergreens. Besides the *Washingtonia filifera*, the park contains *Phoenix* species—relatives of the date palm—from tropical Africa, the Chilean wine palm, the Chinese *Trachycarpus fortuneii* (considered the hardiest palm, tolerating cold of 10°F or lower), the South American pindo and queen palms, and the European fan palm growing in raised beds on the capitol building's west facade.

Surveying the plant collection's geographic extent, these examples point to Capitol Park's underlying theme. It is a public garden with historical, civic, and educational dimensions. It is likewise a showcase of mature trees, as different as the English elm and the Chinese *Ginkgo biloba* but likely to be the largest of their kind to be seen in California without a search. Simply reading a column or two of the species listed in the tree tour guide reveals the twin symbolic statements made by the park's planting scheme. First, the plants have come from all over the globe: Japanese flowering crabapple (*Malus floribunda*), southern European cork oak (*Quercus suber*), Mexican Montezuma cypress (*Taxodium mucronatum*), and Australian bunya bunya (*Araucaria bidwillii*).

Second, Capitol Park emphasizes California natives, from low-growing, defensive cactus to commanding redwoods of the northern coastal forests and southern Sierra Nevada. Many species grow in native habitats nowhere else but California and aside from being botanically unusual, are often of majestic size or great floral beauty. The California redwoods—one appears on the state flag—alone illustrate the significance of native plants to the state's history, economy, and identity.

Capitol Park's beautiful trees, then, illustrate twin themes. California is distinctive because of its openness to the world, allowing people, ideas, and plants to come to the state, take root, and flourish. But California is also unique because of what is native to it—blessings of climate, resources, soil, scenery, water, and natural life. In these ways Capitol Park not only furnishes an appropriate symbolic setting for state government but also incorporates the history and values of California as a place and as a state of mind.

(Capitol Park, in downtown Sacramento, is bounded by N, L, 9th, and 15th sts. The *Capitol Park Tree Tour*, available free in the State Capitol Museum Tour Office, Room B-27 on the ground floor of the capitol building, is highly recommended, as are the legislative chambers, historical rooms, and other exhibits.)

SACRAMENTO
PARKS

N amed for Charles Mathias Goethe, a Sacramento philanthropist and conservationist, the C. M. GOETHE ARBOR-
ETUM flanks the northern entrance to the California State
University, Sacramento, campus. Lushly green and deeply
shaded in summer, much tramping off the paths is necessary to read the
labels of this closely planted small arboretum. The Biological Sciences
Department has posted a permanent map and alphabetical species list.

The tree selection resembles that of Capitol Park, with many nods
toward academic thoroughness. *Liquidambar styraciflua, L. formosana,* and
L. orientalis, for instance, native to North America, China, and Turkey,
respectively, appear near one another for convenient comparison and
contrast. The plan emphasizes underplanted woody shrubs such as
Cotoneaster pannosa or Indian hawthorn. Although the arboretum displays palms, eucalyptus, and a small California native plant garden, it
concentrates on broad-leaved, deciduous trees and shrubs. The effect is
of a quiet, forest setting, woodsy, green, and erudite, the stillness broken
only by the rush of traffic beyond and the occasional avid undergraduates, printed fern-finders and tree identifiers in hand. (C. M. Goethe Arboretum, California State University, Sacramento, next to J St. entrance.)

Set in a shaded park, the McKINLEY PARK ROSE GARDEN,
though modest in size, gives all the pleasures of a formal rose garden
besides having many other trees and flowering plants. Although the
entrance is from H Street at 33rd, the rose garden may be approached
from any direction. Its symmetrical rose beds range along an axis
marked by twin Canary Island palms, towering above vivid maroon
and purple summer poinsettia. Two radial arcs centered on the palms
modify the garden's otherwise rectangular plan. The garden contains
a few standard or tree roses, and the perimeter supports climbing or pillar
varieties. Most of the 800 rose bushes, however, are hybrid teas, labeled
and blooming freshly even at the height of the Sacramento summer.

Flowers aside, the rose's viciously armed, spindly canes make it something less than an attractive plant. Too many rose gardens seem to assume

A small gem: McKinley Park Rose Garden

that if a few roses are good, several thousand must be better, a guiding principle that often creates only busy, monocultural boredom. Annuals and other flowering plants that mingle with the roses redefine the rose garden as McKinley Park welcomes multicolored zinnias, double marigolds, red salvia, vinca, burgundy and amber celosia, and several beds bulging with six-foot-tall cannas, their flowers and tropical purple encouraged by summer heat.

Besides brilliantly colored climbing roses, the perimeter offers trees and shrubs happy in Sacramento: citrus (clipped into umbrella shapes, their topiary complementing the formal rose beds), palms, crepe myrtle, camellias, yews, birch, some fine old oaks, and many other trees and shrubs that define the borders of this agreeable rose garden. Although not large, the McKinley Park Rose Garden is beautifully chosen, planted, and maintained, one of the best of its kind in California.

Established in 1902 as a memorial to the recently assassinated president, the surrounding thirty-six-acre McKinley Park is also worth a look, especially the lake along Alhambra Boulevard which is landscaped with willows, ornamental plums, and a double row of _Washingtonia_ fan palms. McKinley Park also contains the Shepard Garden and Arts Center, which exhibits over two dozen garden, floral, and craft shows annually. (McKinley Park Rose Garden, H and 33rd sts., Sacramento.)

UNIVERSITY OF CALIFORNIA, DAVIS, ARBORETUM

The vast extent of the arboretum at the University of California, Davis, makes the strongest first impression. Undoubtedly other public gardens have more land than its seventy-five acres, but the arboretum extends for two miles along both sides of Putah Creek at the southern edge of the sprawling Davis campus. To see it all requires a commitment of time and energy.

Except at its western end, the arboretum seldom extends far from the serpentine creek that provides its main, linear orientation. The arboretum dates from 1936, when undergraduates planted specimens according to plans by Professor John W. Gregg to be used in teaching plant sciences. Although California native plants were emphasized from the beginning, in the 1950s, the scope broadened to drought-resistant, Mexican, and Australian species. Today the arboretum concentrates on California native and exotic species suitable for the Central Valley climate, generally Mediterranean but with more intense seasonal variations: rainy winters with cold winds and several months of nightly frosts and dry, hot summers.

Although it occupies the true creek bed, Putah Creek has been channelized and lacks an outlet at its western end, where it widens to resemble the lake that it is in fact. (The arboretum's long-range plan proposes returning the creek to its free-running state.) Even as it now exists, however, the arboretum and Putah Creek provide an agreeable landmark, and as the university develops southward it will likely cease to be something of the periphery and become a central campus feature.

As the map (available at arboretum headquarters) reveals, paved paths extend throughout the arboretum. The area sloping down to the creek below the headquarters contains foreign conifers, whose outstanding specimen is a bright green, long-needled *Pinus oaxacana*. Farther east beyond Mrak Hall Drive lies a splendid grove of cork oak, whose bark is harvested for wine bottle corks. That use acknowledges the viticulture and oenology experts at UC Davis. Applying scientific techniques to grape growing and wine making, they have helped to upgrade the California wine industry to international status and have revolutionized the science and art of wine throughout the world, developments summarized in parts of Doris Muscatine et al, eds., _The University of California/Sotheby Book of California Wine_ (1984).

South of a widening in the creek called Lake Spafford looms the deep shade of the T. Elliot Weier Redwood Grove, planted in 1941. (The grove, named for the chairman of the arboretum committee when the redwoods were planted, is considered to be the largest coast redwood grove on interior land.) An "exotic area" at the arboretum's east end contains plants from the world's other Mediterranean climates—southern Europe, Australia, Chile, and South Africa—adapting to a dry landscape with a variety of leaf textures and colors. Along the creek's north side— here the arboretum ends, just before a railway trestle over the creek— lies a eucalyptus collection, established during the late 1950s, with many trees grown to enormous size.

Near Lake Spafford is the Mary Wattis Brown Garden, the first of four specialized gardens. Its self-guided tour of native California plants explores the high rate of endemism among California flora; the Davis area's human history (beginning with the Patwin Indians, whose diet included the California buckeye, toyon and manzanita berries, and oak acorns, all plants grown in the Brown Garden); and distinct hillside vegetation of Mediterranean climates. Known in Italy as "maquis," in southern France as "macchia," and in South Africa as "fynbos," in California this plant community is called "chaparral," from the Spanish _chaporro_, or "short." The most widespread vegetation in California, covering 3.8 million acres on foothills and lower mountains, the chaparral plant community includes forty-three species of ceanothus, toyon, manzanita, chamisa, and tassel bush, each adapted to summer water loss and periodic fires.

An area devoted to acacias (begun in the 1960s to aid the research of Davis biochemistry professor Eric Conn into cyanide-producing compounds derived from the genus) is now considered to be one of the country's most complete acacia collections. It leads into the garden's western section, which makes something of a departure from the rest of the arboretum. Here Putah Creek again widens into a curving lake, and past a Mediterranean section and across a wide lawn are the arboretum's three other specialty gardens.

The Peter J. Shields Oak Grove, fifteen acres devoted solely to oak species, has a self-guided tour. A Sacramento Superior Court judge for forty-nine years, Shields wrote the legislation establishing the University of California's agricultural station at Davis. Eventually Davis would become a full-fledged campus, a development Shields lived to see. He attended the dedication of this commemorative grove, performed one day after his one hundredth birthday, on April 15, 1962. From the native valley oak (*Quercus lobata*, symbol of the arboretum) to exotic oaks from England (*Q. robur*), the Levant (*Q. cerris*), and China (*Q. acutissima*), the grove's two dozen species represent only a fraction of this widespread genus, which has over 450 species. Although less than thirty years old, many of its oaks have already reached statuesque proportions.

Near the oak grove is a garden dedicated in 1966 to Judge Shields's wife, Carolee Shields, whose favorite color was white. This garden can be traced to Gertrude Jekyll's single color gardens and particularly to the Sissinghurst Castle garden of Vita Sackville-West, whose nocturnal habit inspired her to devote a garden solely to white flowers, for viewing at dusk or under a summer moon. In Asia, "moon-viewing gardens" arose both in Japan and Mogul India, where the Hindus taught the ruling Moguls to retreat indoors from ferocious summer heat, only emerging at night to view their garden's pale white flowers that alone retained their hue. White particularly suits hot Central Valley summers, seeming, with the color blue, to set the coolest tone.

Organized as concentric beds and circular paths around a whitewashed wood gazebo, the garden displays white-flowering plants from the spring—*Wisteria sinensis* "Alba" and *Clematis armandii* vines, callas, and flowering quince and peach—through summer and into fall. In September, the garden contains double white hollyhock spires, the flamboyant Matilija poppy (*Romneya coulteri*), the "Delphine Bellotti" and "Honor" roses, and a fine white *Hibiscus syriacus*. The garden also explores the white and gray foliage of Dusty Miller (*Senecio cineraria*) and tactile, velvety lamb's ears (*Stachys byzantina* "Silver Carpet").

Perhaps the most impressive garden at Davis is the Dr. Ruth Risdon Storer Garden, named for the first woman physician on the Davis campus to commemorate her interest in achieving the difficult goals of year-round color with limited water and low maintenance. In the late summer, pink, lavender, and blue seem to predominate, from the tiny blue flowers of bog salvia (*Salvia uliginosa*) through English lavender (*Lavandula angustifolia* "Hidcote") to the dark pink of striped society garlic (*Tulbaghia violacea* "Variegata"), Texas ranger (*Leucophyllum frutescens*), and rose crepe myrtle. The cloud of pink flowers of Macedonian St. Johnswort (_Hypericum cerastoides_), buzzing with bees, blooms vigorously even during a hot September.

The Storer Garden's plants receive three levels of attention. About half the garden receives no summer water; a small zone is kept moist all summer, and the rest receives summer water once or twice monthly. The Storer Garden illustrates how a water-conserving garden can supply color through a hot, dry summer and into fall; one would be hard pressed to find another California garden that succeeds as well in achieving these goals.

The arboretum has traditionally concentrated on trees and plants adapted to this climate, naturalistically cultivated, with floral display a happy accident. Well designed and maintained, the Shields White Flower Garden and the Storer Garden's floral finish, elaborate beds and paths, and consistent labeling suggest a shift, or an expansion, of the arboretum's interests. Besides California natives and drought resistant plants, the arboretum now pursues new goals of artistic interpretation and low maintenance, while devoting resources to agricultural integration, gene pool preservation, and similar topics befitting a research institution. The emerging mix of plants for local climates, aesthetics, practical horticulture, and scientific research indicates the broad scope of the Davis Arboretum.

(The University of California, Davis, Arboretum is open twenty-fours daily, all year, with no admission charge. Arboretum headquarters, located on the south side of La Rue Rd. between Bioletti Way and California Ave., offers a free map and sells self-guided tour brochures. Free tours are on Sundays at 2:00 p.m.; telephone 916-752-4880 for a schedule of topics. Friends of the Davis Arboretum sponsor a lecture series (telephone 916-752-2498). Enter the campus from the south on Old Davis Rd., where a campus map and parking information can be obtained at a kiosk.)

EDDY ARBORETUM, U.S. INSTITUTE OF FOREST GENETICS

The U. S. Institute of Forest Genetics, the world's oldest forest genetics research facility, was founded in 1925 by James G. Eddy, a lumberman from Port Blakely Mill on the Puget Sound. Eddy's experience in New England, the upper Midwest, and the state of Washington convinced him that forests were a finite resource, and he sought to apply scientific breeding and hybridizing methods to commercial timber species. Luther Burbank's success in producing the fast-growing Paradox and Royal walnut hybrids led Eddy to visit him in 1918 to see if he could be interested in applying his techniques to improve timber quality and yields of forest trees. At the age of sixty-nine, and conscious that Eddy's goals could not be reached for decades, Burbank was interested but not willing.

Burbank recommended Lloyd Austin, a young pomologist (an expert in the science of fruit cultivation) from the University of California, Davis. With his own funds, Eddy established the Eddy Tree Breeding Station at Placerville and appointed Austin director. Placerville was chosen for its relatively long growing season and for its proximity to elevations from nearly sea level on the Central Valley floor to the 10,000-foot elevations of the High Sierra. Some years later, during the Depression, Eddy donated the station to the United States, and since 1935 the U.S. Forest Service has operated the facility. Its forestry work has earned the institute an international reputation, and in recognition of its achievements, the institute was placed on the National Register of Historic Places in 1987.

In keeping with Eddy's interests, during much of the institute's history research focused on western pine species. Its scientists' work not only made necessary a revision of pine taxonomy but produced more than ninety new pine hybrids, some with valuable or surprising traits. Manifesting what botanists term "heterosis," hybrids can display greater size, increased disease resistance, or more rapid growth than either parent. The hybrid between the Monterey pine and the knobcone illustrates the phenomenon: although weak wood makes it valueless as a timber tree, this hybrid pine can grow as much as ten feet a year, as a section displayed in the foyer of the institute's administration building demonstrates. This habit suits it for controlling erosion, stabilizing reservoir and stream banks, and providing quick cover around campgrounds, recreational areas, and similar developed forest settings.

As pine hybridization ended in the 1970s, the institute's work has developed in other directions: research into tree selection, genetic engineering, and seedling survival and into tree species, such as eucalyptus, that may prove valuable for planting on marginal land. The Eddy Arboretum, a grove of about seventy of the world's ninety-five pine species, reflects the institute's best-known forestry work. Although the trees are mostly plotted in orchard-style rows, the trail of a half-hour, self-guided tour winds through the grid, pausing at informational plaques giving an overview of the history, hybridizing, and botany of major forest species of the western United States.

The pines range from the Jeffrey, whose bark contains crevices emitting a strong, spicy vanilla fragrance, to the Scotch pine (*Pinus sylvestris*), the world's most widely distributed pine species, growing from Scotland to Siberia and south to Spain and Turkey. Size, resistance to insects or disease, and growth rates reflect considerable genetic diversity within such a widespread species. Races of the Scotch pine, for instance, which are adapted to climates with summer rainfall do not fare well in Placerville's dry summers. Elevation can defeat other species: occasional heavy snows at Placerville's 2,700 feet leave the Mexican weeping pine, *P. patula*, a misshapen failure, even though it thrives in Sacramento.

By contrast, the arboretum contains a fine small grove of a dozen sequoias or Sierra redwoods planted in 1927 and now superb specimens reaching at least 100 feet and over three feet in diameter at the base. Growing densely at higher elevations in the southern Sierra as far as Kern County, these sequoias live near the edge of their natural range. A tiny, isolated grove of sequoias, not far from the institute, is the big tree's northernmost stand.

Each arboretum tree bears a metal tag with a species name, pedigree number, sometimes a place of origin, a "nursery year" (the year the seed went into earth, not necessarily the same year it was set out in the arboretum), and a row and line number. As the tags suggest, the twenty-acre arboretum is only one part of a large scientific enterprise, whose nurseries, greenhouses, laboratories, and growing grounds cover 140 acres. The institute also maintains links to U.S. Forest Service facilities throughout the country as well as to more than 100 plantations in California, some on private land, where cooperative landowners test species in a range of climates, elevations, and soils.

The Eddy Arboretum is a specialized collection, focused not only by concentrating on western forest species but also by its goal of developing trees for use. Work done here could have a positive influence on the future of the planet. While they leave it some distance from the main tourist route, the arboretum's scientific and utilitarian purposes will nonetheless, as the saying goes, interest those to whom they are of interest. The surrounding area, with vineyards, apple orchards, Christmas tree growing, and the historic gold country, can complete a visit to this interesting part of the Sierra foothills.

(2480 Carson Rd., Placerville. Use Schnell School Rd. exit from Highway 50, north to Carson Rd., then east. Free admission; open 8:00 a.m. to 4:30 p.m. Monday through Friday, or telephone 916-622-1225 for appointment. The administration building offers an informational brochure and educational displays.)

CHICO

hico's history and its three horticulturally important sites have many ties to a single figure, General John Bidwell. One of the pioneer generation who came to settle and achieved great things, in late 1841, he led the the first party of Americans across the Sierra Nevada, having left Independence, Missouri, the previous May. After discovering gold in the Feather River, he acquired the 26,000-acre Rancho del Arroyo Chico, employing more than 100 workers growing wheat and fruit, raising livestock, and operating a cannery and saw mill. Bidwell planted the first prune, almond, and cherry trees in the Sacramento Valley, conducted experiments to learn which of 400 fruit and nut trees were adapted to the area, and won the 1878 Paris International Exposition award for producing the world's finest wheat. Governor Leland Stanford appointed Bidwell a brigadier general in the militia, and he served in the House of Representatives. He later ran unsuccessfully for governor and for president (on the Prohibition Party ticket). The multitalented Bidwell also developed a variegated camellia that he named for Mrs. Bidwell, who joined with him in many acts of civic philanthropy.

When Bidwell laid out the town of Chico in 1860, offering free lots to anyone who would build on them, he donated land to churches and schools. In 1887, learning that the choice for the site had narrowed to Red Bluff or his own city, he gave eight acres of his cherry orchard for a State Normal School, since evolved into the 130-acre CALIFORNIA STATE UNIVERSITY, CHICO, campus with 13,000 students and about one thousand faculty members. Nearby, restored and open to the public as a state historic monument, is the mansion General Bidwell commissioned in 1865, designed by Henry W. Cleaveland in the "Italian villa style" and surrounded by exceptional trees. General Bidwell's widow, Annie Bidwell, donated Bidwell Park to the City of Chico in 1905.

Big Chico Creek, a tributary of the Sacramento River, bisects the campus, flowing all summer long through a tree-shaded glade crossed at many points by footbridges. University President Robin S. Wilson designated the campus an arboretum and wildlife refuge in 1982. Even though since that time at least four different maps and numbering schemes have appeared, a revised, unified presentation is now available for a small charge from the Alumni Association office, just off campus at 238 Normal Street.

Near Big Chico Creek are two designated campus gardens. Along a curve of the creek is the Mary Dunbar Lemcke Camellia Garden, shaded by a huge valley oak, a ginkgo, and dense foliage kept green during summers by the slow-moving current. Dedicated in 1969, the garden has azaleas and mature camellias and offers a quiet vantage point for observing the creek's leisurely eddies. Between Trinity and Glenn halls across the creek, the George Patterson Rose Garden, dating from 1957, surrounds a fountain with a small, unlabeled rose display.

The campus retains some link to John Bidwell's property, life, and interests, particularly his passion for trees, which he collected on his travels and planted throughout his property. (He also donated thirty-seven acres in 1888 for a forestry station near Chico Creek.) Lining city streets with shade trees from his own nurseries, Bidwell demonstrated both civic foresight and common sense. Today the mature trees gracing Chico's older neighborhoods add value to property, comfort to the lives of the citizens, and distinction to the city. Like anyone who plants street trees, Bidwell was ahead of his time. So he remains today, when too many of the state's cities, especially in southern California, impoverish their futures by ignoring this elementary aspect of urban design.

Bidwell's tree-planting habit evidently took root at the university. The campus arboretum contains over 100 tree species and thousands of specimens, making possible only the briefest overview. Although elsewhere a fungus blight has decimated the species, American chestnuts (*Castanea dentata*) thrive north of Chico Creek near Holt Hall. Planted by John and Annie Bidwell, their chartreuse, fuzzy seed spheres hang in profusion during late summer near the cut-leaved "tree of heaven." Although known on the eastern seaboard in the eighteenth century, *Ailanthus altissima* arrived in California during the gold rush, accompanying Chinese miners. It has naturalized so well here that it might be condemned as a weed tree but for its ability to provide greenery where little else will survive. (By the 1890s, it had reached St. Louis, where T. S. Eliot grew up to remember "the rank ailanthus of the April dooryard" in "The Dry Salvages.")

Wide lawns in front of Kendall and Trinity halls contain splendid evergreens: atlas cedar, a blue Lawson cypress (_Chamaecyparis lawsoniana "Allumii"_) with its fernlike foliage, and a tall incense cedar (_Calocedrus decurrens_), a Sierra Nevada tree pungently scenting the heavy summer air. In front of Kendall Hall grow southern magnolia, coast redwoods, sycamores, and a giant American linden (_Tilia americana_), among many other imposing trees.

Besides its arboretum, the Chico campus contains many amenities, good maintenance, and a carefully preserved creek ecology. The adjacent BIDWELL MANSION and grounds also add a note of distinction and history to the university. The mansion, painted beige, cinnamon, and dark olive, has twenty-six rooms on two floors, an eighty-foot tower, balustrades, a veranda and porte cochere, and bracketed cornices. A helpful guidebook available inside details the Bidwells' history and includes a tour of the exceptionally well cared for trees on the grounds, some of which—southern magnolia, valley oak, and Ponderosa pine— reach astonishing proportions.

By donating land forming the 2,400-acre BIDWELL PARK along Big Chico Creek for several miles, Annie Bidwell gave Chico the distinction of having within its borders the second largest city park in the United States. Although a few areas have been developed for swimming, golf, and picnics, and State Highway 99 gracelessly disrupts the sylvan atmosphere, Bidwell Park is not a typical park but rather a remarkably unspoiled riparian nature preserve.

Hollywood bestowed its blessing in 1937 by doing location shooting here for _The Adventures of Robin Hood_, starring Errol Flynn as Robin, Olivia de Havilland as Marian, and Bidwell Park as Sherwood Forest. The renowned English taxonomist and plant geographer Sir Joseph Hooker, visiting in 1877 as part of his last major botanical expedition, judged one of the park's oak trees, the "Hooker oak," since damaged, to be the largest oak in the world. During summers the vegetation assumes an almost tropical lushness. Even a leisurely drive through the lanes of Bidwell Park amply reveals the value and beauty that it preserves. Bidwell Park Nature Center at 2968 E. 8th Street provides information and interpretive materials.

TWO
OROVILLE
GARDENS

The gold rushes caused Oroville to become California's fifth largest city by 1856. By the 1870s, the city also had the state's largest Chinese settlement, a community of more than ten thousand living mostly in rudimentary shelters on the Feather River floodplain. Since mechanized gold dredging began in 1898, various schemes to demolish Oroville, dig out underlying gold deposits, and rebuild the town have been floated, so far unsuccessfully. In this century, a citrus, olive, and fruit orcharding industry has taken advantage of Oroville's situation in a thermal belt slightly above the Central Valley floor.

At the LOTT HOUSE IN SANK PARK, a wisteria-covered wood and stucco pergola shades a brick walk leading to the house through beds of ivy and camellias, crepe myrtle, and azaleas. To the east, star jasmine, agapanthus, and miniature roses surround an octagonal fountain and pool. A citrus tree and another rose garden fill the dooryard of the Judge Charles Fayette Lott House, built in 1856 and eclectically ornamented by a balustrade, Gothic revival gingerbread, and an unusual filigreed bargeboard under the peaked second-story eave.

Redesigned by Vernon M. Dean in the 1960s, the grounds feature orchard trees—loquat, persimmon, winter pear, citrus, and pecan—as well as liquidambar, oaks, incense cedar, coast redwood, California fan palm, and southern magnolia. A tour of the Lott House reveals Victorian clothing, dolls, furniture, cooking utensils, and the exhausting paraphernalia of respectability providing the backdrop to a prosperous if strange family. Its oppressive domestic arrangements eventually had a sentimental, happy ending when the spinster daughter, Cornelia, having outlived her father and older brother, finally married her long-suffering suitor, Jess Sank, who built the pergola and later donated the house and grounds to the city. (1067 Montgomery St.; park open daily; $1.50 adult admission for house tours, closed December 1 to January 15; telephone 916-538-2497 for daily tour hours.)

Not far away, across from the Feather River levee, the OROVILLE CHINESE TEMPLE COMPLEX surrounds a courtyard garden. The emperor and empress of China donated funds to build and furnish its oldest building, Confucian and Taoist temple chambers built in 1863. After a 1907 flood swept away its members' fragile homes and dispersed the Chinese community, the Chans, a local family, preserved the temple and deeded it to the city in 1937.

In 1968, the city completed a courtyard garden, designed by Philip Choy in conjunction with Mrs. Cabot Brown. Planted with Chinese species, it includes the familiar kiwi or Chinese gooseberry, the Chinese wisteria, and the equally vigorous Lady Banks' rose, named for the wife of Sir Joseph Banks, director of Kew Gardens. One of several Chinese roses first encountered by Europeans around the turn of the nineteenth century, Lady Banks' rose was first known in Europe in 1807 when William Kerr returned with a plant he found in a Canton garden.

The vines climb on trellises surrounding a paved courtyard on three sides. It contains a _Pinus bungeana,_ native to the central Chinese mountains and called the lace-bark, tissue-bark, or camouflage pine for the patches on its trunk that change color as they ripen from yellow-green to purplish-brown. Nearby is a banana magnolia (_Michelia figo_), not a true magnolia but from a related genus. In late September its contorted, even lurid purple-brown buds begin to swell before blooming with a fragrance said to resemble that of a banana or of port wine.

The memorial to members of the Chan family, a pavilion shelters a small pond with water lilies and waterfowl statuary surrounded by camellias, azaleas, and a pumelo, whose pear-shaped fruit and leaves are used ceremonially during Chinese New Year celebrations. Among the most ancient of the citrus and known in China more than 2,000 years before the birth of Christ, the pumelo is also the largest citrus fruit, as signified in its botanical name, _Citrus grandis._ Its presence here acknowledges not only Oroville's Chinese community but also the area's historically important commercial citrus industry.

The courtyard garden is by no means the only thing to see at the Chinese Temple Complex, set in a grove of ginkgo and other shade trees. Besides the ornate temple chambers, other galleries display Cantonese tapestries, porcelains, lacquerware, objects from Oroville's Chinese community, and nineteenth-century Occidental garments. The complex is unusual both for the garden and for its presentation of an almost forgotten phase of California's cultural history. (1500 Broderick St., Oroville; open daily for $1.50 adult admission; closed between December 1 and January 15; telephone 916-538-2496 for daily hours.)

MICKE
GROVE
PARK

A mid rows of gnarly old grapevines in zinfandel country, a grove of majestic valley oaks (*Quercus lobata*)—reputedly one of the Central Valley's two largest oak groves—shades a Japanese garden donated in 1965 by San Joaquin County residents of Japanese ancestry. Designed by Nagao Sakurai, superintendent of Tokyo's Imperial Palace Garden, the three-acre garden surrounds a Japanese pavilion and a sinuous pond that begins in a waterfall, extends under a fountain and footbridge, and curves past a teahouse before ending in a river stone beach.

Throughout the garden, azaleas and camellias bloom in late winter and spring, and pruned black pines, Japanese maples, ginkgos, acanthus, bamboo, cycads, southern magnolia, dogwood, cryptomeria, and *Aucuba japonica* luxuriate under the oaks. The Japanese garden contains the K. O. Hester Camellia Garden, comprising several hundred camellias. Elsewhere in the park, a small rose garden commemorates William G. Micke, who with his wife Julia deeded the sixty-five-acre oak grove to the county in 1938. Only about one-fourth of the park's 259 acres is developed with a zoo, county historical museum, and other park facilities.

(Micke Grove Park, Micke Grove Rd. [north of Eight Mile Rd. between Highway 99 and Interstate 5, north of Stockton]. Open daily 8:00 a.m. to 5:00 p.m.; $3.00 per vehicle on weekends and $2.00 on weekdays. The Japanese Garden is open 9:00 a.m. to 2:00 p.m., weekends and holidays. Telephone 209-463-0578 for tours of the Japanese Garden; for information, telephone 209-953-8800.)

FRESNO PARKS
AND
GARDENS

The landscaping of the CALIFORNIA STATE UNIVER-SITY, FRESNO, campus ties it closely to local needs: for shade during hot summers, for verticality in flat country, and for the species best adapted for greenery, color, and growth in this climate. *A Guide to the Growing Campus*, with a map and descriptions of 100 tree species, makes the 250-acre campus accessible but omits three specialized gardens from its tour. There is a small rose garden south of the Thomas Administration Building. South of the Conley Art Building, the Hazel Glen iris garden blooms with hundreds of bearded irises. In the middle of a nearby parking area, Robert Boro has designed the newest and most interesting specialty garden, an "allergy-free demonstration garden" displaying nonallergenic plants for home landscapes. Installed in late 1984, maintained and developed by two local Rotary Clubs, and presented to the university in 1989, many plants in the "sneeze-free" garden also bloom dependably, an achievement that in Fresno's hot months is not to be sneezed at.

Residents of this pollen-rich, agricultural area interested in nonallergenic flowering plants will find the species gathered here especially useful. Blooming species include the hot pink trailing verbena (*V. peruviana*); the yellow daisy bush (*Euryops pectinatus* "Green Gold"), named for its abundant, golden yellow daisy flowers; and two lantanas, lavender *Lantana montevidensis*, and *Lantana camara*, a vining shrub bearing yellow flowers with golden centers. The garden also contains fine trees: the Indian bean (*Catalpa bignonioides*), distinguished by fan-shaped, tropical leaves, a smooth trunk, and long, pendulous bean pods; the evergreen *Cryptomeria japonica*; and the purple-leaf plum (*Prunus cerasifera*); among many others.

Otherwise the campus features a significant collection of trees, with long allées of Chinese pistache, Modesto ash (*Fraxinus velutina glabra*), maple, and liquidambar, and mass plantings of single tree species such as an exceptional grove of blue atlas cedar growing east of the Thomas Administration Building. Only a few of the 100 tree species on the tour bear labels, and occasionally individual species can be disappointing or difficult to observe. (A large Mexican palo verde, rare in this area, is hidden in a utility area, screened by Jeffrey pines, and surrounded by chain link.)

For the most part, however, the tour capably presents the arboretum, formally dedicated in 1978. As with many other public universities in California built after 1945, the several thousand trees provide a humane note from which the slabs of campus architecture, so clearly patterned on a warehouse and military model, self-consciously recoil. The trees and plantings mitigate not only the Central Valley's intense summers but also the timid brutalism of institutional building. Here horticulture tries to supply what culture has overlooked; it not infrequently succeeds. (Enter at E. Shaw and N. Maple aves., where a parking kiosk offers *A Guide to the Growing Campus*, briefly describing the origins and culture of one hundred tree species keyed to a campus map.)

The southeastern district of Fresno contains two residential gardens, both Japanese in theme. Dick Duncan, owner of DUNCAN'S WATER GARDENS and a large retail nursery nearby, opens his private garden on weekends during specified hours. Walking up a driveway, entering through a double gate after observantly noting a sign welcoming visitors (if the welcoming sign is not posted, do not enter), and crossing a lawn past a swimming pool, one encounters an extraordinary water garden. In low-lying, flat country, Duncan has dug a three-quarter-acre, 220,000-gallon lake, mounded the excavated earth to create waterfalls, berms, streams, and islands, and planted an extravaganza of trees and flowering shrubs.

Honking to one another, elegant black swans with coral beaks glide decoratively on the pond. The largest of several waterfalls—no Niagara but impressive for a backyard—roars formidably near the garden's botanical centerpiece, a weeping blue atlas cedar (*Cedrus atlantica "Pendula"*) whose limbs dip to meet their reflection in the water. Paths circling the pond wind along inlets and peninsulas through persimmon, birch, azaleas, magnolia, Japanese maple, cryptomeria, crepe myrtle, camellias, deodar, and hibiscus. Meticulously pruned specimens combine with stonework, lamps, bridges, and garden statuary to establish a Japanese tone. As a final touch, the water appears to have been colored a cloudy green, the better to reflect the birds, sky, and plants. The scale of this

A chateauesque oasis on the valley floor: Kearney Park

fifteen-year-old garden reflects both the resources and commitment to make what is in essence a private Eden. Opening it is an act of exceptional public spirit. (Duncan's Water Gardens, at 691 N. Temperance, is actually entered at 6901 E. McKinzie; hours are 9:00 a.m. to 5:00 p.m. Saturdays, 10:00 a.m. to 4:00 p.m. Sundays. *Closed Monday through Friday.* Telephone 209-252-1657.)

Not far away, on a four-acre estate now the site of the TENRI CULTURAL CENTER, is the former residence of Milo Rowell, who lived in Japan just after World War II as a member of General Douglas MacArthur's legal staff involved in drafting the postwar Japanese constitution. The house and garden date from the 1940s and reflect Rowell's interest in Japanese culture as well as his eminence as a camellia fancier and plant connoisseur. Now a religious retreat, the garden is open only by appointment.

Beneath a canopy of bamboo, Japanese maple, oaks, and ginkgo, brick paths lead through beautifully maintained azaleas, camellias, ferns, pittosporum, Japanese irises, acanthus, irises, gerbera, and plumbago. Hedging of box, yew, and holly defines a formal garden that diverges somewhat from the dominant Japanese mode. Bonsai and potted plants surround a reflecting pool near the house, whose eaves shelter subtropical bird of paradise and rhapis palms. A hybridizer of camellias and a plant collector, Rowell cultivated citrus, cycads, Mediterranean fan palms, and deodar cedar south of the house, which extend into plantings of crepe myrtle, persimmon, and grapevines. The garden reflects Rowell's interests in magnolias, succulents and cacti, dwarf conifers, and rock gardening. There are no labels, and the lanterns and statuary associated with Japanese gardens appear only near a small entry pool. Carefully selected, elegantly sited, faithfully maintained plants create an impression of elegance, Japanese and otherwise, in this fine collection. (The Tenri Cultural Center garden is open only by appointment; telephone 209-252-4597.)

Bordering Highway 99 and bounded by Belmont and Olive avenues, ROEDING PARK dates from Frederick C. Roeding's 1903 gift of seventy-two acres to the City of Fresno on the condition that it spend a stipulated amount for the park's development and annual maintenance. Later city purchases and gifts by Roeding and his family brought the park to its present 150 acres. Roeding's son, George C. Roeding (a nurseryman credited with developing the area's fig industry by introducing the fig wasp as a pollinator), acted as park commissioner for many years and supervised its development according to a plan by Johannes Reimas, who was hired to landscape with tall trees in what was then a largely treeless parcel. Although considerably modified by later structures, roads, and other park features, his plan survives in its distinct groves of specimen trees, now grown to great size.

Under their shade, generations of Fresno citizens have gathered during hot valley summers. The park contains several water features (Lake Washington and lily ponds), extensive lawns, and groves of fan palms, dawn and coast redwoods, eucalyptus, cedar, ash, pine, cypress, and maple, many with picnic facilities. Scattered through the park are incense, deodar, and blue atlas cedars, bunya bunya, magnolia, valley and cork oaks, camphors, flowering plums, and several palm species, including the Central Valley favorite, the statuesque Canary Island palm.

A handsome pergola, draped with wisteria and enclosed by Hollywood junipers, covers a path through the heart of the park to an area where the Roeding Line trolley, which was discontinued in 1939, formerly stopped. A map available at the park office near the Belmont Avenue entrance shows these features, although the status of a camellia garden, its diminutive plants fenced off by chain link, remains in doubt, and a rose garden marked on the map is no more. Although a number of attractions—a children's story land, a steam locomotive, a "tot lot" and playland—tend to push its botanical attributes into the background, they reinforce Roeding Park's role as a Fresno tradition. The Fresno zoo, in fact, has added to the park's botanical diversity by its tropical plantings and the Central Valley equivalent of a rain forest habitat, with exotic species that will eventually form an artifically humidified canopy sheltering birds, iguanas, sloths, and monkeys in an ecologically themed educational exhibit. (Roeding Park is bounded by Highway 99, Olive and Belmont aves., and N. Motel Dr.; the park office is north of the Belmont Ave. entrance; telephone 209-488-1551.)

Although originally situated near the edge of the city, Roeding Park now seems almost downtown. With beginnings not unlike that of Roeding Park, a large new park is developing in the northern area into which Fresno has expanded. Ralph Woodward made a large bequest to provide a public park and bird sanctuary, and with additional acreage purchased by Rotary Playland, Inc., and the city, Woodward Park comprises just under 300 acres bordering the San Joaquin River. More than 5,000 trees have been planted and much of the young park has been landscaped. Its southeastern portion, designed as a bird refuge, includes a large lake. Along an inlet on the lake's northern edge lies the three-acre SHIN ZEN "FRIENDSHIP" JAPANESE GARDEN. Begun in 1968, the garden is completely planted but is still adding structures, such as a Japanese teahouse. Its design emphasizes the four seasons, with a winter area of pines, cherry and plum trees and flowering bulbs in spring, the summer shade of broadleafed trees, and fall colors of Chinese pistache and liquidambar.

A string of weeping willows along the lake edge, their tassels drooping almost to the water, offers perhaps the garden's most evocative feature. Asian species—ginkgo, Chinese elm, Japanese maples and dwarf pines, heavenly bamboo, and camellias—contribute to the Japanese atmosphere. This "friendship" garden, however, also contains North American species, such as white alder (growing along one of several watercourses rushing through the garden), coast redwoods, and tulip trees. The rocks, stone lanterns and other statuary, an arched moon bridge across a narrows next to a pond of koi, additional Japanese structures, and the maturing vegetation hold out the promise that this garden will ripen into the serenity characteristic of the Japanese garden. (Woodward Park is entered on Audubon Blvd. between Friant Rd. and Highway 41; $1.00 automobile admission; open daily 7:00 a.m. and 7:00 p.m. during winter and until 10:00 p.m. summers. Shin Zen "Friendship" Garden open weekends, 10:00 a.m. to dusk. Telephone parks division headquarters, 209-488-1551.)

No visit to Fresno would be complete without a drive to KEARNEY PARK, whose 225 acres create a skyline of familiar Central Valley trees: Canary Island palms, bunya bunya, deodar, olives, coast redwood, eucalyptus, and many others. The trees' great size and also their numbers make Kearney Park unusual. Besides the park's several thousand trees, M. Theodore Kearney lined Kearney Avenue with *Washingtonia filifera* palms, making it a landmark on the flat valley floor. A small but choice two-and-a-half-story house (now a museum) in the French manner also distinguishes the park. Kearney died before he could build an elaborate mansion, but drawings remain, as do the thousands of trees in his estate planned by landscape architect Rudolph Ulrich and planted from 1889 to 1905: a fantasy landscape in a featureless plain, a blend of park, forest, and oasis originally intended to surround someone's home. (Palm-lined Kearney Ave., southwest of Fresno, leads to Kearney Park at 7160 W. Kearney Ave.; $3.00 per vehicle admission.)

INDEX

Other Books from John Muir Publications

Adventure Vacations: From Trekking in New Guinea to Swimming in Siberia, Richard Bangs (65-76-9) 256 pp. $17.95

Asia Through the Back Door, 3rd ed., Rick Steves and John Gottberg (65-48-3) 326 pp. $15.95

Being a Father: Family, Work, and Self, *Mothering* Magazine (65-69-6) 176 pp. $12.95

Buddhist America: Centers, Retreats, Practices, Don Morreale (28-94-X) 400 pp. $12.95

Bus Touring: Charter Vacations, U.S.A., Stuart Warren with Douglas Bloch (28-95-8) 168 pp. $9.95

California Public Gardens: A Visitor's Guide, Eric Sigg (65-56-4) 304 pp. $16.95 (Available 3/91)

Catholic America: Self-Renewal Centers and Retreats, Patricia Christian-Meyer (65-20-3) 325 pp. $13.95

Complete Guide to Bed & Breakfasts, Inns & Guesthouses, Pamela Lanier (65-43-2) 520 pp. $15.95

Costa Rica: A Natural Destination, Ree Strange Sheck (65-51-3) 280 pp. $15.95

Elderhostels: The Students' Choice, Mildred Hyman (65-28-9) 224 pp. $12.95 (2nd ed. available 5/91 $15.95)

Environmental Vacations: Volunteer Projects to Save the Planet, Stephanie Ocko (65-78-5) 240 pp. $14.95

Europe 101: History & Art for the Traveler, 4th ed., Rick Steves and Gene Openshaw (65-79-3) 372 pp. $15.95

Europe Through the Back Door, 9th ed., Rick Steves (65-42-4) 432 pp. $16.95

Floating Vacations: River, Lake, and Ocean Adventures, Michael White (65-32-7) 256 pp. $17.95

Gypsying After 40: A Guide to Adventure and Self-Discovery, Bob Harris (28-71-0) 264 pp. $14.95

The Heart of Jerusalem, Arlynn Nellhaus (28-79-6) 336 pp. $12.95

Indian America: A Traveler's Companion, Eagle/Walking Turtle (65-29-7) 424 pp. $16.95 (2nd ed. available 7/91 $16.95)

Mona Winks: Self-Guided Tours of Europe's Top Museums, Rick Steves and Gene Openshaw (28-85-0) 456 pp. $14.95

Opera! The Guide to Western Europe's Great Houses, Karyl Lynn Zietz (65-81-5) 280 pp. $18.95 (Available 4/91)

Paintbrushes and Pistols: How the Taos Artists Sold the West, Sherry C. Taggett and Ted Schwarz (65-65-3) 280 pp. $17.95

The People's Guide to Mexico, 8th ed., Carl Franz (65-60-2) 608 pp. $17.95

The People's Guide to RV Camping in Mexico, Carl Franz with Steve Rogers (28-91-5) 320 pp. $13.95

Preconception: A Woman's Guide to Preparing for Pregnancy and Parenthood, Brenda E. Aikey-Keller (65-44-0) 232 pp. $14.95

Ranch Vacations: The Complete Guide to Guest and Resort, Fly-Fishing, and Cross-Country Skiing Ranches, Eugene Kilgore (65-30-0) 392 pp. $18.95 (2nd ed. available 5/91 $18.95)

Schooling at Home: Parents, Kids, and Learning, *Mothering* Magazine (65-52-1) 264 pp. $14.95

The Shopper's Guide to Art and Crafts in the Hawaiian Islands, Arnold Schuchter (65-61-0) 272 pp. $13.95

The Shopper's Guide to Mexico, Steve Rogers and Tina Rosa (28-90-7) 224 pp. $9.95

Ski Tech's Guide to Equipment, Skiwear, and Accessories, edited by Bill Tanler (65-45-9) 144 pp. $11.95

Ski Tech's Guide to Maintenance and Repair, edited by Bill Tanler (65-46-7) 160 pp. $11.95

Teens: A Fresh Look, *Mothering* Magazine (65-54-8) 240 pp. $14.95 (Available 3/91)

A Traveler's Guide to Asian Culture, Kevin Chambers (65-14-9) 224 pp. $13.95

Traveler's Guide to Healing Centers and Retreats in North America, Martine Rudee and Jonathan Blease (65-15-7) 240 pp. $11.95

Understanding Europeans, Stuart Miller ((65-77-7) 272 pp. $14.95

Undiscovered Islands of the Caribbean, 2nd ed., Burl Willes (65-55-6) 232 pp. $14.95

Undiscovered Islands of the Mediterranean, Linda Lancione Moyer and Burl Willes (65-53-X) 232 pp. $14.95

A Viewer's Guide to Art: A Glossary of Gods, People, and Creatures, Marvin S. Shaw and Richard Warren (65-66-1) 152 pp. $10.95 (Available 3/91)

2 to 22 Days Series
These pocket-size itineraries (4½" × 8") are a refreshing departure from ordinary guidebooks. Each offers 22 flexible daily itineraries that can be used to get the most out of vacations of any length. Included are not only "must see" attractions but also little-known villages and hidden "jewels" as well as valuable general information.

22 Days Around the World, Roger Rapoport and Burl Willes (65-31-9) 200 pp. $9.95 (1992 ed. available 8/91 $11.95)

2 to 22 Days Around the Great Lakes, 1991 ed., Arnold Schuchter (65-62-9) 176 pp. $9.95

22 Days in Alaska, Pamela Lanier (28-68-0) 128 pp. $7.95

22 Days in the American Southwest, 2nd ed., Richard Harris (28-88-5) 176 pp. $9.95

22 Days in Asia, Roger Rapoport and Burl Willes (65-17-3) 136 pp. $7.95 (1992 ed. available 8/91 $9.95)

22 Days in Australia, 3rd ed., John Gottberg (65-40-8) 148 pp. $7.95 (1992 ed. available 8/91 $9.95)

22 Days in California, 2nd ed., Roger Rapoport (65-64-5) 176 pp. $9.95

22 Days in China, Gaylon Duke and Zenia Victor (28-72-9) 144 pp. $7.95

22 Days in Europe, 5th ed., Rick Steves (65-63-7) 192 pp. $9.95

22 Days in Florida, Richard Harris (65-27-0) 136 pp. $7.95 (1992 ed. available 8/91 $9.95)

22 Days in France, Rick Steves (65-07-6) 154 pp. $7.95 (1991 ed. available 4/91 $9.95)

22 Days in Germany, Austria & Switzerland, 3rd ed., Rick Steves (65-39-4) 136 pp. $7.95

22 Days in Great Britain, 3rd ed., Rick Steves (65-38-6) 144 pp. $7.95 (1991 ed. available 4/91 $9.95)

22 Days in Hawaii, 2nd ed., Arnold Schuchter (65-50-5) 144 pp. $7.95 (1992 ed. available 8/91 $9.95)

22 Days in India, Anurag Mathur (28-87-7) 136 pp. $7.95

22 Days in Japan, David Old (28-73-7) 136 pp. $7.95

22 Days in Mexico, 2nd ed., Steve Rogers and Tina Rosa (65-41-6) 128 pp. $7.95

22 Days in New England, Anne Wright (28-96-6) 128 pp. $7.95 (1991 ed. available 4/91 $9.95)

2 to 22 Days in New Zealand, 1991 ed., Arnold Schuchter (65-58-0) 176 pp. $9.95

22 Days in Norway, Sweden, & Denmark, Rick Steves (28-83-4) 136 pp. $7.95 (1991 ed. available 4/91 $9.95)

22 Days in the Pacific Northwest, Richard Harris (28-97-4) 136 pp. $7.95 (1991 ed. available 4/91 $9.95)

22 Days in the Rockies, Roger Rapoport (65-68-8) 176 pp. $9.95

22 Days in Spain & Portugal, 3rd ed., Rick Steves (65-06-8) 136 pp. $7.95

22 Days in Texas, Richard Harris (65-47-5) 176 pp. $9.95

22 Days in Thailand, Derk Richardson (65-57-2) 176 pp. $9.95

22 Days in the West Indies, Cyndy & Sam Morreale (28-74-5) 136 pp. $7.95

"Kidding Around" Travel Guides for Young Readers
Written for kids eight years of age and older. Generously illustrated in two colors with imaginative characters and images. An adventure to read and a treasure to keep.

Kidding Around Atlanta, Anne Pedersen (65-35-1) 64 pp. $9.95

Kidding Around Boston, Helen Byers (65-36-X) 64 pp. $9.95

Kidding Around Chicago, Lauren Davis (65-70-X) 64 pp. $9.95

Kidding Around the Hawaiian Islands, Sarah Lovett (65-37-8) 64 pp. $9.95

Kidding Around London, Sarah Lovett (65-24-6) 64 pp. $9.95

Kidding Around Los Angeles, Judy Cash (65-34-3) 64 pp. $9.95

Kidding Around the National Parks of the Southwest, Sarah Lovett 108 pp. $12.95

Kidding Around New York City, Sarah Lovett (65-33-5) 64 pp. $9.95

Kidding Around Paris, Rebecca Clay (65-82-3) 64 pp. $9.95 (Available 4/91)
Kidding Around Philadelphia, Rebecca Clay (65-71-8) 64 pp. $9.95
Kidding Around San Francisco, Rosemary Zibart (65-23-8) 64 pp. $9.95
Kidding Around Santa Fe, Susan York (65-99-8) 64 pp. $9.95 (Available 5/91)
Kidding Around Seattle, Rick Steves (65-84-X) 64 pp. $9.95 (Available 4/91)
Kidding Around Washington, D.C., Anne Pedersen (65-25-4) 64 pp. $9.95

Environmental Books for Young Readers

Written for kids eight years and older. Examines the environmental issues and opportunities that today's kids will face during their lives.

The Indian Way: Learning to Communicate with Mother Earth, Gary McLain (65-73-4) 114 pp. $9.95
The Kids' Environment Book: What's Awry and Why, Anne Pedersen (55-74-2) 192 pp. $13.95
No Vacancy: The Kids' Guide to Population and the Environment, Glenna Boyd (61-000-7) 64 pp. $9.95 (Available 8/91)
Rads, Ergs, and Cheeseburgers: The Kids' Guide to Energy and the Environment, Bill Yanda (65-75-0) 108 pp. $12.95

"Extremely Weird" Series for Young Readers

Written for kids eight years of age and older. Designed to help kids appreciate the world around them. Each book includes full-color photographs with detailed and entertaining descriptions of the "extremely weird" creatures.

Extremely Weird Bats, Sarah Lovett (61-008-2) 48 pp. $9.95 paper (Available 7/91)
Extremely Weird Frogs, Sarah Lovett (61-006-6) 48 pp. $9.95 paper (Available 6/91)
Extremely Weird Spiders, Sarah Lovett (61-007-4) 48 pp. $9.95 paper (Available 6/91)

Automotive Repair Manuals

How to Keep Your VW Alive, 14th ed., (65-80-7) 440 pp. $19.95
How to Keep Your Subaru Alive (65-11-4) 480 pp. $19.95

How to Keep Your Toyota Pickup Alive (28-81-3) 392 pp. $19.95
How to Keep Your Datsun/Nissan Alive (28-65-6) 544 pp. $19.95

Other Automotive Books

The Greaseless Guide to Car Care Confidence: Take the Terror Out of Talking to Your Mechanic, Mary Jackson (65-19-X) 224 pp. $14.95

Off-Road Emergency Repair & Survival, James Ristow (65-26-2) 160 pp. $9.95

Ordering Information

If you cannot find our books in your local bookstore, you can order directly from us. Please check the "Available" date above. If you send us money for a book not yet available, we will hold your money until we can ship you the book. Your books will be sent to you via UPS (for U.S. destinations). UPS will not deliver to a P.O. Box; please give us a street address. Include $2.75 for the first item ordered and $.50 for each additional item to cover shipping and handling costs. For airmail within the U.S., enclose $4.00. All foreign orders will be shipped surface rate; please enclose $3.00 for the first item and $1.00 for each additional item. Please inquire about foreign airmail rates.

Method of Payment

Your order may be paid by check, money order, or credit card. We cannot be responsible for cash sent through the mail. All payments must be made in U.S. dollars drawn on a U.S. bank. Canadian postal money orders in U.S. dollars are acceptable. For VISA, MasterCard, or American Express orders, include your card number, expiration date, and your signature, or call (800) 888-7504. Books ordered on American Express cards can be shipped only to the billing address of the cardholder. Sorry, no C.O.D.'s. Residents of sunny New Mexico, add 5.875% tax to the total.

Address all orders and inquiries to:
John Muir Publications
P.O. Box 613
Santa Fe, NM 87504
(505) 982-4078
(800) 888-7504